MICHAEL BAIGENT AND RICHARD LEIGH

THE INQUISITION

VIKING

VIKING

Published by the Penguin Group
Penguin Books Ltd, 27 Wrights Lane, London w8 5tz, England
Penguin Putnam Inc., 375 Hudson Street, New York, New York 10014, USA
Penguin Books Australia Ltd, Ringwood, Victoria, Australia
Penguin Books Canada Ltd, 10 Alcorn Avenue, Toronto, Ontario, Canada m4v 3b2
Penguin Books (NZ) Ltd, Private Bag 102902, NSMC, Auckland, New Zealand

Penguin Books Ltd, Registered Offices: Harmondsworth, Middlesex, England

First published 1999
1 3 5 7 9 10 8 6 4 2

Grateful acknowledgement is made to the Mary Evans Picture Library for supplying all the pictures
except for the print of John Coustos which is reproduced by courtesy of the Library of the United
Grand Lodge of England.

Set in 12/16pt Monotype Bembo
Typeset by Rowland Phototypesetting Ltd, Bury St Edmunds, Suffolk
Printed in Great Britain by Clays Ltd, St Ives plc

A CIP catalogue record for this book is available from the British Library

isbn 0–670–88032–9

Contents

Acknowledgements

As ever, we should like to thank Ann Evans and Jonathan Clowes, not only for being our agents, but also for being consultants, managers, counsellors, intercessors, advocates, pagan Cistercians and friends, through whom the puissance of Sainte Quittière is enabled to cast its protection over us.

For their help and support in a diverse spectrum of ways, we should also like to thank Sacha Abercorn, John Ashby, Jane Baigent, Brie Burkeman, Bela Cunha, Helen Fraser, Margaret Hill, Tony Lacey, Alan McClymont, Andrew Nurnberg, Peter Ostacchini, David Peabody, John Saul, Yuri Stoyanov and Lisa Whadcock.

Again, too, our debt to libraries is immense. We should like to thank the staffs of the British Library, St Pancras, the Library of the United Grand Lodge of England, Covent Garden, and the Bodleian Library, Oxford.

Dedication

On n'oubliera le hasard
par un coup de dès
et l'orme detachera
le roi des aulnes.
Une cité rosat abritera
les têtes abattues et le
suaire gêne la lumière.

A contrejour sachant
la cellule, la clarté
entrera la garenne.
Les belles éclaircies du vent
poussent le chat à herisser ses poils.
Ils se refugient dans les bruissements
de la haleine de Mélusine.

JEHAN L'ASCUIZ

Introduction

As the fifteenth century gave way to the sixteenth, Jesus returned. He reappeared in Spain, on the streets of Seville. There were no fanfares attending his advent, no choirs of angels or supernatural spectaculars, no extravagant meteorological phenomena. On the contrary, he arrived 'softly' and 'unobserved'. And yet the passers-by quickly recognised him, were irresistibly drawn to him, surrounded him, flocked about him, followed him. He moved modestly among them with a gentle smile of 'ineffable compassion', held out his hands to them, conferred his blessings upon them; and an old man among the crowd, blind from childhood, miraculously regained the faculty of sight. The multitude wept and kissed the earth at his feet while children tossed flowers before him, sang and lifted their voices in hosannas.

At the steps of the cathedral, weeping mourners were carrying inside a small open white coffin. Within it, almost hidden by flowers, lay a child of seven, the only daughter of a distinguished citizen. Urged on by the crowd, the bereft mother turned to the newcomer and beseeched him to restore the dead girl to life. The procession halted and the coffin was set down at his feet on the cathedral steps. 'Maiden, arise!' he commanded softly, and the girl immediately sat upright, looking about, smiling, with wide wondering eyes, still holding the cluster of white roses that had been placed in her hands.

This miracle was witnessed, as he passed with his entourage of bodyguards, by the city's cardinal and Grand Inquisitor – 'an aged man, almost ninety, tall and upright in stature, with a shrivelled face and deeply recessed eyes, in which, however, there still burned a gleam of light'. Such was the terror he inspired that the crowd, despite the extraordinary circumstances, deferentially fell silent, parted and made way for him. Neither did anyone dare to interfere when, at the old prelate's behest, the newcomer was summarily arrested by his bodyguards and led off to prison.

Such is the opening of Fyodor Dostoevsky's 'Parable of the Grand Inquisitor', a more or less self-contained twenty-five-page narrative embedded in the 800 or so pages of *The Brothers Karamazov*, first published by instalments in a Moscow magazine during 1879 and 1880. The parable's real significance resides in what follows the dramatic prelude. For the reader expects, of course, that the Grand Inquisitor will be appropriately horrified when he learns the true identity of his new prisoner. That, however, is not to be the case.

When the Grand Inquisitor visits Jesus's cell, it is clear that he knows only too well whom the prisoner is; but the knowledge does not deter him. During the prolonged philosophical and theological debate that ensues, the old man remains adamant in his position. In scripture, Jesus is tempted by the devil in the wilderness with the prospect of power, of earthly authority, of secular or temporal dominion over the world. Now, a millennium and a half later, he is confronted by precisely the same temptations. When he resists them, the Grand Inquisitor consigns him to the stake.

Jesus responds only by conferring on the old man a kiss of forgiveness. Shuddering, the kiss 'glowing in his heart', the old man opens the door to the cell. 'Go,' he commands, 'and come no more . . . Come not at all, never, never!' Released into the darkness, the prisoner disappears, never to be seen again. And the Grand Inquisitor, in full consciousness of what has just transpired, continues to adhere to his principles, continues to enforce his reign of terror, continues to sentence other victims – often self-evidently innocent – to the flames.

As can be seen from this perhaps oversimplified summary, Dostoevsky's Grand Inquisitor is no fool. On the contrary, he knows all too well what he is doing. He knows that he carries an onerous and debilitating responsibility on his aged shoulders – to maintain civic order, to uphold the status of the Church founded in the name of the man he has just been prepared to sentence to execution. He knows the Church founded in the man's name is ultimately incompatible with the teachings of the man himself. He knows that the Church has become autonomous, the proverbial law unto itself, no longer rendering unto Caesar but usurping Caesar, presiding over its own imperium. He knows that he has been entrusted with the role of custodian and 'enforcer' of this imperium. He knows that the edicts and acts he promulgates in that capacity will undoubtedly entail what his own theology forecasts will be his eternal damnation. He knows, in short, that he is martyring himself to evil. Because he knows that in functioning as the representative of secular and temporal power, and in tempting Jesus with such power, he is equating himself with the devil.

Since *The Brothers Karamazov* was first published and translated, Dostoevsky's Grand Inquisitor has seared itself into our collective consciousness as the definitive image and embodiment of the Inquisition. We may appreciate the old prelate's agonising dilemma. We may admire the complexity of his character. We may even respect him for the personal martyrdom he is prepared to incur, his self-condemnation to perdition on behalf of an institution he deems greater than himself. We may also respect his secular realism and the brutally cynical understanding behind it, the worldly wisdom that recognises the mechanics and dynamics of mundane power. Some of us may well wonder whether – were we in his position and entrusted with his responsibilities – we might be impelled to act as he does. But for all the tolerance, the appreciation, perhaps the sympathy and forgiveness we might muster for him, we cannot escape the awareness that he is, by any honest moral standards, intrinsically evil – and that the institution he represents is culpable of a monstrous hypocrisy.

How accurate, how representative, is Dostoevsky's portrait? To what extent does the figure in the parable fairly reflect the actual historical institution? And if the Inquisition, as personified by Dostoevsky's aged prelate, can indeed be equated with the devil, to what degree can that equation be extended to the Church as a whole?

For most people today, any mention of the Inquisition suggests the Inquisition in Spain. In seeking an institution that reflects the Roman Catholic Church as a whole, Dostoevsky, too, invokes the Inquisition in Spain. But the Inquisition, as it existed in Spain and Portugal, was unique to those countries – and was accountable, in fact, at least as much to the Crown as it was to the Church.

This is not to suggest that the Inquisition did not exist and operate elsewhere. It did. But the Papal or Roman Inquisition – as it was known at first informally, then officially – differed from the Inquisition of the Iberian peninsula. Unlike its Iberian counterparts, the Papal or Roman Inquisition was not account-able to any secular potentate. Operating throughout most of the rest of Europe, its allegiance was solely to the Church. Created in the early thirteenth century, it predated the Spanish Inquisition by some 250 years. It has also outlasted its Iberian counterparts. While the Inquisition in Spain and Portugal was extinct by the third decade of the nineteenth century, the Papal or Roman Inquisition survived. It exists and continues to function actively even today. It does so, however, under a new, less emotive and less stigmatised name. Under its present sanitised title of Congregation for the Doctrine of the Faith it still plays a salient role in the lives of millions of Catholics across the globe.

It would be a mistake, however, to identify the Inquisition with the Church as a whole. They are not the same institution. Important though the Inquisition has been, and continues to be, in the world of Roman Catholicism, it remains only one aspect of the Church. There have been, and there still are, many other aspects, not all of which warrant the same oppro-brium. This book is about the Inquisition in its various forms, as it existed in the past and as it exists today. If it emerges in a dubious light, that light need not necessarily extend to the Church in general.

At its inception, the Inquisition was the product of a brutal, insensitive and ignorant world. Not surprisingly, it was itself in consequence brutal, insensitive and ignorant. It was no more so, however, than numerous other institutions of its time, both spiritual and temporal. As much as those other institutions, it is part of our collective heritage. We cannot, therefore, simply repudiate it and dismiss it. We must confront it, acknowledge it, try to understand it in all its excesses and prejudice, then integrate it in a new totality. Merely to wash our hands of it is tantamount to denying something in ourselves, in our evolution and development as a civilisation – a form, in effect, of self-mutilation. We cannot presume to pass judgement on the past by the criteria of contemporary political correctness. If we attempt to do so, the whole of the past will be found wanting. We will then be left solely with the present as a basis for our hierarchies of value; and whatever the values we embrace, few of us would be foolish enough to extol the present as any sort of ultimate ideal. Many of the past's worst excesses were caused by individuals acting with what, according to the knowledge and morality of their time, they deemed the best and worthiest of intentions. We would be rash to imagine our own worthy intentions as being infallible. We would be rash to fancy those intentions incapable of producing consequences as disastrous as those for which we condemn our predecessors.

The Inquisition – sometimes cynical and venal, sometimes maniacally fanatical in its supposed laudable intentions – may indeed have been as brutal as the age that spawned it. It must be repeated, however, that the Inquisition cannot be equated with the Church as a whole. And even during the periods of its most rabid ferocity, the Inquisition was obliged to contend with other, more humane faces of the Church – with the more enlightened of the monastic orders, with orders of friars such as the Franciscans, with thousands of individual priests, abbots, bishops and prelates of even higher rank who sincerely endeavoured to practise the virtues traditionally associated with Christianity. Nor must one forget the creative energy the Church inspired – in music, painting, sculpture and architecture – which represents a counterpoint to the Inquisition's bonfires and torture chambers.

During the latter third of the nineteenth century, the Church was compelled to relinquish the last vestiges of its former secular and political power. To compensate for this loss, it sought to consolidate its spiritual and psychological grip, to exercise a more rigorous control over the hearts and minds of the faithful. In consequence, the Papacy became increasingly centralised; and the Inquisition increasingly became the definitive voice of the Papacy. It is in this capacity that the Inquisition – 're-branded' as the Congregation for the Doctrine of the Faith – functions today. Yet even now, the Inquisition does not have things entirely its own way. Indeed, its position is becoming ever more beleaguered as Catholics across the world acquire the knowledge, the sophistication and the courage to question the authority of its inflexible pronouncements.

There have certainly been – and, it might well be argued, still are – Inquisitors of whom Dostoevsky's parable offers an accurate portrait. In certain places and at certain periods, such individuals may indeed have been representative of the Inquisition as an institution. That does not, however, necessarily make them an indictment of the Christian doctrine they sought in their zeal to propagate. As for the Inquisition itself, readers of this book may well find it to have been an institution at once better and worse than the one depicted in Dostoevsky's parable.

1

A Fiery Zeal for the Faith

Inspired by Saint Paul's dextrous salesmanship, Christianity has always offered shortcuts to paradise. Thus did it recruit adherents, even before its emergence as a recognisable religion. Through martyrdom, through self-mortification, through meditation and contemplation, through solitude, through ritual, through penance, through communion, through the sacraments – through all those avenues, the doors to the Kingdom of Heaven were reputedly opened to believers. Some of these access routes may have incorporated elements of pathology, but they were for the most part peaceable. And even when Christians of the first millennium fought – as they did, for instance, under Charles Martel and then Charlemagne – they did so primarily in self-defence.

In 1095, however, a new route to God's domain was officially and publicly made available. On Tuesday, 27 November of that year, Pope Urban II climbed on to a platform erected in a field beyond the east gate of the French city of Clermont. From this eminence, he proceeded to preach a crusade, a war conducted on behalf of the Cross. In such a war, according to the Pope, one could obtain God's favour, and a seat at His throne, by killing.

Not, of course, that the Pope was indiscriminate. On the

contrary, he exhorted Christians to desist from their deplorable, if long established, practice of killing each other. He urged them instead to direct their murderous energies towards the Islamic infidels, who occupied the sacred city of Jerusalem and the Holy Sepulchre, supposed site of Jesus's burial. In order to reclaim for Christendom the city and the tomb, European fighting men were encouraged to embark on a righteous war under the direct guidance of God.

But killing was only one component of an attractive 'package deal'. In addition to a licence to kill, the good Christian could obtain remission from whatever time he might already have been sentenced to serve in Purgatory and from penances to be performed while still on earth. Should he perish in his holy endeavour, he was promised automatic absolution from all his sins. Should he survive, he would be protected against temporal punishment for any sins he might commit. Like the monk or the priest, the crusader was rendered independent of secular justice and subject only to spiritual jurisdiction. Were he to be found guilty of any crime whatever, he would simply have his crusader's red cross removed or confiscated and would then be 'punished with the same leniency as ecclesiastics'. In the years to come, the same benefits were to be made available on a broader scale. In order to partake of them, one did not even have to embark on a crusade oneself. It was sufficient simply to donate money to a crusade.

Quite apart from the spiritual and moral benefits, there were numerous perks to be enjoyed by the crusader on his way through this world, even before he passed through the heavenly gates. He could lay claim to goods, lands, women and titles in the territory he conquered. He could amass as much booty and plunder as he wished. Whatever his status at home – as a landless younger son, for instance – he could establish himself as an august secular potentate, with a court, a harem and a substantial terrestrial estate. Such was the bounty to be reaped simply by embarking on crusade. It was a package whose allure and marketability might well be envied by the insurance salesmen of today.

Thus the crusades ensued. In 1099, the First Crusade established the Frankish Kingdom of Jerusalem – the first instance in history of what would be perceived centuries later as Western imperialism and colonialism. The Second Crusade occurred in 1147, the Third in 1189, the Fourth in 1202. Altogether, there were seven crusades. In between the full-scale campaigns organised and financed from Europe, periods of fighting between Christians and Muslims alternated with lulls of uneasy peace, during which trade – in ideas as well as goods – prospered.

'Outremer', the 'land across the sea' as it was also known, came to comprise a self-contained European principality in the heart of the Islamic Middle East, sustained and supported by European arms and manpower from almost every European kingdom. The city of Jerusalem itself was to be recaptured by the Saracens in 1187. As an outpost of European Christendom, however, Outremer would survive for another century. Only in May 1291 was Acre, the sole remaining fortress, overrun, its last tower collapsing in a cascade of stone, rubble and flame that buried both attackers and defenders.

Whether the insurance salesmen of the time were able to honour their spiritual guarantees – of estates in heaven and a seat by God's side – we do not, of course, know. Fulfilment of temporal promises is easier to monitor. Like a great many package deals and bargain schemes, this one proved a windfall for a few, a disappointment for most. A staggeringly large number of European nobles, knights, men-at-arms, merchants, entrepreneurs, craftsmen and others, including women and children, perished to no purpose whatever, often after bitter ordeals and in gruesome conditions, sometimes eaten by their starving companions. But there were enough who prospered, who obtained land, titles, booty, wealth and other tangible rewards; and they served to provide an inducement for others. If nothing else, one could acquire expertise in arms, in the techniques and technologies of warfare, in fighting and killing; and if the Holy Land failed to offer adequate recompense for a man's newly acquired aptitudes, he could always bring them back to Europe and turn them to account there.

Holy Fratricide

In 1208, while the crusades in the Holy Land were still in progress and the Frankish Kingdom of Jerusalem was fighting for survival, a new crusade was launched by Pope Innocent III. The enemy this time was not to be the Islamic infidel across the Mediterranean, but the adherents of a heresy in the south of France. The heretics in question were sometimes referred to as 'Cathari', denoting 'the purified' or 'the perfected'. By others, including their enemies, they were called 'Albigensians' or 'Albigenses', a designation derived from an early centre for their activities, the southern French town of Albi.

The Cathars are much in vogue today, made topical by current interests in comparative mysticism and by general millennial fever. They have come to be mantled with the romanticism, the poetry and the sympathy often associated with tragically lost causes. But if they do not quite warrant the more extravagant idealisations recently conferred upon them, they must still rank among history's most poignant victims, and they deserve to be recognised as being among the earliest targets of organised and systematic genocide in the evolution of Western civilisation.

Although they might in a loose sense be called Christian (they *did* ascribe a theological significance to Jesus), the Cathars were adamantly opposed to Rome and the Roman Church. As later Protestant denominations were to do, they saw in Rome the embodiment of evil, the biblical 'Whore of Babylon'. Among established Christian congregations at the time, they were closer in some of their teachings to the Byzantine or Greek Orthodox Church. In certain respects – their belief in reincarnation, for instance – they had elements in common with traditions from even further east, such as Hinduism and Buddhism.

Ultimately, however, and despite the sympathy accorded them by recent commentators, the Cathars subscribed to a number of tenets which few people in the West today would find altogether congenial – and which more than a few might well find morbidly unbalanced. Essentially the Cathars were dualist. In other words, they regarded all material creation as intrinsically evil, the work of a lesser and inferior deity. All flesh, all matter, all substance was ultimately to be repudiated and transcended in favour of an exclusively spiritual reality; and it was only in the realm of the spirit that true divinity resided.

To this extent, the Cathars represented a late development of a tradition long established on the perimeters of the Christianised West. They had much in common with the heretical Bogomils of the Balkans, from whom a number of their beliefs derived. They echoed the older third-century heresy of Manichaeanism, promulgated by the teacher Mani in Persia. And they incorporated many elements of the Gnostic dualism which had flourished in Alexandria and elsewhere during the first two centuries of the Christian era, and which probably originated in ancient Zoroastrian thought.

Like the Bogomils, the Manichaeans and the Gnostic dualists, the Cathars emphasised the importance of direct contact with, and knowledge of, the divine. This contact was deemed to constitute 'gnosis', which means 'knowledge' – knowledge of a specifically sacred kind. And by insisting on such direct and first-hand experience of the sacred, the Cathars, like their predecessors, effectively preempted the need for a priesthood, for an ecclesiastical hierarchy. If the greatest virtue was one's own individual and experiential apprehension of the spiritual, the priest became superfluous as custodian and interpreter of spirituality; and theological dogma became irrelevant, a mere intellectual construct which issued from man's arrogant mind, not from any higher or numinous source. Such a position implied a flagrant challenge not only to the teachings, but to the very structure of the Roman Church.

Ultimately, of course, Christianity is itself implicitly dualist, extolling the spirit, repudiating the flesh and the whole of 'unregenerate nature'. The Cathars preached what might be seen as an extreme form of Christian theology – or as an attempt to pursue Christian theology to its logical conclusions. They themselves saw their teachings as being closer to what Jesus himself and his apostles were alleged to have taught. Certainly it *was* closer than what was being promulgated by Rome. And in their simplicity and repudiation of worldly luxury, the Cathars were closer than the Roman priesthood to the lifestyle embraced by Jesus and his followers in the Gospels.

In practice, of course, the Cathars lived in the physical world and had perforce to avail themselves of its resources. Thus, for example, they were forbidden to do violence to the corporeal, to seek a shortcut out of the realm of matter by suicide. Like previous dualist sects, they, too, procreated and propagated, tilled the soil, practised crafts and trades and – despite their nominal pacifism – when necessary resorted to arms. Their rituals and training, however, taught them to regard such activity as a testing ground, an arena in which they could pit themselves against the challenge of evil and, if successful, overcome it. There must obviously have been 'good' and 'bad' Cathars, just as there have always been rigorous and lax adherents of any creed. But on the whole, and regardless of their beliefs, the Cathars were generally perceived by their contemporaries as conspicuously virtuous. In many respects they were regarded as the Quakers would later be regarded. Their qualities earned them considerable respect and made the Roman priesthood all the less attractive by comparison. According to a deposition now in the Vatican's library, a man described how, when he was young, two associates came up to him and said:

> The good Christians have come into this land; they follow the path of Saint Peter, Saint Paul and the other Apostles; they follow the Lord; they do not lie; they do not do to others what they would not have others do to them.[1]

The same witness also reports being told that the Cathars

> are the only ones to walk in the ways of justice and truth which the Apostles followed. They do not lie. They do not take what belongs to others. Even if they found gold or silver lying in their path, they would not 'lift' it unless someone made them a present of it. Salvation is better achieved in the faith of these men called heretics than in any other faith.[2]

By the beginning of the thirteenth century, Catharism had begun threatening to supplant Catholicism in the south of France, and itinerant Cathar preachers, travelling on foot through the countryside, constantly garnered new converts. These preachers did not bully, did not extort, did not traffic in guilt or emotional blackmail, did not tyrannise or terrorise with dire threats of damnation, did not demand payment or bribes at every opportunity. They were noted, like the Quakers after them, for their 'gentle persuasion'.

It is doubtful that all professed converts to Catharism became practising believers. Many, one suspects, took their new faith no more seriously than other Christians of the time took their Catholicism. But Catharism unquestionably exercised an allure. For knights, nobles, tradesmen, merchants and peasants in the south of France, it seemed to offer a congenial alternative to Rome – a flexibility, a tolerance, a generosity, an honesty not readily to be found in the established ecclesiastical hierarchy. More practically, it offered an escape from Rome's ubiquitous clergy, from clerical arrogance and from the abuses of a corrupt Church, whose extortions were becoming increasingly insufferable.

There is no question that the Church at the time was shame-lessly corrupt. In the early thirteenth century, the Pope described his own priests as 'worse than beasts wallowing in their dung'.[3] According to the greatest German lyric poet of the Middle Ages, Walther von der Vogelweide (*c.* 1170–*c.* 1230):

How long wilt thou in slumber lie, O Lord? . . . Thy treasurer steals the wealth that thou hast stored. Thy ministers rob here and murder there, And o'er thy sheep a wolf has shepherd's care.[4]

Bishops of the period were described by a contemporary as 'fishers for money and not for souls, with a thousand frauds to empty the pockets of the poor'.[5] The Papal legate in Germany complained that clergy in his jurisdiction revelled in luxury and gluttony, failed to observe fasts, hunted, hawked, gambled and engaged in commercial transactions. The opportunities for corruption were immense, and few priests made any serious effort to withstand temptation. Many demanded fees even for the performance of their official duties. Weddings and funerals could not proceed until money had been paid in advance. Communion would be refused until a donation was received. Last rites were even withheld from the dying until a sum of money had been extorted. The power to grant indulgences, remission for penances due in expiation of sin, raised immense additional revenue.

In the south of France, such corruption was particularly rife. There were churches, for example, in which no Mass had been said for more than thirty years. Many priests ignored their parishioners and conducted commercial businesses or maintained large estates. The Archbishop of Tours, a notorious homosexual who had been his predecessor's lover, demanded that the vacant bishopric of Orléans be conferred on his own lover. The Archbishop of Narbonne never actually visited the city or his diocese. Many other ecclesiastics feasted, took mistresses, travelled in opulent coaches, employed enormous retinues of servants and maintained lifestyles worthy of the highest nobility, while the souls entrusted to their care were tyrannised and squeezed into ever deeper squalor and poverty.

It is hardly surprising, therefore, that a substantial portion of the region's population, quite apart from any question of spiritual welfare, turned their backs on Rome and embraced

Catharism. Nor is it surprising that Rome, confronted with such defections and a noticeable drop in revenues, began to feel progressively more threatened. Such anxiety was not unjustified. There was a very real prospect of Catharism displacing Catholicism as the predominant religion in the south of France – and from here it could easily spread elsewhere.

In November 1207, Pope Innocent III wrote to the King of France and a number of high-ranking French nobles, urging them to suppress the heretics in their domains by military force. In return, they would be granted rewards of confiscated property and the same indulgences as those conferred on crusaders in the Holy Land. These incentives do not seem to have provided much spur to action, especially in the south. The Count of Toulouse, for example, promised to exterminate all heretics in his fiefdom, but did nothing to implement his promise. Deeming his bloodlust insufficiently enthusiastic, the Papal legate, Pierre de Castelnau, demanded a meeting with him. The meeting quickly degenerated into a furious row, with Pierre accusing the count of supporting the Cathars, and summarily excommunicating him. The count, who may himself have been a Cathar, responded predictably with threats of his own.

On the morning of 14 January 1208, as Pierre was preparing to make his way across the river Rhône, a knight in the count's service accosted him and stabbed him to death. The Pope was enraged and immediately issued a Bull to all nobles of southern France, accusing the count of instigating the murder and renewing his excommunication. The pontiff further demanded that the count be publicly condemned in all churches and authorised any Catholic to hunt him down, as well as to occupy and confiscate his lands.

Nor was that all. The Pope also wrote to the King of France

demanding that a 'sacred war' be undertaken to exterminate the Cathar heretics, who were described as worse than the Muslim infidel. All who participated in this campaign were to be placed under the immediate protection of the Papacy. They were to be freed from the payment of all interest on their debts. They were to be exempt from the jurisdiction of secular courts. They were to be granted full absolution for their sins and vices, provided they served a minimum of forty days.

Thus did Pope Innocent III preach the undertaking subsequently known as the Albigensian Crusade. It was the first crusade ever to be launched in a Christian country, against other Christians (heretical though they might be). In addition to its explicit benefits, it offered, of course, an implicit licence to loot, pillage, plunder and expropriate property. And it offered other advantages as well. The crusader who took up arms against the Cathars did not, for example, have to cross the sea. He was spared the complications and expenses of transport. He was spared, too, the strain of campaigning in the desert and the oppressive climate of the Middle East. If things did not go well, he would not be left isolated in an alien and hostile milieu. On the contrary, he could make his way back to safety easily enough, or even disappear into the local populace.

By late June of 1209, an army of between fifteen and twenty thousand northern nobles, knights, men-at-arms, servitors, adventurers and camp followers had gathered on the Rhône. A minor French baron, Simon de Montfort, was to emerge as their military commander. Their spiritual leader was the Papal legate Arnald-Amaury – a fanatic, a Cistercian and, at the time, Abbot of Cîteaux.

By 22 July, the army had arrived at the strategic city of Béziers, whose population included a substantial number of

Cathars. In the ensuing sack and pillage of the town, Arnald-Amaury was asked how to distinguish heretics from loyal and devout Catholics. The Papal legate replied with one of the most infamous statements in the whole of Church history: 'Kill them all. God will recognise His own.'[6] In the massacre that followed, some 15,000 men, women and children perished. With a triumphalism verging on ecstatic glee, Arnald-Amaury wrote to the Pope that 'neither age, nor sex, nor status had been spared'.[7]

The sack of Béziers terrified the whole of southern France. Even as the crusaders attempted to regroup amid the smoking ruins, a deputation arrived from Narbonne, offering to surrender all their town's Cathars and Jews (who had also by now become 'legitimate targets'), as well as to supply the army with food and money. The inhabitants of other towns and villages abandoned their homes, fleeing to the mountains and forests. But the crusaders were not just intent on restoring the supremacy of Rome. They were also bent on complete extermination of all heretics, as well as on everything they could plunder. In consequence, the campaign dragged on.

On 15 August, after a short siege, Carcassonne surrendered and Simon de Montfort became Viscount of Carcassonne. Throughout the south, heretics were being burned by the score, and anyone else who attempted opposition was hanged. Nevertheless, the Cathars – supported by many southern nobles who sought to resist the depredations visited upon them – struck back, and many towns and castles changed hands repeatedly. The bitterness and the scale of the slaughter increased. In 1213, the King of Aragón attempted to intervene on behalf of the Cathars and southern nobles; but his army was defeated by the crusaders at the Battle of Muret, and he himself was killed. In the autumn of 1217, the crusaders descended on Toulouse, and a siege of nine months ensued. On 25 June 1218, Simon de Montfort himself perished at the city walls, struck by a chunk of masonry which a woman among the defenders had catapulted from a trebuchet.

With Simon's death, the crusaders' army began to melt away and an uneasy peace descended on the ravaged region. It did not last long. In 1224, a new crusade against the south was launched, with King Louis VIII as military commander and the veteran fanatic Arnald-Amaury still presiding as ecclesiastical leader. Despite the French king's death in 1226, the campaign continued until, by 1229, the whole of the Languedoc had effectively been annexed by the French Crown. Further Cathar revolts against this new authority occurred in 1240 and 1242. On 16 March 1244, Montségur, the most important remaining Cathar stronghold, fell after a sustained siege, and more than 200 heretics were immolated on a pyre at the foot of the mountain on which the castle stood.

Quéribus, the last Cathar fortress, fell eleven years later, in 1255. Only then did organised Cathar resistance finally cease. By this time, great numbers of surviving heretics had fled to Catalonia and Lombardy, where they established new communities. Even in the south of France, however, Catharism did not altogether die out. Many heretics simply blended into the local population and continued to embrace their creed and practise their rituals clandestinely. They remained active in the region for at least another half century, and during the first two decades of the fourteenth century there was a Cathar resurgence around the village of Montaillou in the French Pyrenees. By this time, however, an institution as sinister as any crusading army had been established to deal with the heretics.

2

Origins of the Inquisition

While the military campaigns proceeded against Cathar fortresses and towns with large Cathar populations, another development was in progress. Though less obviously spectacular, less dramatic, less epic, it was to be of even greater importance to the history of Christendom, far transcending the immediate context of southern France in the thirteenth century. Its influence was to radiate out across the whole of the Christian world, to shape substantial aspects of Western history and culture, and to endure up to the present day.

In the summer of 1206, a year and a half before the Albigensian Crusade was first preached, the Bishop of Osma in northeastern Spain was passing through southern France on his way back from a visit to Rome. He was accompanied in his journey by one Dominic de Guzmán, sub-prior to the monks attached to the cathedral at Osma. The son of a minor Castilian noble, Dominic was some thirty-six years of age at the time. He had trained for ten years at the University of Palencia and was noted for his rhetorical skills, his aptitude in debate and disputation. Three years earlier, in 1203, he had made his first journey to France, and the threat posed by the Cathar heresy there had spurred him to righteous indignation.

His indignation was intensified by his second visit. At Montpellier, he and his bishop met with the local Papal legates, who complained at length about the heresy 'infecting' the region. To combat the 'infection', Dominic and the bishop conceived an ambitious scheme. The bishop, however, was to die within the year, and the scheme was to be implemented by Dominic alone. If 'credit' is the appropriate word, he was to reap the credit for it.

The Cathars successfully recruited their congregations in large part through itinerant preachers, who commanded respect through their learning, eloquence and theological knowledge. But they also commanded respect through their comportment – their obvious poverty and simplicity, their integrity and probity, their rigorous adherence to the kind of austerity traditionally associated with Jesus himself and his disciples. The Church could not compete in these recognised 'Christian' virtues. The upper echelons of the ecclesiastical hierarchy led lives whose opulence, luxury, sybaritic self-indulgence and shameless extravagance hardly conformed to any established Christian precedent. Local priests, on the other hand, although poor enough, were also appallingly ignorant and uneducated, capable of little more than performing Mass, and certainly unequipped to engage in theological debate. Monks remained restricted to their monasteries, where they engaged primarily in manual labour, religious offices or meditation. The few of them who did possess any aptitude for scholarship had no opportunity to transmit it to the world beyond their cloisters.

Dominic undertook to rectify this situation and, as he conceived it, beat the Cathars at their own game. He proceeded to establish a proliferating network of itinerant monks, or friars – men who were not sequestered in abbey or monastery, but who wandered the roads and villages of the countryside. In contrast to Church dignitaries, Dominic's friars would travel barefoot and live simply and frugally, thus exemplifying the austerity and asceticism ascribed to the early Christians and the original Church fathers. What was more, Dominic's men would be educated, adept at scholarly debate, capable of engaging Cathar preachers or any others in 'theological tournaments'. Their clothes might be plain and their feet bare, but they carried books with them. In the past, other clerical figures had advocated scholarship for its own sake, or for the preservation and monopolisation of knowledge by Rome. Dominic became the first individual in Church history to advocate scholarship as an integral aid and tool for preaching.

During the canonisation process following his death, depositions were taken and compiled from those who had known him personally or witnessed him in action. From these, something of a portrait emerges. Dominic is described as a slender man who prayed almost incessantly through the night, often weeping as he did so. During the day, he would organise public events which enabled him to preach against the Cathars, and he would often burst into tears during a sermon. He hurled himself into the ascetic life and self-mortification with zest. When praying, he would often flail himself with an iron chain, which he wore around his legs. Day and night he lived in the same garb, a rough and coarse hair-shirt which was heavily patched. He never slept in a bed, only on the ground or on a board.

At the same time, he was not without his own unique species of vanity. He seems to have been acutely conscious of his image as an ascetic, and was not above reinforcing it by some all-too-human, if rather unsaintly, prevarications and deceptions. On approaching an inn or roadside hostel where he proposed to spend the night, for example, he would pause first at a nearby spring or stream and drink his fill in private. Once inside the premises, he would augment his reputation for frugality and austerity by drinking almost nothing.

As early as 1206 – during his journey through France with the Bishop of Osma and two years before the Albigensian Crusade was first preached – Dominic had founded a hospice at Prouille. Among the Papal legates he came to know was Pierre de Castelnau, whose murder in 1208 was to precipitate the crusade. A speech at Prouille ascribed to Dominic shortly after the outbreak of hostilities offers some indication of his mentality:

> I have sung words of sweetness to you for many years now, preaching, imploring, weeping. But as the people of my country say, where blessing is to no avail, the stick will prevail. Now we shall call forth against you leaders and prelates who, alas, will gather together against this country . . . and will cause many people to die by the sword, will ruin your towers, overthrow and destroy your walls and reduce you all to servitude . . . the force of the stick will prevail where sweetness and blessing have been able to accomplish nothing.[1]

There are few specific details about Dominic's personal activities during the campaign against the Cathars. It seems clear, however, that he moved with the spearhead of the crusaders' army, operating with a warrant from the equally fanatical Papal legate Arnald-Amaury, Abbot of Cîteaux, who ordered the extermination of the entire population of Béziers on the grounds that 'God will recognise His own'. Even the most apologetic of Dominic's biographers concede that he was often required to pass judgement on suspected Cathars, to convert them to the Church or – if the attempt to do so failed – consign them to the flames. He witnessed the burning of numerous heretics, and appears to have accommodated his conscience easily enough to their deaths.

Not surprisingly, Dominic became a close personal friend, confidant and adviser of the crusade's ruthless military commander, Simon de Montfort, and accompanied him on his trail of carnage and destruction. During part of 1213, when Simon was in residence at Carcassonne, Dominic served as assistant to the city's bishop. He is also believed to have attended the army at the Battle of Muret, where his preaching helped inspire Simon's soldiery to their defeat of the King of Aragón. In 1214, Simon conferred on Dominic the income from at least one freshly conquered town. Dominic also baptised Simon's daughter and officiated at the marriage of his elder son to a granddaughter of the King of France.

By that time, Dominic's activities and his association with Simon had made him something of a celebrity among the crusaders. Thus, in 1214, wealthy Catholic citizens of Toulouse bestowed three houses (one of which still stands) on him and his embryonic order of friars. A year later, he abandoned his original intention of establishing his order at Carcassonne, apparently because of too much adverse, even overtly hostile criticism. Instead, he moved to Toulouse; and it was in the premises donated to him that the Dominican Order was founded, if only as yet unofficially.

Later in 1215, Dominic travelled to Rome and attended the Fourth Lateran Council. At this council, Pope Innocent III echoed Dominic's insistence on the importance of theological study in any preaching of the faith. The Pope also endorsed the official establishment of the Dominican Order, but died before this could be implemented. In December of 1216, the Dominicans were formally established by the new pontiff, Honorius III.

By 1217, the original Dominicans in Toulouse had provoked so much animosity that they were obliged to disperse. In doing so, they proceeded to install themselves in houses as far afield as Paris, Bologna and various localities in Spain. Teachers were now being actively recruited into the Order, and regulations were issued concerning study and the careful handling of books. Every Dominican house had its own teacher, at whose lectures attendance was compulsory. At the same time, the Dominicans pursued the activities that had so alienated them from the citizens of Carcassonne and then Toulouse – spying, denunciation and general intelligence gathering. In such activities as these, the Dominicans demonstrated their worth to the Church. Networks of itinerant friars, wandering the roads of the countryside, were uniquely suited to the gathering of information.

In 1221, Dominic died of a fever at Bologna. He was just over fifty years of age and seems to have burned himself out through sheer expenditure of fanatical energy. The work he had inaugurated, however, continued apace. At the time of his death, there were already some twenty Dominican houses in France and Spain. Members of the Order were known not only for preaching, but for the active and aggressive study of theology. By 1224, at least 120 Dominicans were studying theology in Paris. By 1227, the Pope was beginning to call on them for aid in 'the business of faith'. On specific commission of the pontiff, they became increasingly engaged in the ferreting out and hunting down of heretics, and their zeal in such activities made them ever more indispensable to the Church.

In 1234, with what today might appear unseemly haste, Dominic was officially canonised. Few saints can have had so much blood on their hands. By the time Dominic 'went to his reward', whatever that may have been, his Order numbered nearly a hundred houses. The Dominicans functioned with an insistence on discipline and obedience such as might be associated with certain sects and cults today, and with similar effects on families. Once an individual entered the Order, he was lost thereafter to his relatives and to the world. On one occasion, according to hagiographic accounts, a noble Roman family attempted to reclaim their son from the Order's clutches. The young man was dispatched to another Dominican house, away from Rome. His family pursued him; and he had just crossed a river when they appeared on the opposite bank. At that point the river miraculously flooded, becoming swollen and impassable. The young man remained a Dominican.

The Destruction of Heresy

In 1233, one of Dominic's friends had acceded to the throne of Saint Peter as Pope Gregory IX. It was he who initiated the process that culminated a year later in Dominic's canonisation. At the same time, on 20 April 1233, the new pontiff issued a Bull that conferred on the Dominicans the specific task of eradicating heresy. Addressing his bishops, the Pope wrote:

> We, seeing you engrossed in the whirlwind of cares and scarce able to breathe in the pressure of overwhelming anxieties, think it well to divide your burdens that they may be more easily borne. We have therefore determined to send preaching friars against the heretics of France and the adjoining provinces, and we beg, warn, and exhort you, ordering you . . . to receive them kindly, and treat them well, giving them in this . . . aid, that they may fulfil their office.[2]

Two days later, the Pope addressed a second Bull directly to the Dominicans:

> Therefore you . . . are empowered . . . to deprive clerks of their benefices forever, and to proceed against them and all others, without appeal, calling in the aid of the secular arm, if necessary.[3]

The Pope went on to announce the establishment of a permanent tribunal to be staffed by Dominican brothers. Thus was the Inquisition effectively inaugurated. It became active a year later, in 1234, at Toulouse, where two official Inquisitors were appointed. It is interesting to note that their activities, according to the Papal Bull, were originally to be directed against 'clerks', or clergy – an indication of how many Roman ecclesiastics were in fact secret Cathar sympathisers.

By virtue of the Pope's edict, Dominican Inquisitors were given legal authority to convict suspected heretics without any possibility of appeal – and thus, in effect, to pronounce summary death sentences. The burning of heretics was, of course, nothing new. Simon de Montfort and his army had cheerfully engaged in the practice since the beginning of the Albigensian Crusade in 1209. His actions, however, had been those of a ruthless military commander proceeding on his own initiative, imposing his version of martial law on conquered territory and dealing with his enemies as he saw fit. Now, with the Pope's blessing, the machinery for mass extermination was established on an official legal basis, with a formal sanction and mandate derived directly from the highest authority in Christendom.

Inevitably, given the nature and scale of the administrative apparatus involved, there were hitches. Many clerics grudged the Dominicans their new power and displayed some degree of sympathy for the Cathars, if only on humanitarian rather than theological grounds. Not surprisingly, too, there was a confusion of authority between Inquisitors and local bishops. The Pope had claimed to be lightening the bishops' burden. In practice, he was implicitly divesting them of some of their ecclesiastical jurisdiction, and varying degrees of friction, even overt resentment, ensued. Some bishops insisted that their concurrence was required before heretics could be convicted. Some claimed a right to modify sentences. Some demanded inquisitorial powers of their own.

During the course of the thirteenth century, jealousy and antagonism between Inquisitors and bishops were sometimes to become acute. In theory, the Inquisition's tribunals were supposed to be simply an addition to the bishops' tribunal. In practice, however, episcopal power was gradually being eroded. In 1248, a council was to threaten bishops with being locked out of their own churches unless they complied with sentences handed down by the Inquisition. In 1257, Pope Alexander IV made the Inquisition independent by removing the need for it to consult with the bishops. At last, in 1273, Pope Gregory X would order that Inquisitors should operate in conjunction with local bishops, sharing authority and jurisdiction; and this would gradually become the norm thereafter.

For the first generation of Inquisitors, life was not always easy. It sometimes offered ample opportunity to exult in a sense of tribulation, and to glorify oneself accordingly. Guillaume Pelhisson, for example, was a native of Toulouse who joined the Dominicans around 1230 and became an Inquisitor in 1234, despite his relative youth. Before his death in 1268, he composed a manuscript recounting the activities of the Inquisition in Toulouse between 1230 and 1238. Some three-quarters of a century later, Bernard Gui – one of the most prominent and infamous of all Inquisitors, who figures saliently in Umberto

Eco's novel, *The Name of the Rose* – was to happen upon Guillaume's manuscript and deem it worthy of copying. Bernard's copy has survived in the archives of Avignon and offers a valuable insight into the vicissitudes of the early Inquisition.

Guillaume writes with the declared intention that subsequent generations of Dominicans, as well as other pious Catholics, might

> know how many and what sufferings came to their predecessors for the faith and name of Christ . . . may take courage against heretics and all other unbelievers, and so that they may stand ready to do – or rather to endure – as much or more, if need be . . . For after the numerous, the countless trials borne patiently, devoutly, and with good results by the Blessed Dominic and the friars who were with him in that land, true sons of such a father shall not be wanting.[4]

To demonstrate the difficulties confronting Inquisitors in Albi in 1234, Guillaume writes:

> The lord legate . . . made Arnold Catalan, who was then of the convent at Toulouse, an inquisitor against the heretics in the diocese of Albi, where manfully and fearlessly he preached and sought to conduct the inquisition as best he could. However, the believers of heretics would say virtually nothing at that time, rather, they united in denials; yet he did sentence two living heretics . . . and both were burned . . . He condemned certain other deceased persons and had them dragged away and burned. Disturbed by this, the people of Albi sought to throw him into the River Tarn, but at the insistence of some among them released him, beaten, his clothing torn to shreds, his face

bloody . . . Many misfortunes overtook these people later in the time of Friar Ferrier, the inquisitor, who seized and imprisoned a number of them and also had some burned, the just judgement of God being thus carried out.[5]

Of Toulouse itself, Guillaume complains that

in those days Catholics were harassed and in several locations those who searched out heretics were killed . . . the chief men of the region, together with the greater nobles and the burghers and others, protected and hid the heretics. They beat, wounded, and killed those who pursued them . . . many wicked things were done in the land to the church and to faithful persons.[6]

Guillaume states, in an almost casual, off-hand manner:

The . . . friars made inquisition also in Moissac and sentenced the living John of Lagarde, who, fleeing to Montségur, became a perfected heretic and later was burned there with 210 other heretics.[7]

In 1234 – the year that, in Guillaume's words, 'the canonisation of the Blessed Dominic, our father, was proclaimed'[8] – the Dominicans of Toulouse arranged a celebration Mass for their founder's feast day. Prior to their meal, the participants were washing when 'by divine providence' word came that a woman nearby, dying of fever, had just received the Consolamentum – the Cathar equivalent of the last rites – from certain heretics. Abandoning their ablutions, a number of Dominicans, accompanied by the Bishop of Toulouse, rushed to the sick woman's house and burst into her room.

The bishop . . . seating himself beside the invalid, began to talk to her at length about contempt for the world and for earthly things . . . The lord bishop, with great care, drew from her what she believed on many points and almost all of it was just what the heretics believe . . . Then said the bishop: 'Therefore you are a heretic! For what you have confessed is the faith of the heretics, and you may know assuredly that the heresies are manifest and condemned. Renounce them all! Accept what the catholic church believes.' [The bishop] made these and many like remarks to her in everyone's presence, but he accomplished nothing as far as she was concerned; rather, she persevered all the more in heretical obstinacy. Forthwith, the bishop, who at once summoned the vicar and many other persons, by the virtue of Jesus Christ condemned her as a heretic. Moreover, the vicar had her carried on the bed in which she lay to the count's meadow and burned at once.[9]

Thus did the Dominicans of Toulouse crown their celebration of the newly sainted Dominic's feast day with a human sacrifice.

By 1235, Guillaume reports, hostility to the Dominicans in Toulouse was intensifying. Guillaume appears both mystified and indignant at this attitude, but proudly defiant:

At that time the bodies of certain deceased persons who had been heredicated . . . were dragged through the town and burned. The whole town was excited and aroused against the friars because of the Inquisition and appealed to the count. He came to the inquisitors to ask them, out of consideration for him, to call a halt for a time, adducing his trifling reasons. This they refused to do.[10]

By November of 1235, all Dominicans, and the Inquisition with them, had been forcibly expelled from Toulouse by the city's consuls. The consuls were duly excommunicated by the Inquisition. Shortly thereafter, the Pope demanded the Inquisitors be allowed to return. Once reestablished, they embarked on an orgy of grisly violence:

> At that time, many heretications of prominent men and others, now deceased . . . (were revealed and they were) . . . condemned by sentences, exhumed, and ignominiously were cast out of the cemeteries of the town by the friars in the presence of the vicar and his people. Their bones and stinking bodies were dragged through the town; their names were proclaimed through the streets by the herald, crying, 'Who behaves thus shall perish thus,' and finally they were burned in the count's meadow, to the honour of God and the Blessed Virgin, His mother, and the Blessed Dominic, His servant (who) . . . most happily brought about this work of the Lord.[11]

The Legality of Human Sacrifice

The torture and execution of heretics was nothing new in Christian history. On the contrary, such practices had ample precedent, extending as far back as the fourth century at least. Around AD 385, Priscillian, Bishop of Ávila (381–5), had incorporated in his teachings certain apocryphal material from the Middle East, and possibly elements of Gnostic dualism. Accused of sorcery and heresy, he was brought before Maximus, the Roman emperor at the time, at Trèves, where he was subjected to sustained torture. Convicted of the charges against him, he was beheaded, along with two other clergy, a wealthy woman disciple and a well-known poet associated with him. Tribunes were dispatched to Spain to conduct a further investigation, which resulted in the execution of two additional heretics and the exile of five. Pope Siricus, who occupied the throne of Saint Peter, protested – not about the executions, but about the fact that the trials had been convened in a secular rather than an ecclesiastical court. Priscillian's body was carried back to Spain for burial, where a shrine soon grew up in homage to him – at the site which is now believed to be Santiago de Compostela.[12] The original pilgrimage route to Santiago de Compostela is said to have derived from the itinerary along which Priscillian's body was transported to its final Iberian resting place.

In the 900 years between Priscillian's death and the creation of the Inquisition, there had been other executions of heretics. These had not, however, reflected any coherent or centrally organised Papal policy, but had occurred as isolated intense spasms of violence by local ecclesiastics or strenuously pious secular potentates. Thus, for example, in 1022, the King of France had several allegedly heretical monks of Orléans burned at the stake. In 1126, a solitary heretic was burned at St Gilles. Now, however, under the Inquisition, a formal, more or less smoothly functioning machinery was established for the entire process of investigation, indictment, trial, torture and execution.

Although scant documentation exists to support it, there seems to have been a tradition, dating at least from the ninth century, that Church functionaries were forbidden to shed blood. To draw blood, by lance or sword or dagger, was apparently considered un-Christian. Thus, in *Chanson de Roland*, for example, the ecclesiastic Turoldus, even on military campaign, refrains from carrying pointed weapons. Instead, he wields a mace. It might have been unacceptable to stab a person, but if blood flowed 'incidentally' from a crushed skull, that appears to have been a different and theologically sanctionable matter.

Perhaps in deference to some such tradition as this, the techniques of the Inquisition seemed designed, at least in theory, to keep actual bloodshed to a minimum. Inquisitors had few compunctions or scruples, of course, about inflicting physical pain in the name of spiritual welfare. To accommodate such licence, Pope Alexander IV (1254–61) authorised Inquisitors to absolve each other for any so-called 'irregularities' – the premature death of a victim, for instance. But most forms of torture – such favoured devices as the rack, the thumbscrew, the strappado and water torture – eschewed the deliberate shedding of blood. Devices of this kind would seem to have been contrived to cause maximum pain and minimum mess.

Whatever the other perverse, ingeniously conceived contrivances for inflicting suffering, the supreme instrument of the Inquisition was fire. Fire derived its legal precedent and sanction from the law of Imperial Rome, which was revived in the twelfth century and became the basis for Europe's judicial systems. According to the Roman legal code, death by fire was the standardised punishment for parricide, sacrilege, arson, sorcery and treason. Herein lay the precedent for dealing with heretics. In 1224, the Holy Roman Emperor Friedrich II had passed a law in Lombardy which authorised the burning of relapsed heretics. In 1231, this authorisation was incorporated into Sicilian law. During 1238 and 1239, three legal declarations made the Sicilian judicial code applicable throughout the Holy Roman Empire.

The Emperor Friedrich II was hardly a model Christian himself. He immersed himself in distinctly heterodox teachings. He cultivated an extensive knowledge of Islamic and Judaic thought. He was a practising adept in alchemy, astrology and other aspects of what today would be called 'esoterica'. He had no love for either the Catholic Church or the Pope, who repeatedly accused him of heresy and twice excommunicated him.

But if the Church was consistently at odds with Friedrich, it had no compunction about availing itself of his legal codes, and embraced fire with the rabid zeal of institutionalised pyromania. One of the first actions of the Dominican Inquisition was to exhume the corpses of executed heretics at Albi and to burn them. As has been seen from Guillaume Pelhisson's testimony above, the exhumation and immolation of the dead proved quite as unpopular as the torture and immolation of the living, and such practices often produced a hostile reaction from the local populace, especially in the Languedoc. Many Inquisitors needed armed guards to escort them as they moved about the countryside. A number were assassinated. Such mishaps, however, did not deter their incendiary enthusiasm. The Inquisitor Robert le Petit, for example, burned his way across the whole of northern France. On one occasion in 1239, he presided over the simultaneous death by fire of 180 victims. His excesses were not curbed until two years later, in 1241.

Under the auspices of such men as this, the ancient pagan practice of ritual human sacrifice was effectively resurrected in the guise of Christian piety. The burning of a heretic became an occasion for celebration, a joyous event. The nature of such events was rendered apparent by the designation subsequently associated with them in Spain. Translated literally, the notorious 'auto de fe' — the public trial of which death by fire was the climax — means 'act of faith'.

The Techniques of the Inquisition

The Inquisition quickly developed a methodology of intimidation and control that was impressively effective – so much
so that one can see in it a precursor of Stalin's secret police, of
the Nazi SS and Gestapo. Sometimes an Inquisitor and his
entourage would descend without warning on a city, a town,
a university or, as in *The Name of the Rose*, an abbey. More
usually his arrival would be lavishly prepared in advance. It
would be proclaimed beforehand in church services. It would
be announced in elaborate proclamations on church doors and
public noticeboards; and those who could read would speedily
inform those who could not. When the Inquisitor arrived, he
would do so in a solemn procession, accompanied by his staff
of notaries, secretaries, advisers, assistants, doctors and servants
– as well, often, as an armed escort. Having thus orchestrated
his appearance, he would summon together all residents and
local ecclesiastics, to whom he would preach a solemn sermon
about his mission and the purpose of his visit. He would then
– as if magnanimously proffering invitations to a banquet –
invite all people who wished to confess themselves guilty of
heresy to come forward.

Suspected heretics were given a 'time of grace' – usually
fifteen to thirty days – to denounce themselves. If they did so
within this period, they were generally accepted back into the
Church with no more severe a penalty than a penance. But
they were also obliged to name and furnish detailed information
about all other heretics known to them. The Inquisition was
ultimately interested in quantity. It was quite prepared to be
lenient with one transgressor, even if he were guilty, provided
it could cull a dozen or more others, even if they were innocent.
As a result of this mentality, the population as a whole, and

not just the culpable, was kept in a state of sustained dread conducive to manipulation and control. And everyone, reluctantly or not, was turned into a spy.

Even the most lenient of punishments, the penance, could be severe. The lightest penalty – imposed on those who voluntarily came forward during the 'period of grace' and confessed – was the so-called 'discipline'. Insofar as decency (and the weather) permitted, the self-confessed heretic would be obliged each Sunday to strip and appear in church carrying a rod. At a specified point during the Mass, the priest would then whip him enthusiastically before the entire assembled congregation – 'a fitting interlude', one historian observes drily, 'in the mysteries of divine service'.[13] Punishment did not end there, however. On the first Sunday of every month, the penitent would be compelled to visit every house in which he had ever met with other heretics – and, in each, he would be whipped again. On feast days, moreover, the penitent would be required to accompany every solemn procession through the town and suffer further whippings. These ordeals would be inflicted on the victim *for the rest of his life*, unless the Inquisitor, who would long since have departed, returned, remembered him and released him from his sentence.

Another form of penance, deemed equally light and merciful, was the pilgrimage. This had to be made on foot and could often take several years, during which a man's family might well starve. There were two forms of pilgrimage. The 'lesser' entailed a trek to nineteen shrines scattered about the whole of France, at each of which the penitent would be whipped. The 'greater' pilgrimage involved a longer journey – from the Languedoc to Santiago de Compostela, to Rome, to Cologne, to Canterbury. During the thirteenth century, penitents were sometimes sent on pilgrimage to the Holy Land as crusaders, for anything from two to eight years. If they survived, they were required to bring with them on their return a letter from the Patriarch of Jerusalem or Acre, testifying to their service. At one point, so many heretics were being dispatched on crusade that the Pope forbade the practice, fearing the entire Holy Land might become infected by their thought.

Confessed heretics might also for the duration of their lives be compelled to wear, inside and out, a large saffron cross sewn to the breast and back of all their garments. The penitent was thus exposed to constant social humiliation, ridicule and derision, as well as to occasional violence. People stigmatised with such crosses were ostracised by others, who would be reluctant to do any kind of business with them. Young women would find it impossible to obtain husbands.

Finally, penance could take the form of a fine. Such fines quickly became a source of scandal since Inquisitors often extorted large sums of money for themselves. Bribery and corruption soon became rife. In 1251, even the Pope complained and forbade the imposition of fines. The prohibition did not last long, however, and Inquisitors once again 'won the right to inflict pecuniary penances at discretion'.

Death afforded no release from a penance. If a man died before completing the penances imposed on him, this was interpreted as divine condemnation – an indication that his sentence had not been sufficiently severe in God's eyes. In such cases, the deceased's bones would be exhumed and publicly burned. His property could be legally confiscated, and his surviving family could become liable for his penances, just as they could for his debts.

Such were the more lenient punishments, mercifully imposed on those who confessed their sins voluntarily and informed against others. Information obtained from informers was noted down in comprehensive detail. An immense 'database' was established, to which later interrogations added further documentation; and all this material was efficiently filed and catalogued for easy retrieval. Suspects could thus be confronted with misdemeanours or felonies committed, or allegedly committed, thirty or forty years earlier. In 1316, for example, one woman was shown to have first been arrested for heresy in 1268. Here was a blueprint for the kind of procedures whereby the modern state monitors its citizens. Here was a prototype for the kind of computerised records kept by modern police forces, whereby a youthful transgression – smoking cannabis, for instance, or attending a demonstration – could be invoked years later to discredit a politician or some other public figure.

On arriving in a specific locality, Inquisitors installed themselves in one or another temporary headquarters and here began listening to both confessions and denunciations. The system offered an often irresistible opportunity for evening scores, settling old grudges, plunging enemies into trouble. Wives were frequently encouraged to denounce husbands, children to denounce parents. Witnesses were summoned to support initial testimonies and depositions. If an individual was implicated by two other people, an official would present him with a summons to appear before the Inquisition's tribunal. This injunction would be accompanied by a written statement of the evidence against him. The names of his accusers and of witnesses, though, were never cited.

If the accused attempted to flee, the summons against him was broadcast for three Sundays in succession. If he still failed to appear, he was formally excommunicated and declared an outcast. On pain of their own excommunication, other people were forbidden to provide him with food, shelter or sanctuary.

If, on the other hand, the accused did respond to the

Inquisition's summons, the evidence against him was formally assessed. Should it be deemed sufficient, he was officially placed under arrest and remained, from then on, in the Inquisition's hands. Since no Inquisitor cared to be seen as having erred, every possible subterfuge would be used to extract or extort a confession. Interrogations were often prolonged. According to one functionary, 'there is no need for haste . . . for the pains and privations of imprisonment often bring about a change of mind'.[14] Suspects were sometimes simply kept in strict confinement until they confessed. Sometimes they were chained and denied visitors. Sometimes they were starved. Not infrequently, they were soothingly cajoled. Not infrequently, too, they were tortured.

Under civil law, doctors, soldiers, knights and nobles were not subject to torture and enjoyed immunity. The Inquisition undertook to democratise pain and make it readily available to everybody, regardless of age, sex or social station. Inquisitors were initially prohibited from administering physical torture themselves; they could only act as overseers or supervisors, instructing civil or secular functionaries on what to do, observing and making notes of anything the accused said under duress. Then, in 1252, a Bull issued by Pope Innocent IV formally authorised Inquisitors to administer torture themselves – 'with the restriction that such compulsion should not involve injury to limb or danger of death'.[15] Inquisitors quickly found means of circumventing this restriction. They also complained about it so much that in 1260, the new Pope, Alexander IV, allowed them to grant dispensations to one another for any 'irregularities' that might occur.

The traditional ecclesiastical queasiness about shedding blood remained in force. In consequence, pointed and bladed implements continued to be avoided in favour of the rack, thumbscrews and other devices that caused blood to flow only, as it were, 'incidentally'. Pincers and other such toys constituted a grey area. To tear flesh with pincers was gory enough. If the pincers were red- or white-hot, however, the heated metal would immediately cauterise the wound and staunch the flow of blood. Sophistry of a similar kind was applied to the duration and frequency of torture. Initially, the accused could be tortured only once, and for no longer than thirty minutes. Inquisitors soon began to circumvent this restriction by arguing that there was indeed only one application of torture and that each subsequent thirty-minute session was merely a continuation of the first. Alternatively, a suspect might be tortured for an answer to a single specific point, and answers to a second or third point would justify additional sessions of torture. There are copious records of individuals being tortured twice a day for a week or more.

In practice, the accused was tortured until he was ready to confess – which, sooner or later, he almost inevitably would be. At that point, he was carried into an adjacent room, where his confession was heard and transcribed. The confession was then read back to him and he was formally asked if it was true. If he replied in the affirmative, it was recorded that his confession had been 'free and spontaneous', without the influence of 'force or fear'. Sentencing would follow.

In general, a death sentence was the last resort. Most Inquisitors preferred to keep a 'saved' soul in a more or less intact body, which, through penances or on pilgrimage, testified to the mercy and greatness of the faith. Moreover, as one historian has observed, 'a convert who would betray his friends was more useful than a roasted corpse'.[16]

Inquisitors also recognised that certain heretics could be zealous in their yearning for martyrdom as speedily as possible

– 'and it was no part of the Inquisitor's pleasure to gratify them'.[17]
In such instances, time and constant pain were employed to
dispel the passion for martyrdom. Recalcitrant victims were
consequently subjected to more prolonged and attenuated
ordeals. It was officially recommended that they be kept chained
in a dungeon in solitary confinement, for at least six months,
often for a year or more. The accused's spouse or children
might occasionally be granted visiting rights, in order to induce
a change of heart. Theologians might also be allowed to visit,
to coax or persuade through logical argument and exhortation.

Whatever the reluctance to impose a death sentence, it was
done so frequently enough. Here, clerical hypocrisy flagrantly
displayed itself again. Inquisitors could not themselves perform
executions, which might have made them appear un-Christian.
Instead, they were obliged to enact a ritual whereby the accused
was handed over to the presiding civil or secular authorities,
generally with an established formula: 'We dismiss you from
our ecclesiastical forum and abandon you to the secular arm.
But we strongly beseech the secular court to mitigate its sentence
in such a way as to avoid bloodshed or danger of death.'[18] By
general consent and recognition, this was a deliberately hollow
recitation, which simply enabled the Inquisitor, like Pilate, to
wash his hands of the matter. No one was under the illusion
that the words meant anything other than the stake.

To ensure the maximum number of spectators, executions,
whenever possible, were performed on public holidays. The
condemned would be tied to a post above a pyre of dry wood,
high enough to be visible to the assembled crowd. Later, in
Spain, the victim would sometimes be strangled before the pyre
was actually lit, and would thus mercifully be spared the agony
of the flames. The early Inquisition displayed no such mag-
nanimity, though suffocation from smoke might occasionally

preempt the fire and afford a slightly quicker release. When the ritual was over,

> there followed the revolting process requisite to utterly destroy the half-burned body – separating it into pieces, breaking up the bones and throwing the fragments and the viscera on a fresh fire of logs.[19]

This kind of grisly denouement was deemed especially important in the case of an important heretic, to ensure that no relics were left to be hoarded by clandestine followers.

Inquisitors were assiduous bookkeepers. For the burning of four heretics on 24 April 1323, the accounts of an Inquisitor at Carcassonne show the following itemisation:

> For large wood: 55 sols 6 deniers.
> For vine-branches: 21 sols 3 deniers.
> For straw: 2 sols 6 deniers.
> For four stakes: 10 sols 9 deniers.
> For ropes to tie the convicts: 4 sols 7 deniers.
> For the executioners, each 20 sols: 80 sols.[20]

There is perhaps some macabre poetic justice in these figures. The value of an executioner seems to have been assessed at about the same as eight stakes of wood, and slightly less than a pile of vine-branches.

Like most institutions, nefarious or otherwise, the Inquisition spawned its own celebrities. One of the earliest was the notorious Conrad of Marburg, who regarded mental and physical torture as a rapid route to salvation. Towards the beginning of his career, Conrad had been spiritual adviser to a German princess, the subsequently canonised Elizabeth of Thuringia. Under his sadistic ministrations, she died of self-imposed privations at the age of twenty-four, by which time Conrad had already begun chasing heresies under episcopal authority. Then, in 1227, the Pope commissioned him to preside over the Inquisition in Germany, with virtually limitless powers. These powers went to his head and prompted him, rashly, to accuse a number of high-ranking nobles. They proved more independent-minded and more intractable than their French equivalents. Many of them owed allegiance to the Holy Roman Emperor Friedrich II, who was excommunicated anyway. When Conrad attempted to preach a crusade against them, he was waylaid near Marburg and assassinated.

A year before Conrad met his death in 1233, another Inquisitor, Conrad Tors, had also embarked on a campaign, trooping from town to town, condemning and burning wholesale. 'I would burn a hundred innocents,' he declared, 'if there was one guilty among them.'[21] When Conrad of Marburg was murdered, the Pope ordered Conrad Tors to carry on. He needed no encouragement to do so and continued his activities with relish. He, too, however, allowed his enthusiasm to cloud his judgement. On being summoned before him on a charge of heresy, an unruly noble preempted any untoward verdict by promptly dispatching the Inquisitor.

Among the most famous – or infamous – of the early Inquisitors was Bernard Gui. Bernard was born around 1261 in Limousin, became a Dominican in 1280 and was placed in charge of the Inquisition at Toulouse in 1307. In 1317, he was entrusted by the Pope with a mission to 'pacify' northern Italy, suffering at the time from a serious 'infection' of heresy. He remained an active and zealous Inquisitor until 1324 and died in 1331.

A register survives of the sentences Bernard handed down during his regime as Inquisitor of Toulouse. Between 1308 and 1322, he convicted 636 individuals of heresy – an average of one a week. Forty of his victims were burned at the stake. Some 300 were imprisoned. Thirty-six appear to have escaped his clutches.[22]

Bernard's notoriety derives in large part from the manual of instruction he produced for his colleagues, *The Practice of Inquisition*, completed around 1324. In this text, of which several fourteenth-century manuscript copies survive, Bernard reviews the beliefs of the various heretics the conscientious Inquisitor might encounter – heretics whom he labels 'the Manichaeans of modern times' and 'pseudo-apostles'. He summarises the arguments they might muster in their defence. He provides a methodology for interrogation and offers some sample specimens of how the examination of a suspect should be conducted. His reputation for ruthlessness is reinforced by his obvious relish in inflicting torture – the utility of which he extols for extracting 'truth' not only from accused persons, but from witnesses as well. When the Pope, responding to public outcry, attempted to restrict the use of torture, Bernard promptly complained, arguing that the Inquisition's efficiency would be grievously impaired.

Bernard concludes his book by offering some general guidance on the public deportment appropriate to the well-mannered Inquisitor. Excessive displays of self-congratulation and enthusiasm are implicitly deplored. The Inquisitor should

> so bear himself in passing sentence of corporal punishment that his face may show compassion, while his inward purpose remains unshaken, and thus will he avoid the appearance of indignation and wrath leading to the charge of cruelty.[23]

Even Inquisitors were worried about public relations. In those days, too, image was a problem for prominent individuals.

3

Enemies of the Black Friars

During the twelfth century, most of Europe had experienced a revival of Roman law, which constituted the basis of the prevailing legal system. Roman law – inherited from the old empire nominally Christianised under Constantine in the early fourth century – contained some sixty injunctions against heresy. There thus existed an effective judicial context and sanction for punitive action – and, in consequence, an effective judicial context and sanction for the operation of the Inquisition.

In France, traditionally regarded as 'the eldest daughter of the Church', the Cathar heresy afforded an opportunity for the Inquisition to establish and consolidate its authority. No comprehensive records are available for the first twenty years of the Albigensian Crusade; but in the aftermath of the campaign of 1229, more than 5,000 victims were burned, while innumerable others were subjected to prison, exile or other punishments. By the end of the twelfth century, power on a comparable scale was to be wielded by the Inquisition in Italy.

Later, of course, the Inquisition was to acquire an even greater power, and greater notoriety, in Spain. During the thirteenth century, however, much of Spain and the Iberian Peninsula was still in Islamic hands; and the sheer scale of the conflict between Christians and Muslims left little scope for the Inquisition to pursue its work. In Germany, as the fate visited on Conrad of Marburg and Conrad Tors attests, the Inquisition subsisted on an often tenuous basis. It was in Germany, of course, that the sway of the old Roman Empire had gradually petered out, and Roman legal codes were less firmly rooted in Germany than they were elsewhere. Although ruled in theory by the Holy Roman Empire, Germany, in practice, was subject to no effective centralised authority. Nobles and local potentates tended to be unruly, independent and defiant, frequently resorting to violence to resist any encroachment on their prerogatives. As a result, the Inquisition's activity in Germany was more spasmodic than constant, being pursued only intermittently and only in certain regions. For a decade or so, the Inquisitors might impose their reign of terror in one or another city, one or another principality. They would then provoke a backlash and be driven away.

In England as in Scandinavia, the Inquisition never operated, because the prevailing legal codes did not derive from Roman law. England possessed its own sophisticated legal system, which, at least nominally, upheld the rights of all free men in the kingdom. Guilt was determined by the jury system, and the judicial process made no provision or accommodation for torture. Within this framework, there was neither the tradition, nor the legal and ecclesiastical machinery, geared to maintaining the Inquisition's activities.

Inquisition in the South

In the years immediately following its creation, the Inquisition was kept busy enough. In the south of France and elsewhere, organised Cathar resistance had ceased by the mid thirteenth century; but many small Cathar communities had survived, integrating themselves into the surrounding regions. And there were also many individual Cathars who continued to observe their faith and its rituals clandestinely. Even though such individuals and small communities had ceased to preach and posed no threat of 'infection' to their neighbours, the Church was determined to root them out and exterminate them. They constituted fair game for the hyperactive Inquisitor.

One such was Jacques Fournier, Bishop of Pamiers between 1317 and 1325. In 1326, Jacques became Bishop of Mirepoix and in 1327 a cardinal. In 1334, he was elected Pope as Benedict XII. For this reason, at least some of his records were preserved and subsequently discovered in the Vatican's archives. In 1978, they were edited and published with accompanying commentary in the famous book *Montaillou*, by the distinguished French historian Emmanuel Le Roy Ladurie.

Around 1300, half a century after organised Cathar resistance in the south of France had ceased, Montaillou, a small mountain village in the foothills of the Pyrenees, became a centre for a modest Cathar resurgence. In 1308, the Inquisitor of Carcassonne arrested the entire population of the village apart from very young children. When Jacques Fournier became Bishop of Pamiers in 1317, he was authorised to establish his own 'inquisitorial office'; and it was natural enough that Montaillou, which lay within his jurisdiction, should become the focus of his attention.

Jacques's records testify to the ease and completeness with which Cathar heretics became assimilated into the local population. They testify to cordial enough relations between Cathars and Catholics. They also testify to a degree of understanding, compassion and even sympathy on the part of the future Pope, a preparedness to see the Cathars as fellow human beings.

Unlike Dominic, Jacques Fournier was no rabid fanatic. That, however, did not prevent him from investigating, between 1318 and 1325, ninety-eight cases of heresy involving more than a hundred people, ninety-four of whom appeared before his tribunal. Displaying a Christian tolerance and mercy uncharacteristic of Inquisitors at the time, Jacques sent only five of them to the stake.

It was not only the Cathars who kept the Inquisition occupied. Europe at the time was positively swarming with unorthodox modes of thought, any or all of which constituted ripe targets for the Inquisition. There were, for example, the Bogomils, another dualist sect dating from the tenth century in the old Bulgarian Empire, which during that era stretched from the Ukraine to the Adriatic. From this region, Bogomil thought had spread to Greece and the western Balkans, then further westwards still; and by the twelfth century, it had begun to exercise an influence on Catharism, with which it had much in common. The Bogomils claimed to be the 'true and hidden Christian Church, the Church of Bethlehem and Capernaum'. According to Yuri Stoyanov, probably the definitive modern authority on Bogomil teaching, the heresy 'precipitated the emergence of Catharism and was traditionally recognised by western churchmen and inquisitors as the "hidden tradition" behind Catharism'.[1] Indeed, the Cathars were often called 'Bulgares' or 'Bougres'. Not surprisingly, the Bogomils were soon to incur as assiduous attention from the Inquisition as did the French heretics.

Sharing many tenets with both Cathars and Bogomils were the so-called 'Paterenes' or 'Paterini', who had appeared in southern Italy during the twelfth century. By that time, the Church used the name 'Paterini' almost interchangeably with 'Cathar' or 'Albigensian'. During the first third of the thirteenth century, the Paterini established themselves in the part of the Kingdom of Hungary that comprises modern Bosnia; and in 1235, a crusade was preached against them there similar to that preached in France against the Cathars. The crusade against the Paterini proved conspicuously unsuccessful in extirpating the heresy. In 1325, Pope John XXII complained that many Cathars were fleeing to Bosnia, which was coming to be regarded as a 'Promised Land' for dualist sects.[2] By 1373, the dualist churches in Bosnia were so powerful that Bosnian Catholics were compelled to worship in secret. The Paterini consolidated their position by establishing a close association with regional potentates; and in the fifteenth century, they were to collaborate with the conquering Ottoman invaders. But Bosnia was not the only Paterini stronghold. Even more alarming for the Church of Rome, the heresy proceeded to spread across the entire Italian peninsula. By the early fourteenth century, it was rife in Lombardy, and turning increasingly militant. Specifically to counter this threat, the notorious Bernard Gui was dispatched on his mission to 'pacify' the region.

The dualist sects – the Cathars, the Bogomils and the Paterini – repudiated Rome primarily on theological grounds, and their condemnation of Rome's wealth, extravagance and corruption derived ultimately from theological principles, from a radically different understanding of the nature of spirituality. There were other heresies that had no particular quarrel with Rome's theology, but publicly rejected the wealth, the extravagance and the corruption of the Church and the ecclesiastical hierarchy. Although they would not have thought of themselves as such, they were more akin to the social reformers and revolutionaries of later eras.

Conspicuous among these heresies was that of the Waldensians or Waldenses, founded in the late twelfth century by

Pierre Valdes, a wealthy merchant of Lyons. Having provided for his wife and family, Pierre donated his property to the poor and embarked on the life of an itinerant preacher, extolling poverty, simplicity and other traditional Christian virtues. He soon acquired an entourage of disciples, who accompanied him through the countryside. Some went off to establish their own bands of followers and disseminate their teachings further afield. In many respects, the Waldensians might well have seemed congenial to a man like Dominic, since they, too, condemned the dualism of the Cathars. But they also inveighed against the 'worldliness' of the Church; and they defied the Roman hierarchy by daring to produce copies of scriptural texts in regional languages and dialects. This sufficed to get them stigmatised as a heresy. By the time the Inquisition was established, Peter Valdes himself was dead; but his followers and disciples soon became as subject to persecution as the Cathars, and a great many of them, over the subsequent years, were consigned to the stake.

Among the most tenacious heresies to attract the Inquisition's attention was that of the Brethren of the Free Spirit. The Brethren appear to have originated towards the beginning of the twelfth century in the region of Switzerland and the upper Rhine. In 1212, at least eighty of them were thrown into a ditch outside the city walls of Strasburg and burned alive. That did not prevent them from becoming active by the middle of the century in Swabia, whence they spread across the rest of Germany and eventually reached the Low Countries. By the fifteenth century, their membership in Holland is believed to have included the painter Hieronymus Bosch.

Like the Waldensians, the Brethren of the Free Spirit produced religious books in the vernacular. Unlike the Waldensians, however, their orientation was essentially mystical, even incipiently Hermetic. 'God is everything that is,' they pro-claimed. 'All emanates from him and returns to him.'[3] In consequence, even vermin – rats, for instance – were deemed as divine as human beings. Satan, too, was regarded as an emanation from and a manifestation of God. The Brethren of the Free Spirit contemptuously repudiated Church ritual and the sacraments. 'As the soul thus reverts to God after death, there is neither purgatory nor hell, and all external cult is useless.'[4] Instead, the Brethren spoke of the 'divine internal light', for which they invented the term 'illuminism'.[5] Not surprisingly, perhaps, they were widely accused of devil worship and satanistic practices. They were also accused of sexual licence and abandon – of what later generations would come to call 'free love'. The Inquisition's persecution of them was particularly ferocious.

Among the numerous others to suffer at the Inquisition's hands, it is worth noting Jan Hus in Bohemia. Hus was a member of the faculty at the University of Prague and, from 1401, Dean of Philosophy. At this time, the Church owned 50 per cent of all land in the Kingdom of Bohemia. Like Wycliffe in England, Hus demanded a redistribution of Church property, and insisted on other ecclesiastical reforms as well. He also opposed, bitterly and vociferously, the sale of indulgences – the practice which, a century later, was to elicit such indignation from Martin Luther. At the Council of Constance in 1415, Hus was convicted of heresy for his outspokenness and burned at the stake.

The Destruction of the Knights Templar

In 1304, Pope Benedict XI had died. In the summer of the following year, the King of France, Philippe IV or Philippe le Bel, contrived to install his own candidate, Bertrand de Goth, Archbishop of Bordeaux, on the throne of Saint Peter. The new pontiff took the name of Clement V and proceeded to act as the French monarch's abjectly docile puppet. That, however, did not satisfy Philippe's ambition and compulsive need to control. To consolidate his authority further, he proceeded to kidnap the entire Papacy in 1309 and move it from Rome to Avignon. It was to remain at Avignon for nearly three-quarters of a century, and all seven Popes who presided over it during those years were French. When Gregory XI finally returned to Rome in 1377, the French cardinals elected another Pope, subsequently designated 'Antipope', who remained at Avignon. The 'Great Schism' of 1378 – the conflict between rival Popes, or between Popes and Antipopes – was not to be resolved until 1417.

At the very beginning of the Avignon 'Captivity', when Clement V was first installed as pontiff, the Inquisition faced an entirely new kind of challenge. In the past, it had addressed itself to the ferreting out of heretics. Now, it was to find itself pitted against the single most powerful institution in Christendom at the time, the Knights Templar.

The Templars had originally been established in the Holy Land at the beginning of the twelfth century, shortly after the capture of Jerusalem in the First Crusade. By 1300, they had come to constitute a vast international corporation – a network and a virtual empire second in wealth and influence only to the Papacy itself. If they had consisted initially of fighting men, they now included an even larger number of administrators,

47

bureaucrats, workers and support staff. The Order owned immense estates across the whole of the Christian world – not just in the sphere of Rome's spiritual authority, but also in that of the Greek Orthodox Church of Constantinople. On these estates, the Order's personnel produced timber, farmed, bred horses, raised cattle and sheep. The Order owned ships, too, which trafficked in wool and other commodities, as well as transporting pilgrims and crusaders to and from the Holy Land.

The Templars commanded the most advanced military technology of the era. Their military resources, in expertise, in matériel and in trained manpower, exceeded those of any other European institution. They were also the chief bankers of Europe, adept at the transfer of funds throughout Christendom and complicated financial transactions on behalf of monarchs, ecclesiastics, nobles and merchants. And they were widely respected diplomats, able to act independently of warring factions. Their embassies dealt not only with Catholic potentates, but with the Byzantine Church as well, and with military, political and religious representatives of Islam.

Given their status, it was hardly surprising that the Templars should inspire increasing jealousy and suspicion; and their haughtiness, their high-handed arrogance and lofty complacency elicited further hostility. But there were more serious grounds for antipathy as well, at least so far as the Church was concerned. As early as the beginning of the thirteenth century, at the start of the Albigensian Crusade, Pope Innocent III had criticised the Order, citing allegations of excess and even of apostasy. Among other suspect practices, the Templars welcomed into their ranks excommunicated knights who, in consequence, could receive the burial in consecrated soil that would otherwise have been denied them. The Templars were also notorious for their disrespectful treatment of Papal legates.

They displayed an un-Christian tolerance towards Muslims and Jews. And during the Albigensian Crusade, they provided a refuge in their Order for a substantial number of known Cathars. Indeed, certain of their Grand Masters and regional Masters came from prominent Cathar families.[6]

By the beginning of the fourteenth century, King Philippe IV of France had abundant reasons for disliking the Order of the Temple. He also coveted their wealth, his own fiscal needs being constantly acute. In 1291, he had ordered the arrest of all Italian merchants and bankers in France, whose property he had expropriated. In 1306, he had driven all Jews from his kingdom and confiscated their property as well. It was probably inevitable that Philippe should turn his attention to the Templars as a fresh source of revenue.

But Philippe had reason to fear the Templars, too. Since the loss of the Holy Land in 1291, the Order had been effectively dispossessed, lacking any permanent base or headquarters. For a time, they had settled on Cyprus; but the island proved too small for their grandiose ambitions. They envied the Teutonic Knights, their kindred Order, who had established a virtually independent principality in Prussia and on the Baltic, far to the northeast, well beyond the reach of any enforceable Papal authority. The Templars dreamed of creating a similar principality for themselves, but closer to the hub of European activity. Their designs focused on the Languedoc, still in a devastated condition after the Albigensian Crusade.[7] The prospect of an autonomous, self-contained and self-sufficient Templar state in his own backyard cannot have allowed the French king to sleep very peacefully.

Philippe thus had a number of plausible excuses, and even a few ostensibly valid reasons, for moving against the Templars – and doing so in a manner that would simultaneously neutralise them as a threat and permit him to seize their wealth. It helped, of course, to have a Pope in his pocket. It also helped to have the Inquisitor for France, Guillaume de Paris, as personal confessor and close friend. There was obviously ample latitude for collusion – and for Philippe to proceed with a semblance of unimpugnable legality.

Some time earlier, one of Philippe's ministers had been collecting and collating evidence against the Templars, which was kept under Dominican guard, at Corbeil. From this evidence, it became apparent that the most convenient charge to bring against the Order would be heresy – a charge which may not have been wholly without foundation. On 14 September 1307, letters were accordingly dispatched to royal officials across France, instructing them to arrest, on Friday the 13th of October following, all Templars within their jurisdiction. Personnel of the Order were to be kept under strict guard in solitary confinement, then brought one by one before the Inquisition's commissioners. Each was to have the articles of accusation formally read to him; and each was promised pardon if he confessed to the charges and returned to the bosom of the Church. Should a Templar refuse to confess, he would be sent as promptly as possible to the king. In the meantime, all the Order's property was to be sequestrated and comprehensive inventories of all holdings and possessions were to be compiled. Although issuing from the monarch, these instructions were officially promulgated under the authority of the Inquisitor. Philippe could thus claim to be acting entirely at the Inquisition's behest and deny any personal interest in the matter. To reinforce the charade, the Inquisitor himself, Guillaume de Paris, wrote to his minions throughout the kingdom, listing the crimes of which the Templars were accused and outlining instructions for their interrogation.

During the ensuing months, Inquisitors across France were kept conscientiously busy interrogating hundreds of Templars. A substantial number of victims died in the process – thirty-six in Paris alone, another twenty-five at Sens. But most of the Templars arrested in France were either very young and inexperienced, or elderly. The majority of the fighting men, apparently tipped off by some advance warning, managed to escape. And of the Order's alleged 'treasure', which Philippe had hoped to expropriate, nothing was ever found. Either it had never actually existed, or it was smuggled off to safety in time.

There followed seven years of interrogation, torture and execution, punctuated by trials and retractions of confessions. In 1310, nearly 600 French Templars threatened to retract their confessions and defend their Order to the Pope. Some seventy-five of them were burned by the Inquisition as relapsed heretics. At last, the Order of the Temple was officially dissolved by the Pope; and on 19 March 1314, two of the Order's highest dignitaries – Jacques de Molay, the Grand Master, and Geoffroi de Charnay, his immediate subordinate – were roasted to death over a slow fire on an island in the Seine.

In the years preceding this grisly denouement, action against the Templars was most assiduous in domains where the Inquisition's writ ran most effectively – in France, in Italy, in certain parts of Austria and Germany. Elsewhere persecution of the Order was a rather more desultory affair. In England, for example, where the Inquisition had never previously operated, there was no one to undertake the persecution. Philippe accordingly wrote to his son-in-law, the newly crowned Edward II, and urged him to proceed against the Templars. The English king was shocked by the exhortation – so shocked indeed that he wrote to the monarchs of Portugal, Castile, Aragón and Sicily, encouraging them to ignore the pressure Philippe was bringing to bear on them. Edward asked his fellow rulers to

> turn a deaf ear to the slanders of ill-natured men, who are animated, as we believe, not with the zeal of rectitude, but with a spirit of cupidity and envy.[8]

Subjected to relentless pestering from Philippe, Edward at last relented and, in January 1308, performed the token gesture of arresting ten Templars. There was no serious effort to keep them under guard. On the contrary, they were allowed to wander about in secular apparel, coming and going as they pleased from the castles in which they were supposed to be imprisoned.

Philippe, needless to say, was unhappy. In mid-September 1309, nearly two years after the initial arrests in France, the Inquisition first set foot in England – with the specific objective of prosecuting the Templars. The welcome the Inquisitors received was less than enthusiastic. Their fun was further spoiled when Edward forbade them to employ torture, the one means whereby they might hope to extort the confessions they desired. Aggrieved, the Inquisitors complained to the French king and the Pope. Under pressure from these two sources Edward, in December, reluctantly agreed to sanction 'limited' torture; but the Templars' jailers showed no taste for it whatever, and the Inquisitors continued to feel thwarted.

In their frustration, the Inquisitors proposed alternatives. Perhaps the Templars could be gradually deprived of food until they were subsisting entirely on water. Or perhaps they could be transferred to France, where torture might be properly applied by men with the expertise and the zest for it. Edward continued to be obstructive. At last, in mid 1310, under renewed pressure from the Pope, he grudgingly authorised at least some torture of the requisite intensity to be employed.

In the end, however, less than a hundred Templars were arrested in England and only three confessions were obtained. The three self-acknowledged culprits were not burned. Instead, they were obliged to make a public confession of their 'sins', after which they were absolved by the Church and packed off to a monastery. No other charges were deemed proved against the Templars in England. When the Order was dissolved, those who remained in prison were dispersed to various monasteries – with pensions to support them for the remainder of their days. By that time, a number of English Templars, like many from France before them, had escaped to Scotland.[9] Scotland at the time lay under a Papal interdict, and her king, Robert the Bruce, had been excommunicated. In consequence, Papal writ did not run in the country; and fugitive knights could expect to find there a congenial refuge.

Attacks on the Franciscans

When the Inquisition was called on to act against the Templars, it had already acquired experience in contending with other official Christian institutions. For the better part of the previous century, it had been engaged in an ongoing dispute, a virtual running feud, with the Order that constituted the Dominicans' chief rival for authority and influence. This Order was the Franciscans.

The man later canonised as Saint Francis was born around 1181, the son of a rich cloth merchant of Assisi. If Dominic was a fanatic from the moment he appeared on the stage of history, Francis conformed to a different, though equally familiar, pattern. Like Saint Augustine, Francis spent his youth as a libertine and profligate. Even the most reverential accounts refer coyly to him having done all the things a young man of the time customarily did, and the word 'dissipated' occurs more than once.

Until the age of twenty, Francis worked in the family business. In 1202, he became a soldier, fighting in one of the minor campaigns Assisi was waging against her neighbours. He was captured and spent some months in prison. According to some sources, he suffered a bout of serious illness around this period. There are fragments of evidence to suggest that this illness either was or coincided with some sort of nervous or mental breakdown.

In any case, Francis returned to Assisi disenchanted with his former worldliness. He embarked on a pilgrimage to Rome and discovered in the process a personal exhilaration in poverty. On returning to Assisi, he adopted a lifestyle of austerity and simplicity, caring for beggars and helping to restore a derelict church. He financed the restoration by pilfering some of his father's goods and selling them, together with the horse on which he had carried them off. His father peremptorily disowned him.

All of this was but a prelude to Francis' conversion. The conversion occurred one morning in 1208, as Francis was listening to a biblical text being read in a church near Assisi. The words he heard seem to have resonated for him as a personal call. Immediately thereafter, he discarded his shoes, donned an ascetic dark robe and embarked on a peripatetic life of preaching. As followers began to attend and accompany him, he drew up a rule for his embryonic organisation. According to one clause:

> The brethren shall appropriate to themselves nothing, neither house, nor place . . . but shall live in the world as strangers and pilgrims, and shall go confidently after alms.[10]

Francis and Dominic were almost exactly contemporary. But while Dominic sought power, Francis sought to divest himself of all power. While Dominic sought external adversaries against whom to pit himself, Francis – in a manner much more in keeping with traditional Christian teaching – contended against supposed vice and temptation within himself. Like certain of the heretical sectarians, Francis endeavoured to live in a fashion worthy of that ascribed to Jesus and the 'first Christians'. Had he lived in the south of France, or had the Dominicans not been preoccupied with the pursuit of Cathars there, he himself would very likely have been condemned as a heretic. He and Dominic together reflect two conflicting, diametrically opposed and incipiently schizophrenic aspects of the medieval Church.

In 1209, just as the Albigensian Crusade was gaining bloody momentum, Pope Innocent III approved the rule Francis had drawn up, and the Franciscan Order was established. He and his associates took the designation of 'friars minor'. Three years later, in 1212, the poor Clares, a Franciscan organisation for women, was founded by a member of the Assisi nobility, a lady subsequently canonised as Saint Clare. Francis, in the meantime, began to preach further afield. He wandered through eastern Europe. He then embarked on crusade and, in 1219, was present in Egypt at the siege and capture of the Nile Delta port of Damietta.

So poor and ragged were the early Franciscans that overzeal-ous Dominican Inquisitors sometimes mistook them for Cathars or Waldensians. As a result of one such misapprehension, for example, five of them were executed in Spain. Like the early Dominicans, the early Franciscans were sworn to poverty and forbidden to own property, being forced to subsist entirely by begging. Unlike the Dominicans, however, the Franciscans were committed to manual labour. They were also denied some of the consolations afforded to their rivals. Most Franciscans initially were uneducated, for instance, and thus precluded from the intellectual excitement and distraction of scholarship and theological study. And while the Dominicans could satisfy whatever sadistic or other perverse desires they might harbour by persecuting heretics, the Franciscans were denied this as well.

Not surprisingly, the arduousness of Franciscan discipline proved too much for many members of the Order and many prospective postulants. Even before his death in 1226, the institution created by Francis had begun to mutate. While he was away in eastern Europe and then in Egypt, his stand-in as General of the Order had emerged as a shrewd and skilful politician, extending the influence of the Franciscans and relaxing the strictness of their rule. They continued to engage in manual labour and preaching, as well as running hospitals and tending lepers, but they also now began to accumulate wealth. According to one historian:

> As the Order spread it was not in human nature to reject the wealth which came pouring in upon it from all sides, and ingenious dialectics were resorted to to reconcile its ample possessions with the absolute rejection of property prescribed by the Rule.[11]

When Francis returned from his travels, he made no attempt to regain control, no attempt to resume his position as General. Disowning all interest in politics, organisation and hierarchy, he continued to pursue his simple and untrammelled lifestyle; and the Order, while revering him as its father, proceeded to evolve under other auspices. At its first General Chapter in 1221, five years before Francis' death, it included more than 3,000 brethren, a cardinal and a number of bishops among them.

By 1256, it was to possess forty-nine separate establishments in England alone, with 1,242 friars. During the latter part of the thirteenth century, one of them was to be the famous Roger Bacon.

Within half a century of Francis' death, his Order had become as comfortable and as wealthy as any other clerical institution. It had also in its own way begun to discover the exhilarating intoxication of power. And, as an inevitable corollary, it had become increasingly prone to corruption. In 1257, the man subsequently canonised as Saint Bonaventure was elected General of the Order. One of his first acts was to send a circular letter to all provincial heads, deploring the extent to which worldliness and greed had brought the Franciscans into disrepute. Brethren had fallen increasingly, he complained, into idleness and vice, had indulged in shameful extravagance, had built disgracefully opulent palaces, had extorted excessive legacies and burial fees. Ten years later, nothing had changed, and Bonaventure repeated his indictment, this time even more bluntly: 'It is a foul and profane lie to assert . . . absolute poverty and then refuse to submit to the lack of anything; to beg abroad like a pauper and to roll in wealth at home.'[12]

If the Franciscans, by the end of the thirteenth century, had succumbed to worldliness and corruption, they had also become riven by schisms. Many members of the Order – 'mystical' or 'spiritual' or 'purist' Franciscans – endeavoured to remain loyal to the tenets of their founder. Not surprisingly, their uncompromising position soon led them into conflict with the Dominican-run Inquisition, and more than a few were to incur a charge of heresy. In 1282, for example, the accusation was levelled against Pierre Jean Olivi, the leader of the 'purist' Franciscans in the Languedoc; and though he was subsequently exonerated, his works remained censored.

By the beginning of the fourteenth century, the 'purist' Franciscans were increasingly at odds with the 'mainstream' of their own Order, with the Dominican Inquisition and with the Pope. In 1317, Pope John XXII ruled definitively against the 'purists'. On pain of excommunication, they were commanded to submit to his authority and that of the Order's mainstream. Many refused and turned schismatic, under the name of Fraticelli. In 1318, four Fraticelli brethren were burned by the Inquisition as heretics.

In 1322, a General Chapter of the entire Franciscan Order passed a resolution implicitly sympathetic to the Fraticelli. It stated that Jesus and his disciples had been poor, had renounced personal possessions and repudiated worldliness – and they constituted the ideal model of Christian virtue. Such an assertion entailed a flagrant defiance of the Inquisition, which had only recently issued a ruling attempting to justify ecclesiastical wealth. A reaction was swiftly forthcoming. A year later, in 1323, the Pope denounced the Franciscans' resolution as heresy. The Franciscans as a whole were outraged, many of them accused the Pope himself of heresy and a number defected to the Fraticelli. As friction increased, the General of the Order himself joined the defecting schismatics. For the following two centuries, relations between the Inquisition and the Franciscans – both 'mainstream' and schismatic – were to remain acrimonious. As late as the 1520s, mystically inclined Franciscans continued to be condemned and tried for heresy.

The feud between Franciscans and Dominicans sometimes attained unprecedented dimensions of sublime folly, as well as of infantile literalism and dogmatism. Thus, for example, in 1351, a Franciscan dignitary of Barcelona addressed himself to the blood shed by Jesus immediately before and during the Crucifixion. This blood, according to the Franciscan, had fallen to the earth and had lost its divinity by virtue of its separateness from Jesus's body. It had not, therefore, ascended to heaven when Jesus himself did, but had soaked into the soil.

'The question,' as one historian has observed, 'was a novel one and a trifle difficult of demonstration.'[13] But the Franciscan's assertions deeply outraged Nicholas Roselli, the Dominican Inquisitor of Barcelona, who resented the Franciscans anyway and now felt he possessed fresh grounds for grievance. Welcoming an opportunity to attack the rival Order, he dispatched a detailed account of the matter to the Pope.

The Pope, too, was outraged at the Franciscan's assertions. He promptly convened a conference of theologians to investigate the question of Jesus's shed blood. The conference shared the indignation of Father Roselli and the Pope. The Franciscan's assertions were officially condemned. Instructions were issued to all Inquisitors – anyone who further promulgated such scandalous assertions was to be arrested. The Franciscan who had first enunciated the thesis was compelled publicly to withdraw it.

The matter did not end there, however. Feeling themselves under attack, the Franciscans, though prohibited from any public discussion of Jesus's shed blood, continued to argue their case in private. According to one commentator:

> The Franciscans argued, with provoking reasonableness, that the blood of Christ might well be believed to remain on earth, seeing that the foreskin severed in the Circumcision was preserved in the Lateran Church and reverenced as a relic under the very eyes of pope and cardinal, and that portions of the blood and water which flowed in the Crucifixion were exhibited to the faithful at Mantua, Bruges, and elsewhere.[14]

For the better part of the ensuing century, the dispute quietly rumbled on. Then, in 1448, nearly one hundred years later, a Franciscan professor at the University of Paris brought the problem to the attention of the Faculty of Theology. Renewed discussion resulted in the formation of a board of theologians to investigate the prickly subject further. They spent some years in debate. At last, with great solemnity, they issued their conclusion. It was not contrary to the Church's teachings, they stated, to believe in the original Franciscan thesis – that the blood shed by Jesus during his final days had indeed remained on the earth.

Exhilarated by this victory in their own Hundred Years' War, the Franciscans allowed themselves a measure of triumphalism and grew more audacious. In a sermon at Brescia in 1462, a prominent Franciscan openly endorsed the position of his predecessor. Controversy erupted anew. Curbing his indignation, the local Dominican Inquisitor wrote a politely incredulous letter to the Franciscan. He could not believe, he stated, quietly aghast, that such statements had actually been made. The reports he had received must somehow have misconstrued things. Would the Franciscan kindly assure him that this was indeed the case? When the Franciscan, equally politely, repeated the statements, he was summoned to appear before the Inquisitor the following day.

Alarmed by the prospect of a renewed public spat between Dominicans and Franciscans, the local bishop intervened. He contrived to have the summons withdrawn, but only with the understanding that the matter would be referred to the personal attention of the Pope. In the meantime, Dominicans across the whole of Christendom began fulminating from their pulpits against the Franciscan 'heresy'. Having been kept more or less discreetly quiet for the greater part of a century, the squabble now exploded dramatically before the eyes of a bewildered and bemused populace.

Not wishing to antagonise either Order, the Pope hastened to convene yet another conference to examine the now increasingly pestilential question. He seems to have hoped it would be defused simply by bureaucratic delays and the plodding of administrative machinery. To his discomfiture, participants in the conference exhibited greater eagerness than anticipated for polemical combat.

> Each side selected three champions, and for three days, in the presence of the pope and sacred college, they argued the point with such ardent vehemence that, in spite of the bitter winter weather, they were bathed in sweat.[15]

Neither faction, however, could adduce from the New Testament a single piece of evidence pertaining to the matter in dispute – which remained in consequence unresolved. Across Christendom, controversy between Dominicans and Franciscans continued.

A year later, at the beginning of August 1464, driven to unpontifical impatience and exasperation, the Pope published a Bull. According to this Bull, all discussion of the awkward subject was officially prohibited until it was definitively settled by a pronouncement from the Holy See. As things transpired, the Holy See had no opportunity to issue any such pronouncement, because the Pope died eight days later. The cardinals who then addressed themselves to the matter again failed to reach any agreement. The new Pope contrived to have further disputation indefinitely postponed. As far as the authors of this book are aware, the question of whether or not Jesus's shed blood ascended to heaven remains unsettled to this day, and still hangs unanswered over the Papacy.

4

The Spanish Inquisition

I t is with Spain that the Inquisition is most usually associated. In fact, however, the Inquisition did not become dramatically active in Spain until relatively late. When it did do so, moreover, it was at least in certain respects a very different institution from the Inquisition elsewhere. Yet popular images are not altogether wrong. It was certainly in Spain that the Inquisition attained new dimensions of bigotry, nastiness and terror.

During the thirteenth century, it must be remembered, Spain was not a unified country. Much of the Iberian Peninsula was still controlled by Muslim potentates. And even the Christian part of the peninsula was divided between several autonomous and not always compatible kingdoms. Among the Christian principalities comprising the Iberian Peninsula, the Inquisition was first established in 1238, but only in Aragón. Initially, it operated in a haphazard, inefficient and desultory fashion; and by the beginning of the fifteenth century, it was virtually dormant. In other domains – in Castile, for example, in León and in Portugal – the Inquisition did not even appear until 1376, a full century and a half after its inception in France.

In 1474, the woman known to history as Isabella of Castile ascended the throne of her kingdom. Five years later, her husband, Ferdinand, became King of Aragón. From 1479 on, therefore, they presided as joint rulers of what was in effect a single unified kingdom. During the years that followed, they embarked on a programme of hugely ambitious scope and scale. They undertook to extirpate the last Moorish or Islamic enclaves from their domains – an enterprise that culminated in the capture of Granada in 1492. And they embarked on a ruthless agenda of 'purification' that anticipated National Socialist policies of the twentieth century and the practice of 'ethnic cleansing' implemented in the Balkans during the 1990s. Under Ferdinand and Isabella, Spain was not just to be united. It was also simultaneously to be definitively 'purged' of both Islam and Judaism, as well as of paganism and Christian heresies. To this end, the Spanish monarchs established their own Inquisition in 1478.

In its mechanics and operations – 'in all aspects of arrest, trial, procedure, confiscations, recruitment of personnel'[1] – the Spanish Inquisition emulated the Inquisition elsewhere. Unlike the latter, however, the Spanish Inquisition was not an instrument of the Papacy. On the contrary, it was directly accountable to Ferdinand and Isabella. Because the domains of the Spanish monarchs comprised a species of theocracy with Church and State working in tandem, the Spanish Inquisition was as much an adjunct of the Crown as it was of the Church. It functioned as an instrument not only of ecclesiastical orthodoxy, but of royal policy as well. Addressing the newly installed Inquisitors of Aragón, Ferdinand said to them:

> Although you and the others enjoy the title of inquisitor, it is I and the queen who have appointed you, and without our support you can do very little.[2]

Torquemada

On 1 November 1478, a Bull of Pope Sixtus IV authorised the creation of an Inquisition unique to Spain. Two or perhaps three priests over the age of forty were to be appointed as Inquisitors. The right to appoint and dismiss them was entrusted not to the Dominicans or any other Papal institution, but to the Spanish monarchs. On 27 September 1480, they appointed two Dominicans as Inquisitors. The Inquisitors began their work in the south, adjacent to the still Moorish Kingdom of Granada. The first *auto de fe* was conducted on 6 February 1481, and six individuals were burned alive at the stake. In Seville alone, by the beginning of November, the flames had claimed another 288 victims, while seventy-nine had been sentenced to life imprisonment.

Four months later, in February 1482, the Pope authorised the appointment of another seven Dominicans as Inquisitors. One of them, the prior of a monastery in Segovia, was to pass into history as the very embodiment of the Spanish Inquisition at its most terrifying – Tomás de Torquemada. In the three years following Torquemada's appointment, tribunals of the Inquisition were established in four other locations. By 1492, tribunals were operating in eight major cities.

By this time, too, the Spanish Inquisition was already running amok. Complaints had begun as early as ten years before, within a few months of Torquemada's appointment. In April 1482, responding to aggrieved letters from Spanish bishops, the Pope had issued a Bull deploring the fact that

> many true and faithful Christians, on the testimony of enemies, rivals, slaves . . . have without any legitimate proof been thrust into secular prisons, tortured and con-

demned . . . deprived of their goods and property and handed over to the secular arm to be executed . . . causing disgust to many.[3]

In the same document, the Pope concluded:

The Inquisition has for some time been moved not by zeal for the faith and the salvation of souls but by lust for wealth.[4]

In accordance with this conclusion, all powers entrusted to the Inquisition were revoked, and the Pope demanded that Inquisitors be placed under the control of local bishops. Such measures were, of course, a flagrant challenge to the monarchy, and King Ferdinand was predictably outraged. Pretending to doubt whether the Bull had actually been composed by the Pope, he sent a disingenuous letter back to the pontiff. The missive ended with an explicit threat: 'Take care therefore not to let the matter go further . . . and entrust us with the care of this question.'[5]

Confronted by such defiance, the Pope capitulated completely. On 17 October 1483, a fresh Bull established a council, the *Consejo de la Suprema y General Inquisición*, to function as the Inquisition's ultimate authority. To preside over this council, *la Suprema*, the new office of Inquisitor-General was created. Its first incumbent was Torquemada. All the Inquisition's tribunals throughout Christian Spain were now effectively gathered into the jurisdiction of one centralised administration, with Torquemada at its head.

In the subsequent fifteen years up to his death in 1498, Torquemada wielded a power and influence rivalling that of Ferdinand and Isabella themselves. So far as the Inquisition was concerned, according to one historian, 'he developed the nascent institution with unwearied assiduity'.[6] He did so in a manner 'full of pitiless zeal', and with 'ruthless fanaticism'. His devotion to his role impelled him to decline the proffered bishopric of Seville, and he never discarded the austere garb of a Dominican in favour of fashionable sartorial splendour. He was also rigorously vegetarian. But he kept for himself substantial sums of confiscated wealth, resided in extravagant palaces and travelled with a retinue calculated both to impress and intimidate – fifty mounted guards and another 250 armed men. That did not altogether dispel his paranoia. When he dined, he invariably kept with him 'the horn of a unicorn', which supposedly served to protect him against poison – though there is no indication of how this chimerical talisman worked or what exactly its owner did with it. In other respects he was clearly an intelligent man, one of the supreme machiavels of his age, endowed with profound psychological insight and an aptitude for devious statecraft. In *The Brothers Karamazov*, the Grand Inquisitor is accorded no personal name. There can be little doubt, however, that Dostoevsky had Torquemada in mind as a prototype. And indeed, Dostoevsky's depiction of the Grand Inquisitor is probably as accurate a portrait of Torquemada as any historian's or biographer's. It is certainly not difficult to imagine Torquemada knowingly sending Jesus to the stake for the sake of the Inquisition and the Church.

Under Torquemada's uncompromising auspices, the work of the Spanish Inquisition proceeded with renewed energy. On 23 February 1484, thirty victims were burned alive simultaneously in Ciudad Réal. Between 1485 and 1501, 250 were burned in Toledo. In Barcelona in 1491, three were executed and another 220 condemned to death in their absence. In Valladolid in 1492, thirty-two were immolated at once. The inventory of atrocity goes on, and would run to pages. At one point, the city dignitaries of 'Barcelona wrote to King Ferdinand: 'We are all aghast at the news we receive of the executions and proceedings that they say are taking place in Castile.'[7] In September 1485, the Inquisitor of Saragossa was murdered while at prayer before the high altar in the cathedral; but this only provoked a fresh wave of executions in reprisals. The Inquisition did not traffic only in death, however. In 1499, a year after Torquemada died, the Inquisitor of Córdoba was convicted of extortion and fraud. His successor blithely proceeded to follow in his footsteps, arresting anyone wealthy – even the members of pious Christian families – in order to confiscate and appropriate their property.

The Procedures of the Inquisition

In its methodology and techniques, the Spanish Inquisition emulated the original Papal Inquisition of the thirteenth century. If anything, it implemented its methodology and techniques even more stringently – and even more cynically. Among themselves at least Inquisitors curbed their hypocrisy and spoke with a bluntness that made little accommodation for piety – a bluntness quite worthy of Dostoevsky's fictional creation. In 1578, for example, one Inquisitor went on record to his colleagues, declaring 'we must remember that the main purpose of the trial and execution is not to save the soul of the accused but to achieve the public good and put fear into others'.[8]

In pursuit of this goal, the Spanish Inquisition, like its medieval predecessor, would descend on a town or village at regular intervals – in 1517, for example, every four months – though this frequency gradually decreased as Inquisitors grew lazy, comfortable and reluctant to travel. On arriving at a locality, the Inquisitors would present their credentials to the local

ecclesiastical and civic authorities. A day would then be proclaimed on which everyone would be compelled to attend a
special Mass and there hear the Inquisition's 'edict' read in
public. On the appointed day, at the end of the sermon, the
Inquisitor would raise a crucifix. Those in attendance would
be required to raise their right hands, cross themselves and
repeat an oath to support the Inquisition and its servants. After
these preliminaries, the 'edict' was solemnly read. It adumbrated
various heresies, as well as Islam and Judaism, and called forward
all who might be guilty of 'infection'. If they confessed themselves within a stipulated 'period of grace' – generally thirty to
forty days, although, being at the Inquisitors' discretion, it was
often less – they might be accepted back into the Church
without any unduly serious penalties. They would be obliged,
however, to denounce any guilty parties who had not come
forward. Indeed, this was a crucial prerequisite for being allowed
to escape with nothing more severe than a penance.

> To denounce oneself as a heretic was not enough to be
> able to benefit from the terms of the edict. It was also
> necessary to denounce all those accomplices who shared
> the error or had led one into it.[9]

It is easy to see how the psychological mechanism involved
in this process functioned. In Spain as elsewhere, people would
avail themselves of the Inquisition's apparatus to settle old
scores, to exact personal vengeance on neighbours or relatives,
to eliminate rivals in business or commerce. Anyone could
denounce anyone else, and the burden of vindication would
lie with the accused. People began increasingly to fear their
neighbours, their professional associates or competitors, anyone
with whom they might have a grievance, anyone they might
have alienated or antagonised. In order to preempt a denunci-

ation from others, people would often bear false witness against themselves. Not infrequently, whole sections of a community might confess en masse, thus binding themselves with fetters of paranoia and dread to the Inquisition's control.

In the late fifteenth century, when the Inquisition's edict was read for the first time in Mallorca, 337 individuals denounced themselves. In Toledo in 1486, 2,400 did likewise. But people still lived in terror of business rivals, neighbours, even their own relatives. 'Petty denunciations were the rule rather than the exception.'[10] In Castile during the 1480s, upwards of 1,500 victims are said to have been burned at the stake as a result of false testimony, often unable even to determine the source of the accusation against them. Witnesses for the Inquisition's investigations were kept anonymous, and their testimonies were edited for any items that might betray their identities. The Inquisition thus derived its energy and impetus from the very populace it persecuted. Its power stemmed from a blatant exploitation of the weakest and most venal aspects of human nature.

In theory, each case was supposed to be examined by a conclave of theologians – the visiting Inquisitors and at least one local assessor. Only if the evidence were deemed sufficiently valid was the accused supposed to be arrested. In practice, however, many people were arrested even before their cases were assessed. The Inquisition's prisons were crammed with inmates, a substantial number of whom had not yet had any charges brought against them. They might be incarcerated for years, without so much as knowing the transgression of which they were alleged to be culpable.

In the meantime, they and their families would have been stripped of all property, for an arrest was invariably accompanied by the immediate confiscation of all the accused's belongings

– everything from his house down to his pots and pans. And while he languished in prison, still without any charges being brought against him, his possessions would be sold off to pay for his maintenance in captivity. On occasion, he might be eventually released, only to find himself bankrupt or destitute. And there were instances of the children of rich prisoners dying from starvation as a result of their property having been sequestered. Only in 1561 were the rules modified slightly to allow dependants to be supported, at least in part, from the sale of confiscated goods.

Each tribunal of the Inquisition's twenty-one provincial headquarters possessed its own prison, located in its official 'palace'. Inmates were generally kept in solitary confinement in chains, and allowed no contact whatever with the outside world. If they were ever released, they were required to 'take an oath not to reveal anything they had seen or experienced in the cells'.[11] Not surprisingly, many victims went mad in captivity, died or committed suicide if they could. And yet, paradoxically, the Inquisition's prisons were often considered preferable to those of the secular authorities. There were instances of ordinary common criminals voluntarily confessing to heresy, in order to get themselves transferred from a secular prison to one of the Inquisition's.

At the Inquisition's investigation and interrogation sessions, a notary and secretary would always be in attendance, along with the Inquisitors, a representative of the local bishop, a doctor and the torturer himself, who was usually the secular public executioner. Everything would be noted down punctiliously – the questions posed, the accused's answers and his reactions. The Spanish Inquisition, like its medieval precursor, used lofty rhetoric and hypocrisy to mask and justify the unpalatable reality of torture. The Inquisition's instructions of 1561 stipulated that torture should be applied in accord with

> the conscience and will of the appointed judges, following law, reason and good conscience. Inquisitors should take great care that the sentence of torture is justified and follows precedent.[12]

For the Spanish Inquisition, as for its medieval precursor, a confession extracted in the throes of torture was not in itself deemed valid. Inquisitors recognised that an individual subjected to extreme pain could be persuaded to say anything. In consequence, the accused was obliged to confirm and ratify his confession a day later, so that it could be labelled spontaneous and voluntary, offered without duress. Under the Spanish Inquisition, as under its medieval precursor, a victim was only supposed to be tortured once. And like their predecessors elsewhere, Spanish Inquisitors circumvented this restriction by describing the end of each torture session as a mere 'suspension'. It could thus be claimed that a victim was indeed tortured only once, even if that 'single' instance of torture included a multitude of sessions and suspensions extended over a considerable period of time. And, of course, the victim was deprived of the hope that the end of any given session marked the end of his ordeal.

Whatever sadistic gratification the Inquisitors derived, it must be stressed that their primary objective was less to extract a confession from a single victim than to obtain evidence with which to consolidate control over the populace as a whole. The accused was expected not only to confess his own transgressions, but also to provide evidence, however tenuous, with which to incriminate others. It is hardly surprising that individuals in the anguish of torture would volunteer any name that came to mind – or any name their tormentors wished to hear.

In 1518, *la Suprema*, the governing council of the Spanish Inquisition, decided that torture should not be automatic or routine. In theory at least, its application was to be determined in each specific case by a vote of the presiding local tribunal. In practice, this made little difference, since each local tribunal could vote to apply torture automatically and routinely in every case it tried. When a tribunal had voted to apply torture, the accused would be brought into an audience chamber, with Inquisitors and local ecclesiastical representatives in attendance. The result of the vote would be announced, and the accused would be given another chance to confess. If he still refused to do so, the full formal sentence of torture would be read out.

> It recited that, in view of the suspicions arising against him from the evidence, they condemned him to be tortured for such length of time as they should see fit, in order that he might tell the truth . . . protesting that, if in the torture he should die or suffer effusion of blood or mutilation, it should not be attributed to them, but to him for not telling the truth.[13]

In its attenuation – in the time it took to perform – the ritual would constitute a psychological torture of its own. This would be intensified at each stage of the subsequent proceedings by further delays, further periods of waiting. Anticipation of agony would sometimes produce results as effectively as agony itself.

Inquisitors in Spain, like their medieval precursors, endeavoured to avoid deliberate shedding of blood, and were forbidden to perform executions themselves. Methods of torture were devised to accommodate the prevailing restrictions. In Spain, three were particularly favoured. There was the *toca*, or water torture, whereby water was forced down a victim's throat. There was the *potro*, wherein the victim was bound to a rack by tight cords which could be tightened further by the torturer. And there was the *garrucha*, or pulley, the Spanish version of the Italian strappado. In this procedure, the victim's hands would be tied behind his back, after which he would be hung by his wrists from a pulley in the ceiling with weights fastened to his feet. He would be raised very slowly so as to maximise pain, then dropped a few feet with an abruptness and violence that dislocated his limbs. Not surprisingly, many victims were left permanently maimed, or with their health chronically impaired. It was certainly not unusual for death to occur. If it did, it was deemed to have done so 'incidentally', as an unfortunate concomitant or by-product of torture, rather than as a direct consequence of it.

Later in the career of the Spanish Inquisition, other techniques came into use. A victim might be tied to a rack, for instance, with bindings that were progressively tightened until they cut through to the bone. And there were numerous additional refinements, too obscene to be transcribed. Anything the Inquisitors' depraved imaginations could devise was eventually sanctioned. A regulation of 1561 states that

> in view of the difference in bodily and mental strength among men . . . no certain rule can be given, but it must be left to the discretion of judges, to be governed by law, reason and conscience.[14]

Not surprisingly, there were sometimes great difficulties in finding individuals prepared to enact the Inquisitors' whims and administer the torture. Whenever possible, the municipality's public executioner would be dragooned into the task. In the late seventeenth century, he was paid four ducats for every session of torture – the equivalent of half an ounce of gold, worth around £90 in today's currency. The work he performed for this fee, needless to say, did nothing to endear him to his neighbours. In consequence, he would usually want to conceal his identity. An edict of 1524 forbade the torturer to wear a mask or wrap himself in a sheet. Subsequently, as a compromise, a hood and a change of garments were allowed. By the seventeenth century, complete disguises including masks were again permitted the torturer, 'if it were thought best that he should not be recognised'.[15]

The death penalty itself was reserved primarily for unrepentant heretics, and for those who had relapsed after a nominal conversion to Catholicism. As will be seen shortly, it was reserved most frequently for Jews – for practising Jews and for those suspected of reverting to their faith after having ostensibly embraced the Cross. Like its medieval precursor, the Spanish Inquisition would hand the condemned man over to the secular authorities for execution. If he repented during his last moments at the stake, he would be 'mercifully' strangled before the flames were lit. If he failed to repent, he would be burned alive.

Anti-Semitism and the Inquisition

In methodology, techniques and procedures, the Spanish Inquisition closely copied its medieval precursor. It differed in being accountable not to the Papacy, but directly to the Spanish Crown. It differed in another important respect as well. The primary targets of the medieval Inquisition in France and Italy had been Christian heretics, such as the Cathars, Waldensians and Fraticelli, or putative heretics, such as the Knights Templar. The primary target of the Spanish Inquisition was to be the

Iberian Peninsula's Judaic population. In the virulence and systematic nature of its anti-Semitic activities, the Inquisition in Spain was to anticipate the pathology of twentieth-century Nazism.

In the middle of the fourteenth century, more than a hundred years before the creation of the Spanish Inquisition, Castile had been riven by civil war. Both factions had sought a scapegoat and found one in the Judaic community – particularly numerous in Spain, owing to the laudable tolerance of the earlier Islamic regimes. Pogroms had ensued, and the flames had been further fanned by zealous Christian preachers. The violence had intensified until it attained a climax in 1391, with the murder of hundreds, perhaps thousands, of Jews.

During the last decade of the fourteenth century, many Jewish families in Spain, intimidated by the persecution directed against them, had renounced their faith and embraced Christianity. They became known as 'conversos'. In many cases, however, the enforced nature of their conversion was well known; and it was widely assumed that they continued to adhere to their original faith clandestinely. Undoubtedly, a substantial number of them did; but most seem simply to have become lukewarm Christians to the same extent that they had previously been lukewarm Jews. In any case, and whatever the sincerity of their Catholicism, 'converso' families invariably provoked suspicion and mistrust, and continued to be targeted by anti-Semites. The greatest antipathy was reserved for so-called 'Judaisers' – 'conversos' suspected of still practising Judaism in secret, or, even worse, leading Christianised Jews back to Judaism.

Despite the prejudice around them, many 'converso' families prospered. During the years that followed, a number of them were to rise to prominence in the royal administration, in the civic bureaucracy, even in the Church. In 1390, for example, the rabbi of Burgos converted to Catholicism. He ended his life as Bishop of Burgos, Papal legate and tutor to a prince of the blood. He was not alone. In some of the major cities, the administration was dominated by prominent 'converso' families. At the very time the Spanish Inquisition was formed, King Ferdinand's treasurer was 'converso' in his background. In Aragón, the five highest administrative posts in the kingdom were occupied by 'conversos'. In Castile, there were at least four 'converso' bishops. Three of Queen Isabella's secretaries were 'conversos', as was the official court chronicler. One of Torquemada's own uncles was a 'converso'. Even Santa Teresa, so beloved subsequently for her pathological Catholicism, was not 'untainted'. In 1485, her grandfather was compelled to perform penance for having maintained Judaic practices – an indication that the future saint herself was of Judaic ancestry.

On the whole, 'conversos' and their families tended to be among the best educated people in Spain. As they rose in prominence, they also tended to become some of the wealthiest. Perhaps inevitably, their social and economic status provoked envy and resentment among their neighbours. It was also to exacerbate the hostility of the Inquisition.

From the moment of its creation, the Spanish Inquisition had cast covetous eyes on Judaic wealth. It also regarded Jews themselves with implacable antipathy, simply because they lay outside its official legal jurisdiction. According to its original brief, the Inquisition was authorised to deal with heretics – that is, with Christians who had deviated from orthodox formulations of the faith. It had no powers, however, over adherents of altogether different religions, such as Jews and Muslims. Judaic and Islamic communities in Spain were large. In consequence, a considerable portion of the population remained exempt from the Inquisition's control; and for an institution that sought to exercise total control, such a situation was deemed intolerable.

The Inquisition's first step was to act against so-called 'Juda-isers'. A 'converso' who returned to Judaism after having embraced Christianity could conveniently be labelled a heretic. By extension, so could anyone who encouraged him in his heresy – and this transgression could be further extended to include, by implication, all Jews. But the Inquisition was still handicapped because it had to produce – or concoct – evidence for each case it sought to prosecute; and this was not always easy to do.

The Inquisition enthusiastically endorsed the virulent anti-Semitism already being promulgated by a notorious preacher, Alonso de Espina, who hated both Jews and 'conversos' alike. Mobilising popular support behind him, Alonso had advocated the complete extirpation of Judaism from Spain – either by expulsion or by extermination. Embracing Alonso's pro-gramme, the Inquisition embarked on its own assiduous anti-Semitic propaganda, using techniques that would be adopted some four and a half centuries later by Josef Goebbels. Outrage-ous accusations would be reiterated and repeated, for example, with the knowledge that they would eventually come to be accepted as valid. Citing the anti-Semitism it had thus contrived to provoke in the populace at large, the Inquisition petitioned the Crown to adopt 'appropriate' measures. The proposal to expel all Jews from Spain stemmed directly from the Inquisition. The text advocating the proposal has been described by one historian as 'a ferocious document' which 'reeks of a virulent anti-Semitism'.[16]

King Ferdinand recognised that persecution of Jews and 'conversos' would inevitably have adverse economic reper-cussions for the country. Neither he nor Queen Isabella, however, could resist the combined pressure of the Inquisition and the popular sentiment it had invoked. In a letter to his most influential nobles and courtiers, the king wrote:

> The Holy Office of the Inquisition, seeing how some Christians are endangered by contact and communication with the Jews, has provided that the Jews be expelled from all our realms and territories, and has persuaded us to give our support and agreement to this . . . we do so despite the great harm to ourselves, seeking and preferring the salvation of our souls above our own profit . . .[17]

On 1 January 1483, the monarchs wrote to appease the Inquisition in Andalucia, announcing that all Jews living in the region were to be expelled. On 12 May 1486, all Jews were driven from large tracts of Aragón. But wholesale expulsion had to be deferred for the moment because money and other forms of support from Jews and 'conversos' were urgently needed for the ongoing campaign against the Muslims, pushed back into their ever-contracting Kingdom of Granada.

There is evidence to suggest a clandestine deal was concluded between Torquemada, representing the Inquisition, and the Spanish Crown. Torquemada appears to have accepted the Crown's procrastination in expelling all Jews from Spain until the Muslim Kingdom of Granada was finally and definitively conquered. In other words, Jews would be left unmolested in certain areas until they and their resources were no longer needed. In the meantime, the Inquisition set about preparing the ground for what was to follow. Thus ensued the notorious case of 'the Holy Child of La Guardia', a trumped-up affair as crass as anything perpetrated in our own century by Hitler or Stalin.

On 14 November 1491, two weeks before the fall of Granada,

five Jews and six 'conversos' were sent to the stake at Ávila. They had been convicted of desecrating the host. They had also been convicted of crucifying a Christian child, whose heart they had allegedly ripped out. The purpose of this gruesome exercise had supposedly been to perform a magical ritual intended to neutralise the power of the Inquisition and to send all Christians 'raving mad to their deaths'. The Inquisition assiduously publicised the case in every city of Castile and Aragón, whipping anti-Semitic frenzy up to a peak.[18]

A fortnight later, Granada capitulated, and the last Islamic enclave in Spain ceased to exist. Three months thereafter, in March of the following year, a royal edict ordered all Jews in Spain to convert or be expelled. Those who did neither became fair game for the Inquisition. As Carlos Fuentes has said, Spain, in 1492, banished sensuality with the Moors, banished intelligence with the Jews and proceeded to go sterile for the next five centuries.

Even before the final expulsion, however, Jews and 'conversos' had fallen prey to the Spanish Inquisition in far greater numbers than had heretics. After 1492, the persecution merely intensified, reinforced by a new semblance of legality and legitimacy. Of all those tried by the Inquisition in Barcelona between 1488 and 1505, 99.3 per cent were Jews or 'conversos'. Jews or 'conversos' made up 91.6 per cent of all cases tried by the Inquisition in Valencia between 1484 and 1530. As one historian observes:

> The tribunal, in other words, was not concerned with heresy in general. It was concerned with only one form of religious deviance: the apparently secret practice of Jewish rites.[19]

The End of the Inquisition

With unabated ferocity, the Spanish Inquisition pursued its work for more than 200 years. In England, the reign of William and Mary was followed by Anne's, then by the Hanoverians'. The country was soon to be integrated with Scotland as the United Kingdom of Great Britain, and then to embark on the 'high civilisation' of the Augustan Age. In France, a zenith of cultural achievement had already been attained under Louis XIV, the 'Sun King', who, though elderly, still presided over his *raffiné* court of Versailles. In Spain, 'the seventeenth century closed with a holocaust of conversos'.[20]

The War of the Spanish Succession (1704–15) confirmed the change of dynasty brought about when, in 1701, the Bourbon Philip V ascended the throne formerly occupied by Habsburgs. There seemed to be a fleeting prospect of enlightenment when the new monarch refused to attend an *auto de fe* conducted in his honour. Shortly thereafter, however, the Inquisition reasserted its stranglehold on Spanish society, and the severity of the previous two centuries was resumed. A new wave of repression occurred in the early 1720s.

For some of the Inquisition's intended victims, there was now at least a refuge of sorts close at hand. In 1704, during the War of the Spanish Succession, a British fleet under Admiral Sir George Rooke had launched one of the first amphibious operations of modern times and captured the stronghold of Gibraltar. In 1713, Spain formally ceded 'the Rock' to Britain – on condition 'that on no account must Jews and Muslims be allowed to live or reside in the said city of Gibraltar'. To the frustration of the Inquisition, no attempt whatever was made to observe the Spanish proviso. The Jewish community on Gibraltar rapidly grew, and, by 1717, possessed its own synagogue.

After 1730, the power and influence of the Spanish Inquisition began perceptibly to decrease. There was no shortage of prospective victims, but Spain could not remain altogether insulated from the tolerance coming to prevail elsewhere in Europe. And the Inquisition's functionaries, as one commentator has observed, 'were becoming indifferent and careless, except in the matter of drawing their salaries'. Between 1740 and 1794, the tribunal sitting at Toledo tried only one case a year on average.

During the French Revolution, the Spanish Inquisition lapsed into virtual inertia, cowed by the alarming anti-clerical developments just beyond the Pyrenees. There were, indeed, grounds for misgiving. In 1808, a French army under Napoleon's subordinate, Marshal Joachim Murat, marched into Spain and occupied the country. The Bourbon dynasty was deposed and Napoleon's brother, Joseph, was installed as king. According to the treaty that ensued, the Catholic religion was to be tolerated like any other. Although disgruntled, the Inquisition fancied itself safe; and on this assumption it endorsed the new regime. Certain Inquisitors, however, proved incapable of curbing the zeal of more than three centuries. With touchingly naive imprudence, they arrested Murat's secretary, a classical scholar and self-proclaimed revolutionary atheist. Murat promptly dispatched troops to release the man by force. On 4 December 1808, Napoleon himself arrived in Madrid. That same day, he issued a decree abolishing the Inquisition and confiscating the whole of its property.

In areas of the country remote from French authority, provincial tribunals continued to operate, defying Napoleon's edict, throughout the Peninsular War (1808–14). Their support, however, was haemorrhaging away. They were opposed not only by the Napoleonic regime, but also by the British army under the future Duke of Wellington, then engaged in wresting the Iberian Peninsula back from Imperial France. Even the Spanish forces allied with Wellington's army – Spanish royalists and Catholics, intent on restoring the Bourbon monarchy – were hostile to the Inquisition. In 1813, as Wellington's reconquest of Spain neared its completion, his Spanish allies echoed their French adversaries in decreeing the Inquisition formally abolished.

On 21 July 1814, the Bourbon Ferdinand VII was restored to the Spanish throne. The Inquisition was nominally restored with him; but it had lost most of its archives and documents during the preceding years and could work only in the most desultory fashion. The last prosecution of a Jew in Spain occurred at Córdoba in 1818. Although anti-Semitism was to remain rife in the country, it could no longer be orchestrated by the Inquisition, which had been effectively neutered. In 1820, the people of such cities as Barcelona and Valencia sacked the Inquisition's premises and plundered its archives – the paper from which was bestowed on local fireworks manufacturers and ended as components of skyrockets. At last, on 15 July 1834, a final formal 'decree of suppression' brought the Spanish Inquisition to an end. It had lasted three and a half centuries, and had left Spain in a condition from which she is only now beginning to recover.

5

Saving the New World

W here Spanish explorers, conquistadores, soldiers and settlers set foot, Spanish missionaries swiftly followed. Where the missionaries set foot and planted their crosses, the Inquisition swiftly followed. In addition to its fourteen major tribunals on the Iberian Peninsula, there was one each in outlying Spanish possessions – in the Canary Islands, in Mallorca, in Sardinia and in Sicily, which at the time was ruled by Spanish viceroys. In 1492, the year in which Muslims and Jews were definitively expelled from Spain, Christopher Columbus made his landfall in the West Indies. The conquest of the Americas then began; and the Inquisition was quick to take advantage of the opportunities offered by the New World.

As in Spain, the Inquisition's official brief was to ferret out and punish heresy in order to ensure the 'purity' of the Catholic faith. The Indians encountered in the New World knew nothing, of course, of Christianity. They could not be accused of heresy – of deviating from the faith – because they had nothing of the faith from which to deviate. In consequence, they were declared immune to action by the Inquisition – unless they had been converted to Christianity, then relapsed into their former beliefs and practices. It soon became apparent, however, that punishing Indians who converted and then relapsed effectively dissuaded others from converting at all. This situation threatened to pit the Inquisition against the missionaries, for whom the salvation of 'heathen' souls was paramount. The Inquisition was compelled to give way. It did so more or less willingly, since the persecution of Indians produced little gain anyway – in confiscated goods and property, for example, or in denunciations. All Indians were therefore placed beyond the Inquisition's remit and jurisdiction.

Given the relative dearth of Jews, Muslims and certifiable heretics in the New World, the Inquisition was sometimes pressed to find a *raison d'être* for itself. It found a partial solution to this problem in proliferating bureaucracy and paperwork. Inquisitors wrote dispatches back to Spain on an almost daily basis, summarising events and activities, reporting on the minutiae of the life around them, acting in effect as diarists, chroniclers and operatives in an elaborate surveillance network worthy of a modern secret police force or intelligence agency. The accumulation of paper was immense. The archives in Madrid alone today include more than 1,000 manuscripts and 4,000 bundles of loose pages, all systematically organised. The records of actual tribunals run to a hundred or so volumes, each of 1,000 pages.

This is not to say that the Inquisition in the New World could not find individuals to persecute, put on trial and, often enough, burn. But approximately 60 per cent of the trials conducted in Central and South America were for minor offences, such as the occasional blasphemy, sexual transgression or display of superstition. Most of the remainder were of alleged Judaisers, as well as of Christians suspected of experimenting with Indian rituals or of practising alchemy, astrology, cabbalism and other forms of heterodox or esoteric thought. And Inquisitors in the New World could also roast in their fires a form of delicacy not readily accessible to their colleagues in Spain – that is, Protestants. Protestants, of course, were regarded as the most pernicious and dangerous heretics of all. They were an unknown species in Spain. In the oceans and coastal waters of the Americas, however, they could be found with increasing frequency, often in the shape of English or Dutch pirates and privateers. Their activities in such capacities rendered them all the more desirable as candidates for the stake.

The Tribunal of Mexico

The first missionaries were dispatched to the West Indies in 1500, eight years after Columbus's initial landfall. The first bishop arrived there around 1519 or 1520, just as Hernán Cortés was embarking on the conquest of Mexico. In 1519, two Inquisitors were also appointed. One of them died before his ship sailed. His replacement was not appointed until 1524. The new Inquisitor proceeded to Mexico, by now thoroughly subdued. Here, he found a heretic to burn and promptly returned to Spain. Three years later, in 1527, the first bishops were appointed in Mexico, with authorisation to act as Inquisitors themselves.

The Inquisition did not establish its own tribunal in Mexico until 1570. It did so in Mexico City and immediately commandeered all jurisdiction over heresy from the local bishops. The first *auto de fe* was conducted on 28 February 1574. Two weeks prior to the event, it was announced by an elaborate fanfare of trumpets and drums. The affair was cranked up to the status of a major municipal spectacle, with stadium-style seating being erected for official functionaries and their families, as well as for provincial dignitaries invited to Mexico City for the occasion. The seventy-four prisoners committed to trial consisted largely of Protestants. Thirty-six of them were English – remnants of Sir John Hawkins's crew, captured six years before. At the conclusion of the trials, four Protestants were burned at the stake, two English, one Irish and one French.

The 'high point' of the Inquisition in Mexico came with the 'Great *Auto*' of 11 April 1649. It was directed specifically at the so-called 'New Christians' – the Hispanic-American term for Judaic converts or 'conversos' – who dominated trade between Spain and her colonies almost to the point of monopoly. The evidence against these individuals was tenuous enough. But the Inquisition lusted after their money and their property; and it had even more latitude for spurious prosecution in the New World than it did in Spain.

The 'Great *Auto*' of 1649 was even more of a spectacle than its predecessor of 1574. Like its predecessor, it was announced in advance by solemn processions of trumpets and drums across the whole of Mexico. Crowds began to arrive in Mexico City two weeks prior to the event, some from 600 miles distant. On the afternoon preceding the scheduled trials, an extravagant pageant was arranged. Double lines of opulent coaches moved through the streets of the capital, carrying nobles and notables. Prominent at the head of the parade was the standard of the Inquisition. On arriving at the square where the *auto* was to be conducted, many spectators remained in their coaches all night so as not to lose their places or their view of the proceedings.

Altogether, 109 prisoners were to be tried – representing, reportedly, 'the greater portion of Mexican commerce'. All of them had had their estates and other property confiscated, and none of it was returned, not even to those subsequently reconciled to the Church after the required penances. Twenty individuals were burned in effigy, some of them having previously escaped from prison, some having died there under torture, two having committed suicide. Of the prisoners present in person, thirteen were sentenced to the stake; but after repenting at the last moment and being reconciled to the Church, twelve were accorded the mercy of being garrotted before the flames could reach them. Only one man, a certain Tomás Treviño, was actually burned alive. He had previously denied the charge against him of being a clandestine Jew. The night before his execution, however, he had learned of his conviction and had thereupon openly proclaimed his Judaism, declaring his intention to die in his true faith.

> To silence what were styled his blasphemies, he was taken to the auto gagged, in spite of which he made audible assertion of his faith and of his contempt for Christianity.[1]

At the stake, he remained defiant.

> Undaunted to the last, he drew the blazing brands towards him with his feet and his last audible words were – 'Pile on the wood; how much my money costs me'.[2]

The 'Great *Auto*' of 1649 reflects the Inquisition in Mexico at its peak. On the whole, however, immolations on anything even approaching this scale were rare. For the most part, the Inquisition in Mexico busied itself in amassing wealth, in managing and profiting from the goods and properties it confiscated. Not infrequently, it would trump up charges against individuals for the sole purpose of obtaining their goods and property – which would never be returned, even if the accused were exonerated. In the years immediately preceding the 'Great *Auto*' of 1649, 270,000 pesos' worth of resources were confiscated. Confiscations from the 'Great *Auto*' itself brought in a total of 3 million pesos. In today's money, this sum would be the equivalent of some £30 million, and its purchasing power at the time was significantly greater. In the eighteenth century, a hundred years after the 'Great *Auto*', the currency had already been dramatically devalued. Even then, however, it cost 12,600 pesos to rebuild the Inquisition's palace in Cartagena after its destruction by British guns. At the time of the 'Great *Auto*' then, 3 million pesos would have sufficed to build upwards of 238 major municipal structures. Between 1646 and 1649, the Inquisition obtained enough revenue through its confiscations to sustain itself for 327 years. And this revenue did not include an annual stipend of 10,000 pesos received from the Spanish Crown.

After the 'Great *Auto*' of 1649, the Inquisition in Mexico grew increasingly dormant, content to repose on its wealth. By then it was receiving an immense income, for which it had to do very little. Among its chief problems was that of priests found guilty of sexual transgressions, such as seducing women in the confessional. Culprits of this kind were seldom burned, however, being sentenced to penances of varying severity. By 1702, when the Bourbons succeeded the Habsburgs to the Spanish throne, the Inquisition had lapsed into decadence. In that year, it presided over no more than four cases – three against bigamists, one against a Jesuit who revelled in stripping female penitents naked and whipping them.

Towards the end of the eighteenth century, the American War of Independence and then the French Revolution were to furnish the Inquisition in Mexico with a new *raison d'être*. So-called 'free-thinkers' were regarded as heretics. Anything pertaining to the recently formulated 'Rights of Man', anything that echoed the arguments of Thomas Paine or such French writers as Voltaire, Diderot and Rousseau, was deemed to be tainted by 'free-thinking'. It was also deemed to be seditious

– as inimical to the State as to the Church. The Inquisition therefore began to function not only as an instrument of Catholic orthodoxy, but also as the government's secret police. Its targets now became anyone who bought, sold, printed, circulated, disseminated or even possessed material expounding inflammatory ideas, as well as anyone who promulgated such ideas orally. Revolutionary books and pamphlets, imported from France, from Britain or from Britain's former colonies in North America, became dangerous contraband. Anyone trafficking in such contraband became subject to prosecution.

As governments of our own century have discovered, it is difficult enough to choke off the smuggling of alcohol, tobacco, drugs and pornography. To suppress the circulation of ideas is ultimately impossible. By 1810, moreover, the Inquisition in Mexico had been cut off from its parent in Spain, since Spain now lay under the Napoleonic yoke and the Inquisition there had been dissolved. When insurrection erupted in Mexico, therefore, the authorities lacked the resources to suppress it, and could no longer hope for support from the mother country. And indeed, the royalist factions in Mexico had become as hostile to the Inquisition as the revolutionary forces.

In 1813 Napoleon's suppression of the Inquisition in Spain was reaffirmed by the restored Bourbon monarchy. This measure was applied by extension to Spanish colonies abroad, including Mexico – which by then was itself in the throes of a struggle for independence. As revolution spread across Latin America, the administration in Mexico appropriated all property of the Inquisition. No prisoners were found in its jails. Its palace was thrown open to the populace, who 'gave rein to their contempt'.[3]

In January 1815, the Inquisition in Mexico was temporarily restored when royalist forces in the country gained a brief ascendancy over their revolutionary opponents. The tribunal's property was returned, but only 773 pesos of its former wealth remained, and none of its furniture. In 1817, there was one last prosecution – of a man accused of reading prohibited books. Then, in 1820, as Mexico wrested her independence from Spain, the Inquisition was finally and definitively suppressed.

Lima

Established in 1571, the Inquisition in Mexico had exercised jurisdiction over Central America, over Spanish holdings in North America and across the Pacific to the Spanish dominion of the Philippines. Two years before, in 1569, an Inquisitor had arrived in Peru, and a separate tribunal was established in Lima in 1570. Its jurisdiction extended southwards to Chile and Argentina, and for a time at least northwards to Colombia, Venezuela and the islands of the Caribbean.

The activities of the Inquisition in Peru ran closely parallel to those of its kindred institution in Mexico. As in Mexico, heresy had initially fallen under the jurisdiction of local bishops. When the Inquisition was officially established in 1570, there were more than a hundred cases pending in Lima and Cuzco. As in Mexico, authority over all such cases was transferred from the bishops to the Inquisition's own official tribunal, which launched its regime with the burning of a French Protestant in 1573.

In Lima, too, Indians were exempted from the Inquisition's jurisdiction. But representatives of the tribunal were installed in every locality occupied by Spanish settlers. Cases from Buenos Aires, some 2,000 miles away, as well as from Santiago de Chile, were routinely transferred to Lima. Again, the Inquisition in Peru derived the bulk of its ever burgeoning income from the persecution of wealthy merchants. Many such, mostly of Portuguese descent, were arrested in 1634; they were charged with being clandestine Jews and their property was automatically confiscated. In 1639, a 'Great *Auto*' was conducted, similar to those in Mexico, and millions of additional pesos were pocketed by the Inquisition. This revenue, according to one historian, 'virtually disappeared without anyone knowing where it went'.[4] When Philip IV of Spain learned the scale of the confiscations, he demanded his share of the proceeds. The Inquisition acknowledged the sum it had acquired, but pleaded it had almost nothing left after paying off its creditors – few of whom actually existed.

Like its Mexican counterpart, the Inquisition in Peru had its share of nuisance cases to address, particularly the seduction of women by priests in the confessional. Between 1578 and 1585, there were fifteen such cases. By 1595, twenty-four priests were in prison, charged with the same offence. One of them had displayed sufficient priapic activity to be denounced by forty-three women. On the whole, sentences pronounced on sexually delinquent priests were laughable. Most were simply banned from hearing confessions for a time, or consigned for a year or so to a cloister. One – having seduced twenty-eight women and raped another in church – was banished.

As in Mexico, Protestants were fair game – and less embarrassing than lascivious priests. Among the Englishmen in the *auto* of 30 November 1587 was John Drake, a cousin of Sir Francis. Having sailed around Cape Horn, Drake's ship had been wrecked in the Pacific, off the coast of what is now Chile. He and one companion had made their way over the mountains, then paddled downriver by canoe all the way to Buenos Aires. Here, they were captured and sent over the mountains again to Lima. At his trial Drake capitulated, converted to Catholicism and was sentenced to three years in a monastery. His companion, being more stubborn, was tortured, then sentenced to four years in the galleys followed by life imprisonment.

English prisoners appeared again in an *auto* of April 1592, and three were sentenced to death. Then, in 1593, Richard Hawkins, son of Sir John, mounted a foolhardy expedition against Spanish installations on the Pacific coast, then advanced inland. In the summer of the following year, after a battle near Quito, in modern Ecuador, he was forced to surrender, along with seventy-four others. Sixty-two of these were immediately sent to the galleys. The remainder, including Hawkins himself, were brought to Lima and handed over to the Inquisition. Eight of them, along with seven other English prisoners captured elsewhere, were tried in an *auto* of 17 December 1595. All of them converted to the Church and thereby escaped the stake, although four other victims of different nationalities were burned. Hawkins himself was too ill to appear at his trial. His name, however, and the respect he commanded from his Spanish captors, earned him a special dispensation. He was eventually able to return to England, where he was knighted.

During the latter part of the seventeenth century, the Inquisition in Peru, like its Mexican counterpart, became increasingly desultory, decadent and corrupt. Inquisitors comported themselves like nobles and indulged freely in secular pleasures. One of them, for example, acquired notoriety for keeping two sisters as mistresses.

As in Mexico, the Inquisition in Peru derived a new impetus from the French Revolution and the rise of Napoleon. Peruvian Inquisitors, too, became zealous in their quest for politically seditious material, and in their persecution of 'free-thinkers', Freemasons, putative or real revolutionaries and all other perceived adversaries of the regime. In 1813, however, the Inquisition in Peru was suppressed by the restored Spanish monarchy. It was reestablished in 1814, but nothing of the money it had lost was refunded. In 1820, it was finally and definitively suppressed.

New Granada

Although the first Spanish settlements had been in the West Indies and the islands of the Caribbean, they came under Peruvian authority. Not until 1719 was a new, third, viceroyalty created, that of New Granada, with its capital at Cartagena in what is now Colombia. The subdivision of jurisdiction in Latin America occurred under the Church before it occurred under the Crown. In 1532, the episcopal See of Cartagena was created and a bishop in residence was established. In 1547, Bogotá became a provincial capital. Six years later, it was raised to the status of an archbishopric. Colombia, Venezuela and the islands of the Caribbean fell politically under the authority of the Viceroy of Peru, but they possessed their own ecclesiastical authority. The Archbishop of Bogotá enjoyed powers equal to those of his counterparts in Lima and Mexico City. These included, at least initially, inquisitorial powers. Thus, in 1556, the archbishop ordered that no books could be sold or even owned in his archdiocese unless they had first been examined and approved by the Church.

As has been noted, the Inquisition established its own autonomous tribunal in Lima in 1570, with authority over all Spanish possessions in Latin America south of Panama. In 1577, the Lima tribunal dispatched an Inquisitor to Bogotá. The individual in question quickly became notorious. He feuded bitterly with the archbishop. He regularly kept women in his apartments – and not infrequently violently mistreated them. The local nuns forbade him access to their premises because of his 'licentious conversation'. One of his successors created even greater scandal, becoming infamous for 'adulteries and incests with maids, wives and widows, mothers, daughters and sisters'.[5]

In 1608, the Inquisition in Spain established a new, separate tribunal at Cartagena, invested with powers comparable to those of Lima and Mexico City. Its jurisdiction extended from Panama, through Colombia and Venezuela, to the Guianas and the West Indies. The new tribunal soon became even more corrupt than those of Lima and Mexico City. For more than a century, there was no viceroy within striking distance to keep it in check. And when the viceroyalty of New Granada was finally established in 1719, the Cartagena Inquisition was too firmly entrenched to sanction much interference.

The first *auto de fe* was conducted in February 1614. Thirty victims were paraded through the city and tried for a variety of trivial offences. Desiring to compete with the pomp and pageantry that characterised such events in Lima and Mexico City, the Cartagena Inquisitors took their business very seriously indeed, and 'such was the verbosity that the ceremonies lasted from half-past nine in the morning until after sunset'.[6]

By the seventeenth century, the West Indies and the Caribbean coast of Latin America contained a broader and more diverse cultural and racial mix than Spain's other colonial dominions. In addition to Spanish and Portuguese settlers, there were the Indians, from a diverse number of tribal affiliations; and because of the region's maritime accessibility, there were more Europeans than in Mexico or Peru – Italian, English, French, Dutch. At the time of the initial conquest, Charles V had presided not only over Spain, but over the Holy Roman Empire as well, and many of the early conquistadores had therefore been of German and Austrian extraction. By 1600, their descendants comprised a sizeable Germanic community. Finally, there was a burgeoning population of black slaves from Africa.

In the West Indies and along the Caribbean coast, in cities like Cartagena, Maracaibo and Caracas, people of diverse cultures, races and ethnic backgrounds jostled together in close, often incestuous, proximity. Individuals of mixed blood made up an increasingly significant portion of the population. And the physiological cross-fertilisation was inevitably accompanied by a cross-fertilisation in ideas and religious beliefs, out of which, 'voodoo', in its various guises and manifestations, emerged. So, too, did sometimes bizarre amalgams of Christianity and older Indian traditions. Imported from the non-Catholic parts of Europe, esoteric thought – Rosicrucianism, for example – found the region fertile soil in which to flourish. The result was a hybridisation much more complex than the relative 'purity' of Mexico and Peru.

In theory at least, this situation should have afforded the Inquisition in Cartagena abundant opportunity to run amok. In practice, however, it remained comparatively inert, basking indolently in the fruits of its corruption. Only at sporadic intervals would it bestir itself. Thus, for instance, during the first half of the seventeenth century, witchcraft became a temporary *cause célèbre* – especially, it was alleged, among black slaves employed in the mines. At an *auto* in March 1634, twenty-one putative witches were tried. Most, however, escaped with only whippings and fines. One was tortured for some ninety minutes and died. Two were sentenced to the stake, but La Suprema in Spain refused to ratify the sentences and even released one of the accused.

In March 1622, an Englishman was burned for Protestantism. According to contemporary reports, he was not chained to the stake in the customary fashion, but 'calmly sat on a faggot and remained motionless till life was extinct'.[7] In 1636 and again in 1638, the Cartagena Inquisition, like its counterparts in Lima and Mexico City, turned its attention to wealthy Portuguese merchants – who, as a now standard justification, were accused of Judaising. The confiscations resulting from the trials brought in immense revenues. Content with these, the Inquisition lapsed into profound and prolonged lethargy. Between 1656 and 1818, it did not even bother to publish the annual 'Edict of Faith'.

The lethargy was rudely interrupted in 1697, when French privateers captured Cartagena and sacked the city. One of their first actions was to storm the Inquisition's palace, plunder the tribunal's official regalia and immolate it in a mock *auto de fe*. Demoralised by this trauma, the Inquisition in Cartagena never fully recovered. Forty-four years later, it suffered another debilitating blow. In 1741, the War of Jenkins's Ear,* that most bizarre and surreal of conflicts, was escalating into the War of the Austrian Succession. At the beginning of March, a squadron of the Royal Navy under Admiral Vernon blockaded Cartagena. Having attempted a half-hearted landing and been repulsed, the British admiral contented himself with subjecting the city to a month-long naval bombardment, which left an enduring memory in the minds of the populace. Thus does the event figure in Gabriel García Márquez's short novel, *Of Love and Other Demons*, which offers a revealing insight into the corruption and sexual activity of the Cartagena Inquisition

* An English seaman was captured by a Spanish warship, accused of theft and punished by having an ear lopped off. Britain promptly declared war, but apart from the shelling of Cartagena the conflict did not extend beyond sporadic exchanges of naval gunfire.

during the last third of the eighteenth century. During the British naval bombardment of Cartagena, the palace of the Inquisition was totally demolished. It was not to be rebuilt for twenty-five years. By that time, revolution was already looming on the horizon – and, with it, the Inquisition's demise.

But the Cartagena Inquisition proved sluggish even in opposing the revolution that threatened its extinction. In 1789, a Spanish translation of the French Declaration of the Rights of Man was published. Not surprisingly, it was promptly banned, being perceived as inimical to the stable order of society and conducive to that most insidious form of subversion, tolerance. In 1794, as the Reign of Terror swept France, the viceroys of New Granada and Peru wrote to their respective Inquisitions, demanding that all copies of the offending text be ferreted out and destroyed. After what purported to be a lengthy and diligent search, the Cartagena Inquisition claimed not to have found a single copy.

It hardly mattered whether this futility stemmed from torpor or from covert revolutionary sympathy. The Inquisition in Cartagena was soon to incur the same fate as its counterparts in Mexico and Peru. In 1810, the first popular uprising occurred, and the Cartagena Inquisition, despised as it was by virtually the entire city, became a primary target. After being briefly restored, it was suppressed again in 1820, along with its counterparts elsewhere. In 1821, the revolutionary forces emerged triumphant, and the vice-president of the newly established United States of Colombia officially declared the Inquisition abolished. Shortly thereafter, the Congress of the fledgling country pronounced the Inquisition 'extinguished forever and never to be re-established'.[8]

6

A Crusade Against Witchcraft

While smoke from the Spanish Inquisition's fires cast a malodorous pall from the Iberian Peninsula to the New World, the original, older Papal Inquisition was keeping productively busy elsewhere in Europe. It had found a new target, which it harried with fresh impetus. Its enthusiasm in doing so during the centuries that followed was to claim more lives than had the Albigensian Crusade.

Conventional history, popular assumptions and tradition to the contrary, the Church had never really established as complete authority as it wished over the peoples of western Europe. Admittedly, its writ ran everywhere. It could call anyone, peasant or monarch, to account. It could divide the continent into dioceses and bishoprics, could bully individuals into purchasing indulgences, could extort tithes. It could punish anyone who defied its teachings, or whom it chose to accuse of doing so. It could dragoon whole communities into attending Mass and observing its other statutory rites and rituals, holy days, feast days and festivals. And it could, indeed, elicit a significant degree of voluntary allegiance in exchange for the solace and consolation it offered, the reassurance and posthumous rewards it promised. But in what is now called 'the battle for hearts and minds', it had not met with unqualified success. While many hearts and minds did take seriously the Virgin and the saints, there were many others for whom the Virgin and the saints were simply new masks, new guises, new manifestations of much older deities or principles. And there were many other hearts and minds that remained at least in part devotedly and unabashedly pagan.

As early as the twelfth century, the Church had preached crusades against the pagan tribes of Prussia and the Baltic coast – the territory that subsequently comprised Pomerania, Lithuania, Latvia and Estonia. Within its own established sphere of influence, however, the Church had conducted at best only a sequence of holding actions against what it perceived to be the forces of darkness – the brooding, sinister, malevolent energies apparently lurking in the gloomy forests that still covered much of the land. For pious Christians, these forests and the darkness associated with them concealed innumerable forms of evil, and provided an impregnable refuge for the demonic. Surrounded by such forests, villages and towns, not to mention isolated abbeys and monasteries, were like spiritual outposts or forts, stranded in the wilderness of hostile country and often beleaguered or besieged.

In fact, the forces concealed by the forests were simply those of nature and the natural world – which were 'unregenerate' in the Church's eyes. It is a cliché that the gods of any religion tend to become the devils of the religion that supplants it. Before the advent of Christianity, the domains of the Roman Empire had recognised the god Pan as the supreme deity presiding over the natural world. Pan was the goat-horned, goat-tailed, goat-hoofed figure who reigned over the natural world's vigorous, tenacious, ruthless and ostensibly chaotic life. He enjoyed particular prerogatives in matters of sexuality and fertility. Under the authority of the Church, Pan was officially

demonised and characterised as satanic. There was ample precedent for such procedures. Centuries earlier, to cite but one
instance, the Phoenician mother goddess Astarte had been
subjected to a forcible sex change and transformed into the
demon Ashtaroth.

With the collapse of the Roman Empire, most European
peasantry continued to acknowledge Pan, or his sometimes
older regional equivalents, in one form or another – as Herne
the Hunter, for example, as the horned god Cernunnos, as the
Green Man, as Robin of the Greenwood or Robin Goodfellow,
who became conflated eventually with Robin Hood. Nor was
it Pan alone who received such homage. Along the borders of
modern France and Belgium, the Roman moon goddess of the
hunt, Diana, was known as Diana of the Nine Fires, and
fused with her ancient antecedent, Arduina, from whom the
Ardennes derives its name. Such deities retained their currency
despite the advent of Christendom. European peasants might
attend church on Sunday, hear Mass and assimilate on one level
the rites and teachings of Rome. At the same time, however,
they would still leave milk in saucers and make numerous other
kinds of offering to placate the older forces lurking in the forests
around them. And they would sneak out at the appropriate
dates of the year for the *Walpurgisnacht* or 'Witches' Sabbath',
for the pagan observance of solstices and equinoxes, for fertility
rites, for festivals and carnivals in which the gods of the old
religion figured prominently, albeit in disguised and Christianised form. In almost all communities, moreover, there was
invariably at least one elderly woman revered for her wisdom,
her capacity to tell fortunes or see into the future, her knowledge
of herbal and meteorological lore, her skill as a midwife. They
were often trusted and consulted, especially by other women,
more readily than the local priest. The priest represented powers

that might determine one's posthumous fate and destination. But there were many matters for which these powers often seemed too majestic, too awesome, too sternly judgemental, too abstract or remote to be pestered. The typical village crone, on the other hand, would provide a conduit to powers more immediate and readily accessible. It was she, rather than the priest, who would be consulted on such issues as weather and crops, the welfare of livestock, personal health and hygiene, sexuality, fertility and childbirth.

From the time of its first introduction into Europe, the Church had had to contend with pagan residues and vestiges, from elves, gnomes, trolls and fairies to the august horned god himself. On occasion, it had attempted to demonise them and stamp them out. A document of the ninth century, for example, mentions 'the demon whom the peasants call Diana' and asserts: 'Some wicked women, reverting to Satan . . . profess that they ride at night with Diana on certain beasts.'[1] More frequently, the Church came to an uneasy accommodation with its pagan antecedents and sought to hijack them when possible. For instance, the Irish goddess Brigit, patroness of fire, was effectively subsumed by a putative saint of the same name. Thus churches and Christian shrines were habitually built on sites previously sacred to pagan believers. In AD 601, Pope Gregory I established this practice almost as official policy. In a letter to an abbot, the Pope wrote that he had

> come to the conclusion that the temples of the idols among that people should on no account be destroyed. The idols are to be destroyed, but the temples themselves are to be aspersed with holy water, altars set up in them and relics deposited there. For if these temples are well-built they must be purified from the worship of demons and

dedicated to the service of the true God. In this way, we hope that the people, seeing that their temples are not destroyed, may abandon their error and, flocking more rapidly to their accustomed resorts, may come to know and adore the true God. And since they have a custom of sacrificing many oxen to demons, let some other solemnity be substituted in its place, such as a day of Dedication or the Festivals of the Holy Martyrs whose relics are enshrined there.[2]

The Inquisition enabled the Church to adopt a more aggressive policy, to take the offensive against the vestiges of paganism. In consequence, the former reluctant tolerance was to be officially abrogated giving way to persecution. Elves, gnomes, trolls and fairies were to be condemned and castigated as demons or demonic powers. The horned god of nature – the Green Man in his various manifestations – was to be transformed into Satan. Participation in the old pagan rituals was to be labelled witchcraft or sorcery. And belief in witchcraft or sorcery was to be formally classified as a heresy, with all the punishments accruing thereto. According to the historian Keith Thomas:

> Witchcraft became a Christian heresy, the greatest of all sins, because it involved the renunciation of God and deliberate adherence to his greatest enemy.[3]

Through what the historian Hugh Trevor-Roper calls 'the device of an extended definition of heresy',[4] the pagan foundations of European civilisation were to be brought under the Inquisition's jurisdiction.

By implication this jurisdiction was to extend even to natural disasters. Famine, drought, flood, plague and other such phenomena were no longer to be attributed to natural causes, but to the working of infernal powers. Not only madness, but even outbursts of temper or hysteria were to be ascribed to demonic possession. Erotic dreams were to be attributed to visitations by incubi or succubi. Midwives and traditional village 'wise women' – those familiar with herbal lore or adept at dispensing advice – were to be branded as witches. Fear and paranoia were to be promulgated until they clamped the entirety of Europe in a vicelike grip. And in this atmosphere of pervasive terror, tens of thousands, perhaps even hundreds of thousands, were to become victims of official ecclesiastical murder.

The Hammer of the Witches

For centuries, the Church was profoundly confused in its attitude towards witchcraft. Most priests, especially in rural areas, were poorly educated and seldom left the local population in which they themselves were rooted. In consequence, they would share the local population's unquestioned belief in the reality of witchcraft – in the capacity of the village crone, for example, to exercise occult powers, to blight a crop, produce diseases in livestock, cause mysterious deaths. Whether they observed their vow of celibacy or not, they would hardly have much knowledge of gynaecological matters; and many of them were undoubtedly rendered queasy by what must have seemed the unclean complexities of female plumbing. In her aptitude for dealing with such things, in the trust and confidence she inspired in other women, the village crone would almost daily confront the priest with empirical and demonstrable proof of his own inadequacy and inferiority. For such priests, witchcraft was an unimpugnable reality, and one that fostered a sense of rivalry and resentment.

Until the late fifteenth century, however, official Church dogma denied the reality of witchcraft. The blighted crop, the diseased cattle, the unexplained death might be ascribed to the work of the devil or to natural causes, but not to the village crone. So far as the Church was concerned, witchcraft was a delusion disseminated by the devil. The sin, therefore, was not witchcraft itself, but belief in witchcraft, and the practices attending such belief. By virtue of belief in witchcraft,

> the witch has abandoned Christianity, has renounced her baptism, has worshipped Satan as her God, has surrendered herself to him, body and soul, and exists only to be his instrument in working the evil ... which he cannot accomplish without a human agent.[5]

As early as the ninth century, accounts of witches flying to their Sabbath had been declared fantasy by the Church – but anyone subscribing to such fantasy was deemed to have lost his faith, and thus to be proved 'an infidel and a pagan'. This position was subsequently to be enshrined as an article of Canon Law. Those who believed in witchcraft had supposedly lost their faith and slipped into a delusion. Because it resulted from loss of faith, such delusion was held to constitute heresy.

Around the mid fifteenth century, the Church's position began to change. In 1458, one Inquisitor, a certain Nicholas Jaquerius, argued that 'the existing sect of witches' was altogether different from the heretics cited in the relevant sections of Canon Law.[6] In other words, the Inquisitor insisted, the power exercised by witches was very real, and not to be dismissed as fantasy. In 1484, the Church performed a complete and dramatic about-face. A Papal Bull of that year completely reversed the former position and officially recognised the putative reality of witchcraft. In this Bull, the Pope declared:

It has indeed lately come to our ears . . . that in some parts of Northern Germany, as well as in the provinces . . . of Mainz, Cologne, Trèves, Salzburg and Bremen, many persons . . . have abandoned themselves to devils, incubi and succubi, and by their incantations, spells, conjurations, and other accursed charms and crafts, enormities and horrid offences, have slain infants yet in the mother's womb, as also the offspring of cattle, have blasted the produce of the earth, the grapes of the vine, the fruits of the trees.[7]

Seven years later, in 1491, the University of Cologne issued a warning that any argument against the reality of witchcraft 'was to incur the guilt of impeding the Inquisition'.[8] By dint of flamboyant circular reasoning, the position was rendered unassailable shortly thereafter by the Inquisitor of Como, who stated that

numerous persons have been burned for attending the Sabbat, which could not have been done without the assent of the Pope, and this was sufficient proof that the heresy was real, for the Church punishes only manifest crimes.[9]

According to a modern historian:

No longer content with accusations of sorcery, or even with the suggestion that sorcery inherently entailed demonic magic, judges now wanted to portray the magicians as linked in a demonic conspiracy against the Christian faith and Christian society. The sorcerer, intent only on specific acts of malice against particular enemies, gave way before the company of witches committed to the destruction of Christendom.[10]

In the past, it had been heresy to believe in witchcraft. Now, at a single stroke, it became heresy to disbelieve. A mechanism had been established from which – for anyone the Church wished to find inimical – there was no escape. A prevailing atmosphere of wholesale paranoia was generated. And scapegoats could now be called to account even for natural disasters, thus exonerating both God and the devil. Given the raging misogyny of the Inquisitors, almost invariably the scapegoats in question would be women.

In the Bull of 1484 which officially recognised the reality of witchcraft, Pope Innocent VIII specifically mentioned two individuals by name:

> And although Our dear sons Heinrich Kramer and Johann Sprenger . . . have been by letters Apostolic delegated as Inquisitors . . . We decree . . . that the aforesaid Inquisitors be empowered to proceed to the just correction, imprisonment and punishment of any person, without let or hindrance.[11]

Heinrich Kramer was a Dominican who, around 1474, had already been appointed Inquisitor for Salzburg and the Tyrol. At Salzburg, he served as spiritual director of the Dominican church. In 1500, he was to be appointed Papal Nuncio and Inquisitor for Bohemia and Moravia. His colleague, Johann Sprenger, was also a Dominican, the prior of the Order's convent at Cologne. In 1480, he became Dean of the Faculty of Theology at the University of Cologne. A year later, he was appointed Inquisitor for the provinces of Cologne, Mainz and Trèves. In 1488, he became head of the Dominican Order's entire German province.

Around 1486, some two years after being cited in Pope Innocent VIII's Bull, Heinrich Kramer and Johann Sprenger produced a book. This text must surely rank among the most notorious and – in the deepest moral sense of the word – most obscene works in the entire history of Western civilisation. It was entitled *Malleus Maleficarum*, 'Hammer of Witches', meaning a hammer to be used against witches; and, at more than 500 pages in modern editions, it did indeed constitute, quite literally, a hammer. So popular was it that by 1520, a mere thirty-four years after its appearance, it had gone through thirteen editions. It has remained in print ever since; and perversely enough there are still people who take it seriously. As recently as 1986, it was newly translated into English and extolled in a rhapsodic panegyric by Montague Summers, an eccentric would-be esotericist and self-appointed expert on vampires and werewolves. According to Summers, the *Malleus* is 'among the most important, wisest, and weightiest books of the world'.[12] In case such praise should prove too tempered or too moderate, Summers concludes:

> It is a work which must irresistibly capture the attention of all men who think, all who see, or are endeavouring to see, the ultimate reality behind the accidents of matter, time and space.[13]

In legal, lurid and often pornographic detail, the *Malleus* undertakes to adumbrate supposed manifestations of witchcraft. It purports to be a definitive do-it-yourself manual not only for Inquisitors, but also for judges, magistrates, secular authorities of all kinds and by extension every sufficiently deranged up-standing citizen who has reason or unreason enough to suspect the presence of witchcraft around him. In fact, it constitutes a compendium of sexual psychopathology, and is an illuminating illustration of pathological fantasy running exuberantly out of control. With an obsessiveness that would betray itself immediately to any modern psychologist, the text focuses – indeed, dotes – on diabolic copulation, on intercourse with incubi and succubi, on sundry other forms of erotic experience and sexual activity (or inactivity) attributable by the infected imagination to demonic forces. It offers techniques of diagnosis and prognosis. It adumbrates therapeutic procedures and supposedly remedial punishments. It furnishes formulae and recipes for exorcisms. In its treatment of its subject matter, it aspires to positively encyclopedic scope and scale. And it became, in effect, a species of surrogate Bible for Inquisitors, and not for Inquisitors alone. As Montague Summers says – correctly, on this one occasion – in his misplaced encomium, the *Malleus*

> lay on the bench of every judge, on the desk of every magistrate. It was the ultimate, irrefutable, unarguable authority. It was implicitly accepted not only by Catholic but by Protestant legislature.[14]

The *Malleus* begins by asserting explicitly

> the belief that there are such beings as witches is so essential a part of the Catholic faith that obstinately to maintain the opposite opinion manifestly savours of heresy.[15]

Here is a flagrant echo of the Papal Bull of 1484, which reversed the Church's previous position by officially recognising the supposed reality of witchcraft.

Having stated its basic premise, the *Malleus* proceeds to elaborate:

> This then is our proposition: devils by their art do bring about evil effects through witchcraft, yet it is true that

without the assistance of some agent they cannot make any form . . . and we do not maintain that they can inflict damage without the assistance of some agent, but with such an agent diseases, and any other human passions or ailments, can be brought about, and these are real and true.[16]

In other words, the infernal forces are powerless in themselves. They can only work their evil through the conduit of some human agency. In consequence, human beings are now to be blamed for misfortunes previously ascribed to God's unfathomable behaviour, to the processes of the natural world or to demonic malevolence beyond the Inquisition's reach. Should anything go wrong in the well-ordered functioning of things, there will now be someone to punish for it.

According to the *Malleus*'s free-associative logic, witches at their most powerful can raise hailstorms and tempests. They can invoke lightning and cause it to strike men and animals. They can cause impotence and sterility in men and animals. They can also cause plagues. They can murder children as offerings to demonic forces. When no one is watching, they can make children fall into bodies of water and drown. They can prompt a horse to go mad under its rider. They can cause either great love or great hatred in men. They can kill men or animals with a glance – the so-called 'Evil Eye'. They can reveal the future. They can travel through the air, 'either in body or imagination'.

The *Malleus* recognises that some Inquisitors may prove diffident about dispensing punishment, if only through fear of demonic attacks or counterattacks on themselves, demonic preemptive strikes or reprisals. It accordingly offers reassurance that witches cannot injure Inquisitors and other officials because they dispense public justice. Many examples could be adduced to prove this, but time does not permit it.[17]

Time was obviously pressing. The authors of the *Malleus* still had some 500 pages to write, developing and amplifying their thesis. They therefore contented themselves with only a modicum of further reassurance:

> There are three classes of men blessed by God, whom that detestable race cannot injure with their witchcraft. And the first are those who administer public justice against them, or prosecute them in any public official capacity. The second are those who, according to the traditional and holy rites of the Church, make lawful use of the power and virtue which the Church by her exorcism furnishes in the aspersion of Holy Water, the taking of consecrated salt, the carrying of blessed candles . . . the third class are those who, in various and infinite ways, are blessed by the Holy Angels.[18]

In other words, the Church possesses its own superstitions, its own magical rituals and practices, which are intrinsically superior simply because they stem from the Church. And in the 'Holy Angels', the Church has its own disincarnate occult allies, who are intrinsically more powerful than the disincarnate occult allies of the witch.

> For the exorcisms of the Church are for this very purpose, and are entirely efficacious remedies for preserving oneself from the injuries of witches.[19]

The *Malleus* is militantly – indeed, psychopathically – misogynistic. Intrepid though they might be in contending with

The standard of the Inquisition in Spain. Founded in 1478, the Spanish
Inquisition was not finally abolished until 1834.

A procession of Inquisitors and victims to an *auto de fe* in Goa,
the Portuguese colony in India.

The conclusion of an *auto de fe* in Goa, with public
burnings of those convicted.

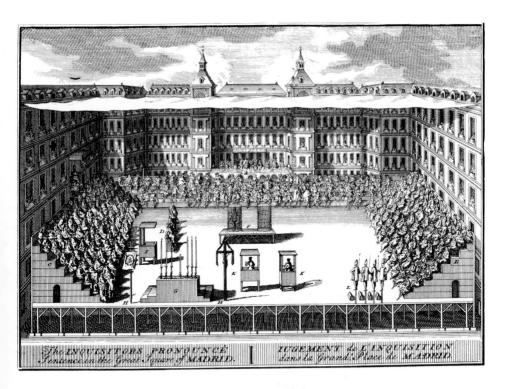

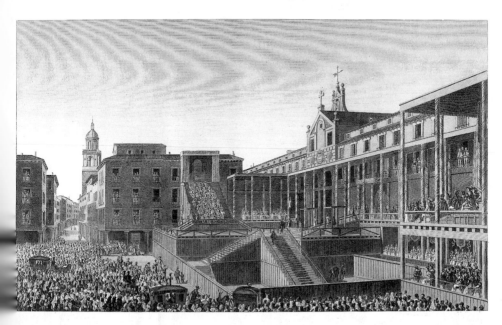

Two ornate and theatrical *autos de fe* of the Spanish Inquisition in Plaza Mayor, Madrid (*top*) and Valladolid (*above*).

On 30 June 1680 an *auto de fe* was held in Madrid in the presence of King Carlos II of Spain and his young bride. Fifty-one people were burned alive or in effigy.

Conrad of Marburg, the ruthless and notorious head of the
Inquisition in Germany from 1231. His excesses led to his denunciation
by bishops and princes and to his murder in 1233.

ENGRAVED
for the
PRIMITIVE MARTYRS.

The Martyrdom of JOHN HUS.

Jan Hus, the Bohemian ecclesiastical reformer, who was excommunicated by the
Pope in 1411. Refusing to recant, he was burned alive in Constance in 1415.

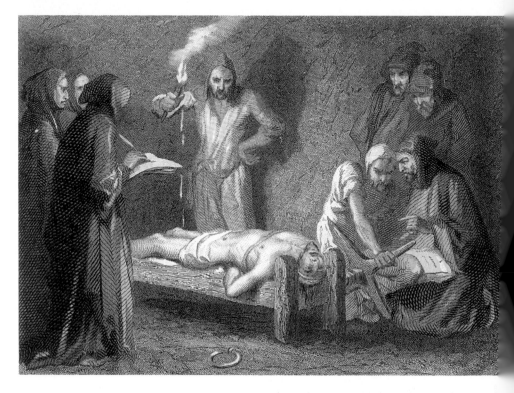

Opposite and above The Inquisition put their victims to the
'question' – they tortured them. If found guilty, they were handed over
to the secular authorities to be 'relaxed' – that is, burned.

Top and above Freemason John Coustos was arrested by the Inquisition in Lisbon in 1743, where he was tortured and interrogated for his crime of Freemasonry. After his release, he published a book in England in 1746 that described and illustrated his experience, *The Sufferings of John Coustos for Freemasonry*.

invisible powers, the authors of the text were terrified of women to a degree verging on dementia. Women are regarded as inherently weak and, almost by definition, 'fallen'. A woman 'is an imperfect animal, she always deceives'.[20] She is 'quicker to waver' in religious faith. She is 'a liar by nature'. She is 'beautiful to look upon, contaminating to the touch and deadly to keep'.[21] She is to blame, in effect, for virtually everything: 'All witchcraft comes from carnal lust, which is in women insatiable.'[22]

If beautiful women were particularly suspect, so, too, were midwives, with their intimate knowledge and experience of what the Inquisitors perceived as feminine mysteries. Stillborn children were routinely believed to have been murdered by a midwife as an offering to the devil. Deformed, disfigured, sickly or even badly behaved children were similarly ascribed to the midwife's witchcraft. By virtue of the confidence she inspired in other women, and the competition for authority she entailed for the priest, the midwife was an ideal target. On the midwife, the Inquisitor could practise, hone and refine his warped skills with impunity.

The *Malleus* is merciless in its treatment of girls who had been seduced and then jilted:

> For when girls have been corrupted, and have been scorned by their lovers after they have immodestly copulated with them in the hope and promise of marriage with them, and have found themselves disappointed in all their hopes and everywhere despised, they turn to the help and protection of devils.[23]

But no stigma whatever is attached to the seducer himself – who, if anything, the *Malleus* implies, is likely to become a victim.

The *Malleus* is quick to interpret as witchcraft any behaviour its clerical authors cannot explain – behaviour that might entail nothing more sinister than the effects of drugs, such as ergot or 'magic mushrooms', or female masturbation, or simple sensual sunbathing:

> the witches themselves have often been seen lying on their backs in the fields or in the woods, naked up to the very navel, and it has been apparent from the disposition of those limbs and members which pertain to the venereal and orgasm, as also from the agitation of their legs and thighs, that, all invisibly to the bystanders, they have been copulating with Incubus devils.[24]

And the book offers, too, a rationalisation that must have assuaged the bruised pride of many a cuckolded husband:

> It is certain also that the following has happened. Husbands have actually seen Incubus devils swiving their wives, although they have thought that they were not devils but men. And when they have taken up a weapon and tried to run them through, the devil has suddenly disappeared, making himself invisible.[25]

The *Malleus* addresses itself to sundry other manifestations and practices of witchcraft as well. It deals with the alleged killing, cooking and eating of children. It describes the various ways in which witches bind themselves to demonic forces. It discusses the sticking of pins into wax images. Again and again, however, with the obsessive single-mindedness of a guided missile, it returns to matters of sexuality. Not infrequently, the book's sexual obsessions take wing into fevered fantasy. It speaks, for instance, of witches who . . . collect male organs in great numbers, as many as twenty or thirty members together, and put them in a bird's nest, or shut them up in a box, where they move themselves like living members, and eat oats and corn.[26]

Such images as this are ascribed to demonic illusion, caused 'by confusing the organ of vision by transmuting the mental images in the imaginative faculty'.[27] But one cannot help wondering whether the work's authors, simply to conceive of such things, have not partaken of some psychotropic substance themselves, or possessed imaginations more tortured and twisted even than Bosch's.

The *Malleus* is particularly obsessed by copulation with disincarnate demonic entities – with incubi (male) and succubi (female). Such sexual relations with incorporeal beings might often entail nothing more than a wet dream. In consequence, the book's authors are much preoccupied with semen. In clinical detail, they explore the question of precisely how demons consummate the sexual act. They consider whether it is 'always accompanied by the injection of semen'.[28] If so, they query where the semen comes from – whether, for example, it is intrinsically demonic, or whether it has been stolen from mortal men. The quality of the semen is then subjected to minute scrutiny. By what criteria do demons choose men from whom to pilfer seed? Can semen ejaculated during 'innocent' wet dreams be collected by demons and, so to speak, recycled? No possibility is left unstudied.

For the authors of the *Malleus*, copulation with a disincarnate entity was an especially grievous and heinous transgression. It represented for them a blasphemous parody of the Virgin Birth, the process whereby Jesus himself was conceived by the Holy

Spirit or Holy Ghost. Four centuries later, the novelist Joris-Karl Huysmans was to speculate about the mysterious, supposedly unmentionable and ultimately unpardonable 'Sin against the Holy Ghost' – the one sin for which there was reportedly no forgiveness. Huysmans identified this sin – the nature of which was kept scrupulously secret by the Church – as precisely the blasphemous parody of the Virgin Birth entailed by sexual relations with a disincarnate entity. He may well have been right, and the portentous secret may not have been quite as secret as it purported to be. In Marlowe's *Doctor Faustus*, for instance – composed when the *Malleus*, first published a century before, was still widely in use – Faustus employs demonic agencies to conjure up the incorporeal shade of Helen of Troy. By definition, Helen's shade would be classified as a species of succubus. And it is only after his sexual union with her that his ultimate fate is sealed, and he is irrevocably and irretrievably damned.

Witch Trials

Armed with the *Malleus Maleficarum*, the Inquisition embarked on a reign of terror across the whole of Europe. In its investigations and interrogations, the rule of evidence was simple. Anything to which two or three witnesses testified on oath was accepted as wholly true and definitively proven. Much use was made of trick questions calculated to trap both suspect and witness. One might be asked, for instance,

> whether he believes that there are such things as witches, and that . . . tempests could be raised or men or animals bewitched. Note that for the most part witches deny this at first.[29]

If, witch or not, one does deny belief in witchcraft, the next question follows with the impact of a trap snapping shut: 'Then are they innocently condemned when they are burned? And he or she must answer.' No matter what the victim replies, he or she is already doomed, since disbelief in witchcraft is itself a heresy.

When a witch was captured, elaborate precautions were taken to neutralise her powers. In order to deny her contact with the earth, and through it with the infernal regions, she would be carried aloft on a plank or in a basket. She would be presented to her judge with her back turned, to prevent any attempt to bewitch him with her gaze. Judges and all other personnel involved in a trial 'must not allow themselves to be touched physically by the witch, especially in any contact of their bare arms or hands'. Judges were also advised to wear – sealed in specially blessed wax and hanging from a thong or chain about their necks – some blessed herbs and a quantity of salt consecrated on Palm Sunday. Despite the reiterated reassurances of immunity enjoyed by Inquisitors and judges, no chances were to be taken.

The trial would proceed with a fairly sophisticated understanding of psychology. The techniques employed reflect considerable experience in the process of extracting or extorting information. Inquisitors recognised that the mind can often be its own worst enemy – that fear can breed in solitude and isolation, and can often produce results as satisfying as physical brutality. Fear of torture, to cite the most obvious example, would thus be generated, stoked and fuelled to a pitch of panic that precluded the need for torture itself. If the accused did not confess promptly, she would be told that examination by torture would follow. It would not follow immediately, however. Instead, the *Malleus* advises, let the accused be stripped, or if she is a woman, let her first be led to the penal cells and there stripped by honest women of good reputation.[30]

Her judges might then 'question her lightly, without shedding blood', but only

after keeping the accused in a state of suspense, and continually postponing the day of examination, and frequently using verbal persuasions.[31]

The Inquisitor is encouraged to utilise such now familiar techniques as that of 'hard' and 'soft' policemen:

let him order the officers to bind her with cords, and apply her to some engine of torture; and then let them obey at once but not joyfully, rather appearing to be disturbed by their duty. Then let her be released again at someone's earnest request, and taken on one side, and let her again be persuaded; and in persuading her, let her be told that she can escape the death penalty.[32]

The *Malleus* advocates flagrant duplicity. A witch might be promised her life, but the life would be life in prison, on bread and water.

And she is not to be told, when she is promised her life, that she is to be imprisoned in this way; but should be led to suppose that some other penance, such as exile, will be imposed.[33]

And even to obtain this dubious dispensation, she must denounce and reveal the identities of other witches. Nor, the *Malleus* hastens to qualify, need the original promise of life actually be kept. There is no obligation to treat a witch with honour, and many Inquisitors think that, after she has been consigned to prison in this way, the promise to spare her life should be kept for a time, but that after a certain period she should be burned.[34]

Alternatively,

the Judge may safely promise the accused her life, but in such a way that he should afterwards disclaim the duty of passing sentence on her, deputing another Judge in his place.[35]

When a witch is returned to her cell following a torture session,

the Judge should also take care that during that interval there should always be guards with her, so that she is never left alone, for fear lest the devil will cause her to kill herself.[36]

In other words, a suicide or attempted suicide produced by agony and despair is also to be interpreted as demonically inspired, and therefore a further proof of guilt. Thus did the Inquisitors exculpate themselves. When women attempted suicide by stabbing themselves in the head with the pins fastening their headcloths, 'so they were found by us when we had risen, as if they had wished to stick them into our own heads'. Even such acts of frenzied desperation would be ascribed to malevolent intent and twisted to serve as evidence.

In any case, suicides or attempted suicides were obviously fairly common. The *Malleus* observes of witches that 'after they have confessed their crimes under torture they always try to hang themselves'. And, 'when the guards have been negligent, they have been found hanged with their shoe-laces or garments'.[37]

If, despite sustained torture, a witch still refuses to confess, the *Malleus* counsels more baroque deceptions. A witch might be taken to a castle, for example, whose owner might

> pretend he is going on a long journey. And then let some of his household . . . visit her and promise that they will set her entirely at liberty if she will teach them how to conduct certain practices. And let the Judge note that by this means they have very often confessed and been convicted.[38]

As a last resort, the *Malleus* advocates the most blatant and breathtakingly shameless treachery:

> And finally let the Judge come in and promise that he will be merciful, with the mental reservation that he means he will be merciful to himself or the State; for whatever is done for the safety of the State is merciful.[39]

The Spread of Mass Madness

In our own era, we have all experienced the way in which one or another public 'scare' can escalate, as if by some psychological contagion, and assume the proportions of mass hysteria. In the United States during the 1950s, there was Senator Joseph McCarthy's paranoically obsessive crusade to ferret out putative Communists. In *The Crucible*, the playwright Arthur Miller attacked McCarthy's campaign by analogy, through the metaphor of the Salem witch trials of the seventeenth century. As a result of Miller's work, the term 'witch hunt' has become an accepted modern idiom for any attempt to winkle out supposed enemies through the instillation and dissemination of collective fear. More recently, we have experienced other forms of mass panic as well. Following Ronald Reagan's bombing of Libya, we saw dramatic numbers of American tourists alter their travel plans and refrain in terror from international flights. We have seen whole communities in Britain swept by allegations of child abuse for satanic rituals, causing scores of parents to be forcibly separated from their children. Given these modern instances of public scares, it is easy to understand how the fear of witchcraft could assume proportions of panic on an epidemic scale, when promulgated by the supreme religious authority of the time – could become, in effect, the psychological equivalent of plague. According to one historian:

> This witch-madness was essentially a disease of the imagination, created and stimulated by the persecution of witchcraft. Wherever the inquisitor or civil magistrate went to destroy it by fire, a harvest of witches sprang up around his footsteps.[40]

In speaking of the Church, the same historian observes:

> Every inquisitor whom it commissioned to suppress witchcraft was an active missionary who scattered the seeds of the belief ever more widely.[41]

The frenzied persecution of witchcraft began under the auspices of the Inquisition, when the Church still exercised undisputed supremacy over Europe's public religious life. Indeed, so obsessed was the Inquisition with witchcraft that it was soon to be caught altogether off guard by the advent of a much more serious threat – in the form of an apostate monk named Martin Luther. Within thirty years of the publication of the *Malleus Maleficarum*, however, the 'witch-madness' was to spread to the fledgling Protestant churches.

By the mid sixteenth century, both Protestants and Catholics alike were burning witches not by twos or threes, but by the hundreds; and this incendiary frenzy continued for more than a century, attaining a climax during the carnage of the Thirty Years War between 1618 and 1648. Between 1587 and 1593, the Archbishop-Elector of Trèves burned 368 witches, the equivalent of more than one a week. In 1585, two German villages were so decimated that only one woman was left alive in each. During a period of three months, 500 alleged witches were burned by the presiding Bishop of Geneva. Between 1623 and 1633, the Prince-Bishop of Bamberg burned more than 600. During the early 1600s, 900 were burned by the Prince-Bishop of Würzburg, including nineteen priests, one of his own nephews and a number of children accused of having sexual relations with demons. In Savoy during the same period, upwards of 800 were burned. In England during the Protectorate, Cromwell had his own 'Witchfinder-General', the notorious Matthew Hopkins. By the end of the seventeenth century, the hysteria had spread across the Atlantic to the Puritan colonies of New England, there engendering the infamous trials at Salem that provided the backdrop for Arthur Miller's play.

But not even the worst depredations of Protestantism could equal those of Rome. In this respect, the Inquisition's record was unrivalled. The Inquisition itself boasted that it had burned, at very least, some 30,000 witches during a period of 150 years. The Church had always been more than a little prone to misogyny. The campaign against witchcraft provided it with a mandate for a full-scale crusade against women, against all things feminine.

7

Fighting the Heresy of Protestantism

The crusade against witchcraft enabled the Church to indulge its propensity for misogyny – and to impose an authoritarian control over women that rendered them subordinate and kept them in what it deemed their appointed place. Ultimately, however, something of less immediately obvious consequence was involved as well. For the witch, as custodian of feminine mysteries and of the old pagan religion, was also an embodiment of the natural order, with which she enjoyed a much closer, much more intimate rapport, than did the priest. And the natural order – nature herself – was inherently 'unregenerate'. Nature still existed in a 'fallen' state and had yet to be redeemed, had yet to be brought into docile accord with divine law – or at any rate with divine law as the male intellects of the Church sought to interpret it. Nature had yet to be tamed and ordered. Only then would it cease to provide a refuge, a sanctuary and a conduit for the demonic. Unfortunately for the Church the problem was not quite that simple.

From the very beginning – from the days when a recognisable and definable 'Christian' thought had emerged out of Judaism and paganism – Church theologians had had difficulty in delineating the demonic. In periods of social, cultural, political or intellectual anarchy, when the Church constituted a bastion of order and coherence, the demonic could safely be identified as any manifestation of disorder. During such periods, the devil was indeed the lineal descendant of goat-horned, goat-hoofed, goat-tailed Pan, lord of 'unregenerate nature' in all its unbridled and seemingly chaotic energy – which, of course, also included sexuality. During such periods, faith was yoked to rationality, and the demonic was its antithesis – the frenzied, the possessed, the orgiastic, the irrational. Thus the demonic was thought to manifest itself in witchcraft and especially in the *Walpurgisnacht* or 'Witches' Sabbath'. And it was thus in witchcraft, and in the irrational, often sexual rites of pagan religion, that the Inquisition sought to identify the traditional archetypal 'adversary' of Christianity.

There were other instances, however, when the Church itself trafficked in unreason, and faith was yoked not to rationality, but to the irrational. If the volcanic and tempestuous energy of the *Walpurgisnacht* could be channelled into piety – into the hysteria associated with certain Church festivals, for example, or with the abandonment often apparent in evangelical sects today – it could be sanctioned and endorsed. A visitation from a succubus in the form of Helen of Troy might serve to damn Faustus; but the same psychological mechanism, if it generated an apparition of the Virgin instead, could confer sainthood.

If the Virgin, rather than Helen, appeared in a vision, the demonic became that which questioned the vision's validity. By extension, the demonic became the sceptical intellect which questioned the validity of anything promulgated by the Church. If the devil could sometimes take the form of frenzied Pan, he could also take the form of cold, cunning, silkily seductive and persuasive Lucifer, the wily logician and tempter whose subtle skill in sophistry and casuistry could outwit the most adept theologian. It was in this form, as the serpent in the Garden of

Eden, that the devil had supposedly first manifested himself in the Old Testament. And according to Christian propagandists, it was in this form that Lucifer, as a consequence of his intellectual pride, was first supposed to have been expelled from heaven and his seat by God's side. If the devil could sometimes be wildly irrational, then, he could also be hyper-rational, hyper-intellectual. When faith depended on irrational belief and unquestioning adherence, the devil became the principle which dared to question – in other words, any defiantly independent thought. During the Renaissance and the Lutheran Reformation, according to the Inquisition, it was in this form that the devil manifested himself; and it was in this form that the Inquisition sought to locate and extirpate him.

This is not to say that persecution of the irrational demonic ceased. The ferreting out of witches, warlocks and other adherents of the old pagan religion continued, even gained momentum; and the newly established Protestant churches were as zealous in harrying them as Rome. Luther himself inveighed against the devil and against witchcraft, and Protestant religious leaders of all denominations quickly followed suit. Protestantism could be as intolerant, as narrow-minded, as bigoted, ignorant and brutal as the Inquisition itself.

But while Catholic and Protestant thought-police jointly pursued the traditional irrational forms of the demonic, the Inquisition now had to contend as well with the demonic in its antithetical form – the form of intellectual pride, of independent thought, of investigation and inquiry that openly defied the priesthood and pursued an agenda of its own. For the Inquisition of the Renaissance and the Reformation, Satan might be discernible in the aged midwife or wise woman of one or another village; but he could also be discerned – and more dangerously so – in the guise of such figures as Martin

Luther, Galileo Galilei, Giordano Bruno and Tommaso Campanella.

What, then, was the demonic? In practice, *anything* deemed to be hostile or inimical to the Church could be labelled so. The infernal powers could be held responsible not only for extreme manifestations of rationality or irrationality, but also for books, philosophies, political movements and anything else that might be construed as disobedience of Papal authority. Learning itself would soon come to be regarded as demonic.

Throughout the Middle Ages, the Church had comprised a bastion of learning in a world of untutored barbarism. As Umberto Eco illustrates in *The Name of the Rose*, however, the Church also exercised a monopoly on learning which effectively ensured that the world around it remained untutored and barbaric. Knowledge, so the cliché goes, is power; and the Church wielded power largely through the knowledge it monopolised, commanded, controlled and made available to the lay populace only, as it were, by drip-feed.

With the Reformation, this situation was to change dramatically. The Reformation was to witness a veritable explosion of knowledge. It was to issue from secular sources. It was to issue from the newly established Protestant 'heresies', such as Lutheranism. It was to issue from the recently reinvigorated esoteric tradition of Hermeticism. And it was to be disseminated on an unprecedented scale by the advent of printing and the circulation of printed material. Luther's translation of the Bible into the vernacular, and other translations that followed such as the Geneva Bible and the English-language King James Version, were to make scripture available for the first time to the layman – who could read it for himself, without the interpretation and filtering apparatus of the priesthood. All such learning was to be stigmatised by the Church as demonic, and in consequence to attract the attention of the Inquisition.

In the past, there had been very few learned men outside the Church, and fewer still who could hope to receive a hearing without incurring dire, even fatal, consequences. Now, an entire and imposing edifice of learning was being erected that arrogantly ignored, and sometimes flagrantly defied, Rome's authority. If the devil was manifest in the orgiastic irrationality of witchcraft, he was now becoming equally manifest in the eloquence of the printed word – and in the audacity of the inquiring, questing and independent mind, which rushed boldly in where angels, fools, ecclesiastics and even saints had previously feared to tread.

The Counter-Reformation

For Rome, the new situation posed new demands. Without conceding any more ground than it was forced to, the Church sought to adapt – and to adapt the Inquisition with it. In the thirteenth century, during the Albigensian Crusade, the Dominicans had constituted a major innovation by virtue of being learned – by virtue of being trained in theology and thus able to dispute with Cathar and other heretics on their own terms. Over the subsequent three centuries, however, the Dominicans, like their rival Orders, had become increasingly idle, self-indulgent, reposing on their laurels, clinging to the power and privileges they possessed, making scant effort to confront the new challenges that had arisen. Their position in relation to the proliferating Protestant heresy was defensive at best. More often than not, they were simply passive, hoping it would go away. Persecuting hapless women for witchcraft required little effort, little discipline, little organisation. To

counter the influence of knowledgeable and articulate heresi-
archs like Luther, Calvin and Zwingli was rather more
troublesome.

To contend with Protestantism, the Church needed a sixteenth-century equivalent of what the Dominicans had been
300 years before – a cadre of highly trained and dedicated
individuals who could actually dispute with their adversaries
on a basis of equal learning and intelligence, equal subtlety,
equal psychological sophistication. And if Protestantism was
indeed – as appeared ever more likely – going to withstand all
attempts at extirpation, the Church had at least to establish
some sort of quantitative or numerical superiority, in the size
of its congregation and in the territory over which it exercised
spiritual dominion. Among other things, it had to consolidate
its position in parts of the world that were only just beginning
to be explored, had to convert whole regions and continents
of heathen before Protestantism could get to them. In other
words, the Church needed an institution or organisation of
highly skilled, highly intelligent, highly trained and highly
motivated missionaries – a new soldiery of Christ or 'Milice
de Christ', who, with military discipline and fortitude, could
crusade in the sphere of the intellect the way the Templars and
Hospitallers had done on the battlefields of the Holy Land.
The institution that rose to this challenge was the Society of
Jesus, or the Jesuits.

The Society of Jesus was created by a Spaniard, Ignatius
Loyola (c. 1491–1556), whose original ambition had been to
win military glory. During a siege of the fortress of Pamplona
in 1521, Loyola was seriously wounded. While convalescing,
he became increasingly studious and introspective. He
embarked on a pilgrimage to Montserrat, hung his weapons at
the shrine there, then retired to live in a cave for a year as a

hermit. In this seclusion, he wrote his manual, *The Spiritual Exercises*, which outlined a new and rigorous programme of Christian meditation. In 1523, he embarked on a second pilgrimage, this time to Jerusalem. When he returned to Spain, he took up studies at the University of Alcalá.

By 1526, Loyola had begun to preach in public – and to incur suspicions of heresy from the Spanish Inquisition, who arrested him and kept him in chains for some three weeks while *The Spiritual Exercises* was examined and investigated. He was duly exonerated of the charges against him and released, but ordered to cease all public discussions of theology for four years. To escape this prohibition, Loyola moved to Paris in 1528. Here, he gathered a small circle of devoted followers who were to become the original Jesuits. In 1534, all of them took an oath of allegiance at a church in Montmartre.

On 27 September 1540, Pope Paul III officially established the Jesuits under their original name, the 'Company of Jesus'. Although they carried no arms, their training, discipline and nomenclature conformed to essentially military patterns. It has even been suggested, and not without some credibility, that Loyola modelled the Jesuits' hierarchy and organisation on those of the Knights Templar.

In the century and a half that followed, the Jesuits were to become the spearhead of the Counter-Reformation, the Church's methodical efforts to establish new spheres of influence, as well as to regain at least some of the ground lost to Protestantism. Like military planners, the Jesuits organised their campaigns in accordance with strategic thinking. In order to establish currency and credibility, they were quite prepared to join in the general persecution of witchcraft. According to Hugh Trevor-Roper, if the Dominicans had been the evangelists of the medieval Counter-Reformation, the Jesuits were the evangelists of the sixteenth-century Counter-Reformation, and if Protestant evangelists carried the craze to the countries which they conquered for reform, these Catholic evangelists carried it equally to the countries which they reconquered for Rome. Some of the most famous of Jesuit missionaries distinguished themselves in propagating the witch-craze.[1]

Ultimately, however, witchcraft was of secondary importance to the Jesuits. Their primary interests lay elsewhere. Bohemia and Poland, for example, both of which had proved fertile soil for Protestantism, were soon to be reclaimed for the Church. And within a few years, the network of Jesuit missions, like the old preceptories of the Templars and Hospitallers, encompassed the known world. They extended westwards across the Atlantic to the Americas, eastwards to the Indian subcontinent, to China, Japan and the islands of the Pacific. Closer to home, the Jesuits were instrumental in reforming, repackaging, rebranding and relaunching the Inquisition.

By 1540, when Pope Paul III officially established the Jesuits, the 'Babylonian Captivity' at Avignon had ended, and the Great Schism that had rent the Church for more than a century had finally been resolved. Within five years, the Council of Trent was to formulate a blueprint that would determine the Papacy's status, administrative apparatus, orientation and hierarchy of priorities for the next three and a quarter centuries. And for the newly reunified Church, the paramount concern was, of necessity, the crusade against the heresy of Protestantism.

As a prelude to the Council of Trent, Pope Paul embarked on a radical reform of the Papacy's government and administration. A number of separate offices or departments was created to preside over the various subdivisions of the Church's affairs. All functioning under direct Papal control, they were designated 'congregations' and 'councils'. The Inquisition was now to become one such 'congregation'. Having suffered personally at its hands, Loyola may not have harboured much love for the Spanish Inquisition, but he admired its discipline, its efficiency, its smoothly working machinery. Instigated in large part by the Jesuits, the old Papal or Roman Inquisition was reconstituted, and modelled specifically on its Spanish counterpart. Just as the Spanish Inquisition served as an instrument of Spanish royal policy, the Papal or Roman Inquisition was to become an instrument of Church policy. In other words, its chief priority was no longer to be the supposed 'purity' of the faith, but the stability and welfare of Papacy and Church. Its official title was the 'Sacred Roman Congregation and Universal Inquisition, or Holy Office'. In 1908, its name was to be changed again to the 'Congregation of the Holy Office'. For most commentators, a more abbreviated form – simply the 'Holy Office' – was subsequently to suffice. Seldom has so innocuous, even ostensibly laudable, a title managed to acquire such sinister associations. In an effort to purge these and sanitise the institution further, the Inquisition was once more renamed in 1965 as the 'Congregation for the Doctrine of the Faith'. It operates under that appellation today, a direct lineal descendant of the original Inquisition created in 1234 and reconstituted in 1542.

Loyola and the Jesuits were one major influence in the creation of the revamped Inquisition, or Holy Office. Of comparable importance was an ambitious and fanatical Dominican, Giovanni Caraffa. Between 1515 and 1522, Caraffa had served as Papal Nuncio to Spain, where he, like Loyola, had been impressed by the Spanish Inquisition's efficiency. On his return to Italy, he had become the leader of a pious circle of high-ranking ecclesiastics devoted to restoring the Church's purity and moral integrity.

One means of doing so for Caraffa, and of attracting attention to himself in the process, was to launch a campaign against Michelangelo's painting of the Last Judgement in the Sistine Chapel. When the painting was unveiled in 1541, Caraffa and his circle proceeded to turn it into a scandal. They were outraged by Michelangelo's overt phallic symbolism, by his depiction of one man being dragged by the genitals and others kissing, and vociferously condemned the work as indecent. Their indignation was soon being echoed by like-minded colleagues, and criticism rumbled on for the next twenty-four years. In 1551, for example, a prominent Dominican wrote that Michelangelo 'is admirable in depicting the naked bodies of men and their pudenda', and complained that 'it is most indecent to see all these nudities everywhere, on the altars and in the chapels of God'.[2] Eventually, the Council of Trent decreed that 'corrections' be made to the painting. In 1565, an artist was specifically commissioned for this purpose and modestly shrouded all offending protuberances in loincloths and robes. The receipt he received for his efforts still exists, detailing 'the sum of 60 scudi due . . . in payment for the work done by him in 1565 in covering the pudenda of the figures in the Chapel of Pope Sixtus'.[3]

By that time, Caraffa himself was dead. But his original attacks on the painting in 1541 had attracted the sympathetic interest of Pope Paul III, who raised Caraffa and five other members of his circle to the status of cardinals. Eventually, in 1555, Caraffa himself became Pope, taking the name of Paul IV and occupying the throne of Saint Peter until his death in 1559.

Supported by Loyola and the Dominican Cardinal Archbishop of Burgos, Caraffa, on earning the favour of Paul III,
advocated the establishment of a permanent tribunal of the
Inquisition, modelled on that of the Inquisition in Spain. It
was thus that the Holy Office was created in 1542. Caraffa
was appointed the first Inquisitor-General of the reconstituted
institution. The Pope reserved for himself the right of pardon.
Apart from that, the new Papal Inquisition, or Holy Office,
was given virtually unrestricted powers, including the right to
delegate authority to other ecclesiastics and invoke the aid of
the secular arm if necessary. Immediately on receiving his
appointment, Caraffa commandeered a substantial house in
Rome and fitted it with prison cells. He then issued four
procedural rules to be implemented by all Inquisitors. They
were to 'punish even on suspicion'. They were to 'have no
regard for the great'. They were to be severe with any who
'shelter behind the powerful'. And they were to 'show no
mildness, least of all towards Calvinists'. Of these injunctions,
Caraffa in private conversations particularly stressed the need
to strike at men in high places, 'for . . . on their punishment,
the salvation of the classes beneath them depends'.[4] What he
had no need to say, of course, was that such an onslaught against
the powerful effectively neutralised any prospective rivals or
challengers to his authority.

There ensued a purge of the kind that anticipated those
perpetrated in our own century by Hitler, Stalin and other
more petty tyrants of their ilk. According to one historian, the
whole of Italy 'became paralysed'. The head of the Capuchin
Order fled to Geneva. Other prominent figures, both secular
and ecclesiastic, sought refuge elsewhere. In 1546, the entire
University of Modena disbanded itself. Yet Caraffa still chafed
against Pope Paul's preparedness to pardon and the extent

to which this vitiated the Holy Office's capacity to terrorise.

It was not until he himself became Pope in 1555 that Caraffa at last possessed the licence he had long sought. To exploit this fully, he delegated his right-hand man, the Dominican Michele Ghislieri. In 1557, Ghislieri was appointed cardinal and, a year later, Grand Inquisitor. Subsequently, in 1566, Ghislieri was to become Pope in his turn, taking the name of Pius V.

No sooner had Caraffa ascended the throne of Saint Peter than the new reign of terror began in earnest. In 1556, twelve converted Jews were burned at Ancona, their conversion presumably being deemed insufficiently complete. In 1557, a cardinal was imprisoned. During the same year, a number of Venetians were convicted of heresy, delivered to Rome and consigned to the stake. When Caraffa died in 1559, he was so loathed by the populace of Rome that they attacked the Holy Office's premises, demolished the buildings, looted and burned all records. Undeterred, however, the Holy Office continued about its business. In 1562, some 2,000 Waldensians were brutally massacred in southern Italy. In 1567, a prominent Florentine humanist was beheaded. In 1570, a professor of rhetoric was garrotted at Siena. In 1573, the Holy Office undertook to 'investigate' Veronese's painting, *The Feast in the House of Levi*, and Veronese himself was summoned before the tribunal for questioning. He escaped punishment, but was ordered to alter the painting at his own expense.

In the meantime, the Church had undergone a significant transformation. As early as 1523, the rapid spread of Protestantism had made the need for reform painfully apparent. It was suggested that such reform might best be effected by a general Church Council. The Papacy and the Curia were at first alarmed by the proposal, fearing that any Council might proclaim itself greater than the Pope. Indeed, no sooner had the prospect of a Council been publicised than the price of saleable ecclesiastical positions in Rome dropped dramatically. Eventually, however, in 1545, Pope Paul III did convene the Council of Trent.

Trent was one of the supremely important Councils in Church history, playing a crucial role in defining both the Church and the Papacy as they have come down to us today. Punctuated by interruptions and sporadic adjournments, the Council extended over a total of eighteen years, from 1545 until 1563. It outlasted both Paul III and Caraffa in his papal identity of Paul IV.

The Council opened with an attempt – admittedly half-hearted in the most influential quarters – to conciliate and accommodate Protestantism. It quickly became apparent, however, that any such attempt was doomed. Thereafter, the assembled ecclesiastics addressed themselves to means of contending with Protestantism, and, in order best to do so, to adapting their own Church for struggle. The Council proclaimed, for example, 'the equal authority of scripture and tradition'.[5] In other words, the Church, as embodiment of tradition, was decreed to possess an authority equal to that of scripture itself. This, of course, was intrinsically inimical to Protestantism, which recognised the authority only of the Bible. The rupture with Protestantism was rendered even more definitive by other measures – the formulation of the Doctrine of Original Sin, for example, and a repudiation of Luther's insistence on Justification by Faith.

At the same time, the Council of Trent undertook to clarify the position of the Papacy in relation to bishops and to Church Councils. Thus, for instance, certain reformers initially endeavoured to 'affirm the superiority of the Council even to the Pope, and so declare its supreme authority'.[6] In the end, however, it

133

was the Papacy that emerged as supreme authority, exercising control over bishops as well as Church Councils. A millennium earlier, the Church had been largely decentralised, and the Pope had simply been Bishop of Rome, the proverbial 'first among equals'. During subsequent centuries, his power had become progressively more centralised, but it had not been officially ratified as such. After the Council of Trent, the Church became the equivalent of an absolute monarchy, with the Pope enjoying the status of sovereign. From this point on, the Jesuits, the Holy Office and all other Roman Catholic institutions were dedicated less to the supposed 'purity' of the faith than to the stability of the Papacy and the Church.

That stability had already suffered from the proliferation of heretical and secular learning. In regions where Protestantism held sway, little could be done to repair the damage. Elsewhere, however, the Church attempted to regain and reestablish something of its former monopoly over knowledge. To this end, a new form of censorship was introduced. It assumed the form of the Holy Office's notorious 'Index of Prohibited Books'.

As early as 1554, local tribunals of the Holy Office – in Venice and Milan for instance – had drawn up their own lists of forbidden works. In 1559, in his capacity as Pope Paul IV, Caraffa published his own definitively authoritative *Index Librorum Prohibitorum*. It included not only heretical texts, but also those the Holy Office deemed immoral. Among them were works by Hermeticists, such as Heinrich Cornelius Agrippa von Nettesheim, and by humanists, such as Erasmus of Rotterdam. All works by Martin Luther were banned, as were those of Jan Hus. Books pertaining to magic, alchemy and astrology were condemned. So were a compilation of texts purporting to have been composed by King Arthur and a collection of prophecies ascribed to Merlin. The Judaic Talmud was forbidden, along with thirty translations of the Bible in its entirety and eleven of the New Testament. There was also a list of sixty-two printers to be shunned, most of them in Protestant Basle.

In 1564, Caraffa's Index was officially approved by the Council of Trent and reissued with a number of additions. In 1571, Michele Ghislieri – Caraffa's former lieutenant and Grand Inquisitor, now installed as Pope Pius V – created, under the auspices of the Holy Office, a special 'Congregation of the Index', whose sole task was to oversee, maintain and update the list of prohibited works. This institution continued in existence until 1917, when its duties were again placed under the direct control of the Holy Office. For four centuries, the Index was issued in updated form at sporadic intervals. Printed at Vatican City, the last complete edition appeared in 1948. Among the authors and texts condemned were (in alphabetical order) Johann Valentin Andreae, Balzac, the Church of England's Book of Common Prayer, Giordano Bruno, Descartes, Dumas (both *père* and *fils*), Fenelon, Flaubert, Robert Fludd, Frederick the Great of Prussia, Victor Hugo, James I of England, John Locke, Michael Maier, John Stuart Mill, Montaigne, Henry More, Ernest Renan, Rousseau, Spinoza, Stendhal, Laurence Sterne, Swedenborg, Voltaire, Zola, all histories of Freemasonry and all histories of the Inquisition itself. During the 1950s, a number of other authors were added as afterthoughts – Sartre, Alberto Moravia, Gide, Kazantzakis, Unamuno and Simone de Beauvoir.[7]

Such a list posed daunting problems for Catholic historians and literary scholars. One of the authors of the present book recalls his first year of graduate school at the University of Chicago, where a basic course required for the degree programme included Stendhal as mandatory reading. In the class at the time, there were a handful of seminarians and two or three nuns. In order to obtain permission to read *The Red and the Black*, they were obliged to petition the Holy Office through the local archbishop, and receive special dispensation in writing.

By that time, however, the sluice gates had already opened. *Ulysses*, *Lady Chatterley's Lover*, *Lolita* and other major works previously banned by secular authorities had become readily available. So, too, had a number of lesser but still consequential books – by William Burroughs, for example, Henry Miller and Hubert Selby. Libraries at convents and seminaries were being duped by practical jokers into purchasing multiple copies of Genet's *Our Lady of the Flowers*, which was also being mischievously recommended to unsuspecting nuns. For the moral and theological sentinels of the Holy Office, the mere process of keeping up with supposedly depraved texts, still more of banning them, must have seemed a task for a veritable squadron of Sisyphae. At last, in 1966, the Index was officially abolished – an act, one would like to imagine, of capitulation and despair.

Persecution of the Renaissance Magi

The Church emerged from the Council of Trent with a new consolidation of pontifical authority and with two institutions – the Jesuits and the Inquisition in its modernised guise as the Holy Office – to spearhead the Counter-Reformation. In reclaiming such territories as Poland and Bohemia for Rome, as well as in spreading the Church's message overseas, these institutions displayed an energy, a resourcefulness and a zeal of often epic proportions. Ultimately, however, the war was already lost, and with only occasional exceptions the battles fought were defensive battles – holding actions conducted to retain an ever-diminishing dominion. In the beginning, for example, Protestantism had meant solely Lutheranism, the creed promulgated by Martin Luther in Germany. But the new heresy of Protestantism had quickly proved to be hydra-headed, and other Protestant sects had appeared with alarming rapidity. Luther had been followed by Calvin in Geneva, Zwingli in Zurich, John Knox in Scotland. Although his reasons for doing so were hardly theological, Henry VIII had created the Church of England and severed its connection with Rome. There had also been a resurgence of certain old heresies in new forms, and a number of messianic or millenarian movements and eruptions – the self-styled Anabaptists, for instance, who had emerged in Protestant Holland and then proceeded to capture the German city of Munster in 1534, proclaiming their own 'Kingdom of Zion' and inaugurating a regime of anarchic licence and orgiastic frenzy. Even Catholic scholars had become increasingly 'infected' by heterodox thought.

When the Council of Trent ended in 1563 the world had changed. Through printing and the dissemination of ideas, both secular learning and Protestantism had become established facts, which the Church could neither accommodate nor extirpate. In less than half a century, Rome's previous hegemony over Europe's spiritual life had effectively been shattered, and Catholic dominion reduced by something like a third. The mass persecution of witches continued, by Protestantism as fanatically as by the Church. Apart from this, however, the work of the Holy Office became more focused, more specialised, more precisely delineated, intellectually disciplined and surgically conducted. From the mid sixteenth century on, the history of the retitled Inquisition became a history less of wholesale terror and indiscriminate persecution than of specific individual cases, but certain of these involved some of the most distinguished names in the evolution of Western civilisation.

Among the chief targets of the Holy Office were the Faustian figures who have come to be known as 'Renaissance Magi', men whose thirst for knowledge, audacity of spirit and visionary aspirations encompassed the arts, the sciences, theology, philosophy, medicine, technology and the spectrum of disciplines collectively regarded as 'esoterica', including astrology, alchemy and magic. During the first third of the sixteenth century, the most important of these figures had been Aureolus Philippus Theophrastus Bombastus von Hohenheim, subsequently known simply as Paracelsus, and Heinrich Cornelius Agrippa von Nettesheim, the primary model for both Marlowe's Doctor Faustus and Goethe's Faust. Both Paracelsus and Agrippa had a number of rancorous encounters with the Inquisition. During their lifetimes, however, the Inquisition in question was the old Inquisition, prior to its relaunch as the Holy Office. In consequence, both of them, though incurring sporadic short terms of censure or imprisonment, escaped largely unscathed. Agrippa castigated the Inquisitors of the time as 'bloody vultures' and condemned the stupidity whereby heretics 'are to be convinced with Faggot and Fire, not with Scriptures and Arguments'.[8] On one occasion, while serving as a functionary for the Free City of Metz, he defended a woman accused of witchcraft against the local Dominican Inquisitor, whom he confronted, faced down and out-argued in open court.

The 'Magi' who followed Paracelsus and Agrippa, and who found themselves pitted against the modernised Holy Office, were not so fortunate. In 1591, for example, Tommaso Campanella, a mystical Dominican with what would later be seen as 'Rosicrucian' tendencies, published a book advocating the validity of empiricism, as well as faith, in the study of philosophy. The book was condemned by the Holy Office and Campanella was imprisoned for heresy. In 1599, shortly after his release, he was again in trouble, this time for subversive political activity.

He was accordingly arrested, tortured and sentenced to life imprisonment. A friend who visited him in his cell later reported

> his legs were all bruised and his buttocks almost without flesh, which had been torn off bit by bit in order to drag out of him a confession of the crimes of which he had been accused.[9]

During his incarceration, Campanella produced his most famous book, *La città del sole* (*The City of the Sun*), a blueprint for an ideal Utopian community of the sort being extolled at the time by mystical writers. In another work, he argued that all nature was alive and that the world possessed a soul 'created and infused by God'.[10] This provoked the wrath of the Inquisitors, who complained that if Campanella's contention were valid, the world soul would imbue with its qualities 'vermin and other unworthy objects'.[11] In 1626, after more than a quarter of a century in prison, Campanella was at last released. By 1634, he was again under threat and fled to France.

A more dramatic case than Campanella's was that of Giordano Bruno (1548–1600). Like Paracelsus and Agrippa before him, Bruno was the very archetype of the 'Renaissance Magus'. Among numerous other things, he was a poet, a dramatist, a philosopher, a theologian, a scientist, a visionary and a self-proclaimed magician. In certain respects, such as his megalomania, he may well have been more than a little mad; but he was also unquestionably a genius, one of the most profound, brilliant, original and extraordinary minds of his age, whose thinking has reverberated down to our own century and influenced such figures as James Joyce.

After thirteen years in a Dominican monastery at Naples, Bruno absconded in 1576 and embarked on a peripatetic career, promulgating his own mystical system through preaching, teaching and lecturing, as well as through print. By 1581, he had become an eminent figure in Paris and enjoyed the favour of the court. In 1583, he arrived in England, residing at the lodgings of the French ambassador. He engaged in a prominent public debate at Oxford, expounded on Copernicus's theory that the earth moved around the sun and produced a discernible influence on such figures as the poet Sir Philip Sidney. During the subsequent eight years, he travelled around Germany, Switzerland and Bohemia, and in Prague made the acquaintance of the Holy Roman Emperor Rudolf II.

Unfortunately for Bruno, his success fostered an excessive self-confidence and a misplaced sense of immunity. In 1591, at the invitation of a Venetian noble, he imprudently returned to Italy. A year later, he was denounced to the Holy Office, arrested, transferred to Rome and imprisoned. For the following seven years, despite the most extreme and protracted torture, he argued tenaciously with the Inquisitors. To their demands that he retract, he stubbornly and repeatedly refused. At last, in 1600, he was officially convicted of heresy and sentenced to death. On 17 February of that year, he went to the stake. He went gagged, lest his continuing defiance prove embarrassing to his executioners or unsettling for the assembled spectators.

For modern readers, the most famous victim of the Holy Office during the Counter-Reformation would undoubtedly be Galileo Galilei (1564–1642), who today is a household name, familiar to every schoolchild. The telescope having been invented only shortly before, Galileo in 1609, constructed his own more powerful version of the instrument and began using it, for the first time, to study the heavens. His astronomical observations enabled him to demonstrate empirically that Copernicus's theory had been correct – that the earth and the other planets of the solar system did indeed revolve around the sun and that the earth, therefore, was not the centre of the universe. This was contrary to Church teachings, which rested on the Biblical account of the creation in Genesis, with all the implications attending thereto. In consequence, Galileo was arrested by the Holy Office and spent the last eight years of his life in prison, convicted of heresy. As a somewhat belated afterthought, he was absolved of his sins by the Vatican in 1992, three and a half centuries after his death.

8

Fear of the Mystics

I n *The Brothers Karamazov*, Dostoevsky's Grand Inquisitor is ruthlessly prepared to send Jesus himself to the stake in order to preserve the stability and efficiency of the Church. To understand this mentality – to understand, that is, the Inquisition's role in European history and culture, as well as its own priorities – one must confront the distinction between religion and 'spirituality'. Or, to phrase the matter slightly differently, one must confront the distinction between 'a religion' and 'the religious experience'. This distinction is crucial, indeed essential, to any comprehension of religious issues. Yet it is almost invariably overlooked, blurred or deliberately muddled. For most people, the words 'religion' and 'spirituality' mean the same thing and are used interchangeably, indiscriminately.

The point in question can be illustrated by a simple, even ostensibly frivolous, analogy. Let us imagine an individual who has never encountered electricity as we know it today – a force regulated, tamed and subject to human control, rendered active or dormant at the flick of a switch. This hypothetical individual might be from a so-called 'primitive' society, like those of certain Pacific islands during the Second World War – adherents of a 'cargo cult', for example, who regarded Allied servicemen as veritable gods descending from the skies in great metal birds, and continued long after hostilities had ceased to worship at altars constructed from derelict aircraft components, abandoned Jeeps, rubber tyres or even Campbell soup cans. Alternatively, our hypothetical individual might be from the past – an American Indian before the advent of the white man, or even one of our own medieval ancestors – teleported, as in some science fiction scenario, into the present.

Such an individual would be dazzled, even terrified, by the surroundings in which he suddenly found himself. But with all the spectacular marvels confronting him, he would probably not be unduly impressed by the serpentine wires connecting our lamps, our refrigerators, our televisions and other appliances to electrical sockets in the wall. If told that these sockets were a source of immense power, our hypothetical individual might well be sceptical. If, however, he poked his finger into one such socket, he would undergo a species of revelation. In the contemporary vernacular, he would 'get zapped'. Something dramatic, even traumatic, would happen, of an immediacy and an intensity that brooked no questioning, no act of belief or disbelief. Assuming he were not summarily electrocuted, our hypothetical individual would be catapulted for a matter of seconds into an 'altered state of consciousness'. His hair would stand up on end. His faculties would be scrambled. He would be incapable of any coherent thought, still less of any coherent speech. Without any voluntary assent on his part, a yell or a cry might well be wrenched from his lips. He would be torn out of himself, out of his accustomed mental habitat, and projected into some other dimension of experience.

To an onlooker or a bystander, our hypothetical individual's ordeal would certainly be real enough, 'objectively' real. He would not merely have imagined what was happening, not have hallucinated it. A recognisable mechanism or dynamic would be involved, not just physiologically, but psychologically as well. Yet it would be perfectly explicable in rational terms. To our hypothetical individual himself, however, his experience would be of an altogether different order. The reality he was encountering within his psyche would be very different from that of the onlooker or bystander. That reality would usurp all other realities, would fill and overbrim his consciousness to the exclusion of everything else. It might even eclipse his consciousness entirely.

Assuming he survived his experience, our hypothetical individual would undoubtedly emerge from it in a state of profound disorientation. When he had regained command of his faculties, he would want to know what had happened to him, what had produced that extraordinary moment of 'otherness'. He could not gainsay the experience, could not dispute it or deny it, but he would be incapable of explaining what it meant, what it signified. At this point, there would arise the problem that attends any religious experience, any attempt to make sense of it, to establish its relevance to everyday existence and to society as a whole – the problem of *interpretation*.

Since he himself would have no framework or context to explain what he had undergone, we could offer our hypothetical individual an interpretation – which he would probably be inclined to accept for want of any alternative. We could tell him he had just established direct and immediate contact with the Great God Electricity. We could expound eloquently on the powers of this deity. We could explain how this deity provided us with an inexhaustible source of divine energy – which lit our homes and our cities and enabled us to turn night into day, which permitted us to receive magical sounds from the air through our radios and magical moving pictures through our televisions, which governed the functioning of our cars, our refrigerators, our telephones, our washing machines and all the other appliances and accoutrements of modern civilisation. We could then devise and adumbrate an elaborate theology based on the Great God Electricity. We could describe how the god should be propitiated and rendered docile. We could explicate and demonstrate how the god might be persuaded to serve us. And we could then send our hypothetical individual back to his own milieu, equipped with, say, a portable generator and the other apparatus required to introduce the god to his society.

In his own milieu our hypothetical individual could establish a cult without too much difficulty and install himself as high priest. With his portable electrical kit, he could 'initiate' those around him – perhaps many, perhaps an elect few – into his 'mysteries'. For the majority, it would be sufficient simply to witness a friend, neighbour or relative getting 'zapped' by the new god. One would then readily accept the new god as an act of faith, without having to undergo the experience oneself.

By virtue of the power he had demonstrated and controlled, our hypothetical individual could impose his own theology – and with it his own cosmology, his own dogma, his own code of ethics, his own commandments, his own catalogue of sanctions and prohibitions. In the absence of any other, his interpretation would be regarded as definitive, and his authority would be absolute. Until one day, wandering in the forest during a thunderstorm, or flying a home-made kite as Benjamin Franklin supposedly did, some other individual might establish his own unique contact with the Great God Electricity, independent of the prevailing theology and dogma. He would discover that the experience itself was just that – an experience undergone at first hand, to which all the intellectual baggage, all the *a posteriori* interpretations, were irrelevant.

Suspicion of the Christian Mystics

This analogy may well appear frivolous. It does, however, serve to illustrate the distinction between the 'religious experience' on the one hand, and, on the other, the combination of faith and intellectual interpretation involved in 'religion'. The 'religious experience' – which can indeed be equated with 'spirituality' – is above all an experience. It does not require or involve 'belief' or 'faith'. It entails what the individual undergoing it at the moment can only apprehend as a form of direct and self-validating knowledge; and knowledge precludes any necessity for belief. If one *knows*, directly and immediately, one has no need to believe. If one touches one's hand to a hot stove or an open flame, one does not need to 'believe' in pain. Pain is experienced, immediately and directly, with an intensity that usurps the foreground of consciousness, preempting both belief and intellectual interpretations, rendering them irrelevant, secondary and subsequent to the direct apprehension or knowledge. During the first century or two of the Christian era, such direct apprehension was referred to as 'gnosis', which means simply 'knowledge'. Those who sought or experienced 'gnosis' were called, or called themselves, 'gnostics'. Today, we might call them mystics and ascribe their experience to a psychological dynamic or an 'altered state of consciousness'. But whatever the terminology attached to it, there remains the raw and undiluted experience itself, dissociated from all rational interpretations appended after the fact.

In contrast, a religion is based not on 'gnosis', but on a theology, which is the intellectual interpretation attributed after the fact to the direct apprehension of 'gnosis'. A theology attempts to explain the religious experience, to determine what the experience 'means' – even though it may 'mean' nothing at all, at least in intellectual terms. Theologies involve dogma, articles of faith, moral codes, prohibitions and sanctions, rites and rituals. The more complex and elaborate these things become, the more divorced and dissociated they become from the original experience that initially inspired them. Eventually, a theology loses all contact with the original experience and becomes an intellectual edifice in its own right, self-justifying and self-sufficient. The religion based on such a theology no longer has anything to do with 'spirituality'. It has been transformed into nothing more than an instrument for conditioning and control. It is then merely a social, cultural and political institution, responsible for legislating morality and maintaining – or in some cases challenging – civic order. And for the hierarchical power structure presiding over such an institution, 'gnosis' constitutes a threat, because it renders the power structure superfluous. In order to protect the power structure, its custodians must turn themselves into Dostoevsky's Grand Inquisitor.

The theology and the organised religion based upon it are represented by the priest. The religious experience is represented by the mystic. The priest promulgates faith and traffics in intellectual dogma, in the business of interpretation and codification. In short, he deals with the *exoteric* dimension of what is generally called the 'spiritual'; and all too often this dimension ceases to be 'spiritual' in the process, becoming instead a matter of docile belief accepted at second hand, or of rationality and intellectuality. In contrast, the mystic confronts the *esoteric*, the private or personal or 'hidden' dimension of the 'spiritual'. He undergoes it as an experience and apprehends it as a form of direct knowledge, with an intensity and an immediacy that preempt both interpretation and belief.

Given these distinctions, it is hardly surprising that most established and organised religions tend to be nervous about their own mystical traditions, about the mystics among their congregations. The mystic always remains a potential maverick, a potential renegade or apostate, a potential heretic – and therefore a potential candidate for persecution. Because of his insistence on direct experience, he does not require or even necessarily want a priest as interpreter. In effect, the mystic renders the priest and the entire ecclesiastical hierarchy superfluous. And the mystics of the world's various religious traditions will generally have more in common with each other than any of them will with their own official priesthoods. The esoteric experience of the mystic involves a common denominator, a common psychological dynamic. The exoteric theology of a priesthood will invariably differ from those of other, rival priesthoods – and the difference will often culminate in violence. Throughout human history, believers have waged war against one another. Gnostics or mystics have not. People are only too prepared to kill on behalf of a theology or a faith. They are less disposed to do so on behalf of knowledge. Those prepared to kill for faith will therefore have a vested interest in stifling the voice of knowledge.

It was thus inevitable that Christian mystics, even those within the bosom of the Church, should find themselves regarded as suspect. And it was inevitable, in consequence, that some of them at least – those who bore conspicuous public witness to their experiences – should find themselves subject to harassment and persecution. Such was the fate that befell the figure whom many would regard as the greatest mystic of the Middle Ages, Johannes Eckhart.

Eckhart – now generally known as Meister Eckhart – was born in Germany around 1260. Having entered the Dominican Order, he obtained a Master's degree from the University of Paris in 1302, and was appointed first Prior of Saxony two years later. In 1307, he was made head of all Dominican houses in Bohemia. In 1311, he was teaching theology at the University of Paris. He returned to Germany in 1313 and remained there as a teacher until his death in 1327.

Eckhart's vision was typically mystical. Although he lectured on theology, his own mystical experiences had convinced him that nothing, ultimately, was separate from God. God encompassed, subsumed and suffused the entirety of creation, including humanity. In other words, there was no distinction between God and man. To convey his sense of the omnipresence of the divine, Eckhart coined the famous term '*Istigkeit*', which can best be translated as 'is-ness'. In extolling the supremacy of such personally experienced immanence, he explicitly rejected all 'external cult'.

To the Inquisitors among his fellow Dominicans, as well as to the presiding Archbishop of Cologne, Eckhart's statements appeared dangerously close to a form of pantheism, which was deemed heretical. Indeed, Eckhart was suspected of being secretly in league with certain heretical sects condemned precisely because of their pantheism. In 1326, complaints were made to the Pope that Eckhart was preaching erroneous doctrine, and a special Inquisitor was appointed to investigate the allegations. As things transpired, the Inquisitor proved to be mystically oriented himself and sympathetic to Eckhart's vision. A prolonged controversy erupted between Eckhart's critics and his supporters, and his case dragged on for the better part of a year, into 1327. Before it could be resolved, Eckhart himself died, but the proceedings continued for two years after his death. At last, in 1329, his teachings were officially adjudged to contain seventeen examples of heresy and eleven of suspected heresy. Only through complicated legal wrangling was he spared the posthumous indignity of having his remains exhumed and burned.

In England the Inquisition did not operate and possessed no permanent tribunals. During the trials of the Templars, which coincided with Meister Eckhart's career, Inquisitors had to be brought into the country from abroad, only to be received with a distinctly frosty welcome and, at best, grudging cooperation. In consequence, an English mystical tradition was able to flourish, and mystics such as Mother Juliana (or Julian) of Norwich were left unmolested. Yet even English mystics recognised the inimical mentality of the Inquisition. Among the most important of English mystical texts is the anonymously authored fourteenth-century work, *The Cloud of Unknowing*, which contains statements that are often virtually interchangeable with those of Meister Eckhart. Like Eckhart, *The Cloud of Unknowing* exhorts the reader that 'yes, you and God are so one that you . . . may in a sense truly be called divine'.[1] And, further:

> The humility engendered by this experiential knowledge of God's goodness and love I call perfect . . . For sometimes people well advanced in the contemplative life will receive such grace from God that they will suddenly and completely be taken out of themselves and neither remember nor care whether they are holy or sinful.[2]

But from the safety of Inquisition-free England, *The Cloud of Unknowing* could dare to be explicit in condemnation of the Inquisitors, even going so far as to castigate them as agents of the infernal:

Again, the fiend will deceive some people with another insidious plot. He will fire them with a zeal to maintain God's law by uprooting sin from the hearts of others . . . he incites them to assume the role of a zealous prelate supervising every aspect of the Christian life . . . he maintains that the love of God and the fire of fraternal charity impel him. But really he lies, for it is the fire of hell in his brain and imagination that incites him.[3]

If English mystics escaped persecution unscathed, those in Spain attracted particularly assiduous attention from the Inquisition there. Despite this, however, Spain seems to have fostered mysticism on a scale unequalled elsewhere in western Europe. Indeed, during the sixteenth and seventeenth centuries, a veritable epidemic of mysticism occurred in Spain. Those who had supposedly succumbed to the 'infection' were known collectively as 'Alumbrados', which translates as 'Illuminati'.

It is important to recognise that the Spanish Alumbrados were quite different from the later, eighteenth-century Illuminati of Bavaria. Unlike their subsequent German namesakes, the Spanish Alumbrados were not an organised and hierarchically structured secret society dedicated to social or political revolution. On the contrary, they were merely a number of disparate individuals, most of whom had no formal contact with one another and no programme or agenda. Some of them had unquestionably undergone the 'altered state of consciousness' that constitutes the mystical experience. Others, without having undergone it, simply *believed* in the supremacy of the mystical experience over the conventional act of faith – and in so doing performed their own, somewhat less conventional, act of faith. In any case, and whatever their first-hand experience or lack of it, the Alumbrados would characteristically speak of an inner light, of the unity of all creation, of the oneness of man with God, of the need to abandon oneself to all impulses deemed to be divine in origin. In many respects, their statements echo those of a much older and more organised heresy, the Brethren of the Free Spirit, which had been prevalent in Germany, Flanders and Holland since the Middle Ages. Holland, of course, was the Spanish Netherlands at the time. During the sixteenth century, it was occupied and devastated by Spanish troops. It is not impossible that principles originating with the Brethren of the Free Spirit found their way back to Spain with the returning soldiery.

The Spanish Inquisition was particularly severe with Alumbrados. All Alumbrado writings were placed on the Index. In 1578, the Inquisition modified its official declaration of faith in order to label a number of Alumbrado assertions as heresy and theological error. From then on, the persecution of Spanish mystics acquired a new momentum and ferocity. More lenient penalties – fines, penances, imprisonment, even torture – began increasingly to lead to the stake.

Probably the most celebrated Spanish mystic of the period is Teresa Sánchez de Cepeda y Ahumada, better known today as Santa Teresa de Jesús or Saint Teresa of Ávila (1515–82). Born into a noble family, Teresa received a modicum of formal education, which enabled her to spend much of her girlhood immersed in chivalric romances – the kind of romances that Cervantes would satirise in *Don Quixote* some three-quarters of a century later. These were soon to be replaced as her literary fare by devotional works. Throughout her life, Teresa was plagued by a number of nervous illnesses which affected her both physically and psychologically and which may have included a form of epilepsy. In the Spain of her time, her unstable health would have disqualified her from a secular existence of marriage and childbearing. In any case, she felt a religious calling and in 1535, at the age of twenty, entered a Carmelite convent at Ávila. Twenty years later while praying in a chapel, she underwent her first mystical experience. From then on, the mystical or visionary experience – what she herself called 'the rapture' – was to be a regular and recurring feature of her life.

On the advice of her confessors, she composed an autobiography which described her experiences. The Inquisition forbade its publication during her lifetime, perhaps fearing that a cult might grow up around her, like that which had grown up around Saint Francis two and a half centuries before. Instead, Teresa was allowed to pursue her desire for a simpler and more austere lifestyle by founding a convent of her own. She called her sisterhood the Discalced – that is, Barefoot – Carmelites. From within their cloister, she continued to write. She completed her autobiography, describing the successive stages whereby union with God was attained as 'mansions'. She wrote an account of the foundation of her convent, which was soon to have some seventeen sister houses. She produced a spiritual guide for the nuns of her Order and a manual of spiritual exercises. She also produced an impressive corpus of poetry. Of her copious correspondence, more than 400 letters survive.

Later commentators have made much of the erotic nature of Teresa's mystical experiences. With strikingly explicit sexual imagery, for example, she will describe herself as being 'ravished' by a divine lover, or by divine love; and her ecstasy will sometimes convey the impression of a spiritual – or spiritualised – orgasm. There is unquestionably a pathological element to Teresa's mysticism, which a Freudian would ascribe to the sublimation of repressed sexuality. It would be a mistake, however, to reduce her mysticism to nothing more than that. The mystical experience and the erotic experience have always been closely related in their psychological dynamics, and each has often expressed itself in the imagery of the other. Behind Teresa's sexual imagery, there remains an experience which mystics of all ages, of all religious traditions, have consistently endeavoured to express, even the most sexually well adjusted. Thus, for instance, Teresa describes how, during her state of 'rapture', the soul is dissolved in God, to a point at which all distinction is eradicated. The soul, God says to her, 'dissolves utterly . . . to rest more and more in Me. It is no longer itself that lives; it is I.'[4]

As mystics have traditionally done, Teresa recognises the ultimate futility of attempted communication: 'The glory that I felt within me cannot be expressed in writing, nor yet in words; it is inconceivable to anyone who has not experienced it.'[5] And she confesses:

There was one thing that I was ignorant of at the beginning. I did not really know that God is present in all things; and when He seemed to me so near, I thought that it was impossible.[6]

Any attempt to dismiss Teresa as a mere neurasthenic or hysteric would be negated by her autobiography and her letters, which display a surprising secular shrewdness, an admirable pragmatism and commonsense, a refreshing sense of humour. They also show an acute awareness of the dangers posed by the Inquisition. Teresa is clearly nervous about her testimony being condemned as heretical. She writes to her confessor that he should only accept her work

so long as my tale is consistent with the truths of our holy Catholic Church. If it is not, your Reverence must burn it immediately, and I agree to its destruction. I will set down my experience, so that, if it conforms to Christian belief, it may be of some use.[7]

She states in her autobiography that certain clerics were unwilling to hear her confessions. Some of those who did, she says, declared her to be possessed by demons and in need of exorcism. One, she reports, concluded definitively that she was being deceived by the devil. And she speaks, too, of friends coming to warn her 'that some charge might be raised against me, and that I might have to appear before the Inquisitors'.[8]

There were certainly grounds for such concern. Teresa's radical mysticism was intrinsically inimical to the Church's hierarchal structure, implicitly challenging the relevance of the established priesthood. She addresses head-on the distinction established at the beginning of this chapter between the mystical experience and any *a posteriori* interpretation of it. She recognises that 'in spiritual matters we often try to interpret things in our own way, as if they were things of this world, and so distort the truth'.[9] She states boldly that 'the wearing of a habit is not enough to make a man a friar, and does not imply that state of great perfection which is proper to a friar'. And then, turning abruptly cautious, she adds: 'I will say no more on this subject.'[10]

No less controversial are Teresa's assertions that mere adherence to the forms of ritual, however assiduously performed and for however long, do not render God's grace – that is, the mystical experience – any more certain: 'Sometimes we attach a pitiful importance to things we do for the Lord which could not really be considered important even if we did them very often.'[11] And:

We think we can measure our progress by the number of years during which we have been practising prayer. We even think that we can find a measure for Him who bestows immeasurable gifts on us at His own pleasure, and who can give more to one person in six months than to another in many years.[12]

And again:

it is dangerous to keep counting the years that we have practised prayer. For even though it may be done in humility, it always seems liable to leave us with the feeling that we have earned some merit by our service . . . any spiritual person who believes that by the mere number of years during which he has practised prayer he has earned these spiritual consolations, will, I am sure, fail to reach the peak of spirituality.[13]

More dangerously still, Teresa militantly opposed the holding of possessions, not only by monks, friars and nuns, but by other ecclesiastics as well:

Someone once asked me to inquire of God whether he would be serving Him by accepting a bishopric. After Communion, the Lord said to me: 'Tell him that when he truly and clearly understands that true dominion consists in possessing nothing then he can accept it.' By this He meant that anyone who is to assume authority must be very far from desiring to do so. At least he must never strive to obtain office.[14]

Teresa was no doubt fortunate in that by the time she came to prominence, Torquemada was long dead. Apart from being forbidden to publish during her lifetime, she escaped all moles-tation from the Inquisition – which must probably be ranked as much of a miracle as anything else in her life. In 1622, forty years after her death, she was canonised.

But if Teresa evaded the Inquisition's clutches, there were many other mystics – some of them personally known to her – who did not. Chief among these was one of the most important poets of the period, Juan de Yepes y Alvárez, who adopted the name of Juan de la Cruz (John of the Cross). Of humble origins, Juan was born more than a generation after Teresa, in 1542. In 1563, at the age of twenty-one, he joined Teresa's reformed Order of Barefoot Carmelites and became spiritual director of her convent at Ávila in 1572. In the great mystical poems that constitute his legacy to posterity, he addressed both the numinous experience and the 'dark night of the soul' that precedes it.

Juan also wrote that

> church observances, images and places of worship are merely for the uninstructed, like toys that amuse children; those who are advanced must liberate themselves from these things which only distract from internal contemplation.[15]

Not surprisingly, such assertions caused him to be repeatedly denounced to the Inquisition. He was investigated at regular intervals and subjected to persecution. In 1576, he was imprisoned for nine months under particularly stringent conditions by the Inquisition's tribunal at Toledo. In the years immediately preceding his death in 1591, he was banished to a so-called 'desert house' in Andalucia. He was finally rehabilitated and canonised in 1726.

9

Freemasonry and the Inquisition

In the Europe of the early seventeenth century – a Europe no longer subject to the Church's hegemony – heresies, mysticism and mystically oriented philosophies were proliferating. There were a number of ultimately futile attempts to institutionalise the mystical experience and establish it as a new, all-encompassing world religion – with, inevitably and paradoxically, its own accompanying dogma diluting and distorting it. And there were attempts as well to adapt mysticism to politics, and establish an ideal Utopian state resting on mystical foundations. Such, for example, was the vogue of so-called Rosicrucian thought that began to appear around 1614 and was hailed by its exponents as a harbinger of a new Golden Age. Although Rosicrucianism was more 'gnostic' in its approach, more all-embracing, more tolerant, more psychologically sophisticated and more spiritually honest than either Catholicism or Protestantism, it, too, involved an intellectual *interpretation* of an empirical experience; and the more complex the interpretation became, the more the experience itself receded into the background, becoming supplanted by yet another theology.

The Church unquestionably felt threatened by Rosicrucianism, and the Holy Office duly added suspected Rosicrucians to its list of deviants. Like witches, Rosicrucians were to be hunted down, ferreted out and vigorously prosecuted. But the chief culprit in Rome's eyes remained Protestantism, with which Rosicrucianism was more or less tenuously associated. It was, after all, Protestantism that had created the circumstances and the spiritual climate in which Rosicrucianism, along with other forms of heterodox thought, could thrive. And thus Protestantism remained the primary target of the Counter-Reformation. If the Jesuits and the rechristened Holy Office represented the Counter-Reformation in the sphere of thought, teaching and doctrine, the corresponding social, political and military offensive was conducted – at least initially and ostensibly – by the Catholic armies of Habsburg Spain and the Habsburg Holy Roman Empire.

This offensive occurred in the form of the Thirty Years War (1618–48) – a conflict akin to a world war in the modern sense, and the most appalling, costly and catastrophic conflict to be fought on European soil prior to the twentieth century. In this war, the Church was not only ultimately thwarted, but, in its own eyes, scandalously betrayed. By the time hostilities ended, Rome's authority was even more fragmented and precarious than it had been before. Having been engaged in her own civil war, England, under Cromwell's Protectorate, was even more securely Protestant than ever. The Protestantism of Scandinavia and the North German states was equally unassailable; and Protestant Holland had emerged as a major world power, at least at sea and abroad. The Protestant naval powers of England and Holland now fought each other for control of the oceans, and of the colonies, formerly dominated exclusively by Catholic Spain and Portugal.

Worst of all for the Church, France had supplanted Spain as the supreme military power on the continent; and she had done so by aligning herself with the avowed enemy. French policy during the Thirty Years War had been orchestrated not by the apathetic Louis XIII, but by his chief minister, Cardinal Richelieu. And Richelieu, a Catholic cardinal implementing policy for a predominantly Catholic country, proceeded to deploy Catholic troops on behalf of the Protestant cause. Although other countries, especially Sweden, had repeatedly thwarted the Church's military power, it was ultimately the army of Catholic France that shattered the martial supremacy of Catholic Spain. The Thirty Years War had commenced as a predominantly religious conflict, with Catholic armies endeavouring to extirpate Protestantism in Bohemia and Germany. By the time the war ended, it had turned into a conflict of vested interests fought for the sake of the balance of power; and religion had become both incidental and subordinate to secular concerns. France, once regarded as 'the eldest daughter of the Church', now dominated Europe; but her priorities had come to revolve less around the throne of Saint Peter than around that of the 'Sun King', Louis XIV, and his court at Versailles. The regime jealously guarded its independence of Papal control. It even possessed the right to appoint its own bishops.

Such was the situation in the aftermath of the Thirty Years War and during the latter half of the seventeenth century. By 1725, the Church's authority on the continent had become even more eroded, its position even more precarious. In 1688, James II of England had converted to Catholicism, and the Papacy was able for a brief moment to envisage itself reinstated as the official religious power of the British Isles. But Britain remained obdurate in her opposition to 'Popery' and James was repudiated by his subjects, who offered the crown to his son-in-law, William of Orange. There ensued the Siege of

Londonderry and, in 1690 and 1691 respectively, the two decisive battles of the Boyne and Aughrim. As a result, James was deposed and Parliament enacted legislation that prevented a Catholic from ever sitting on the British throne. The now Catholic Stuarts fled into exile, whence they repeatedly attempted to foment rebellions in Scotland, culminating with the campaign of Charles Edward Stuart, Bonnie Prince Charlie, in 1745–6. Nothing was to come of any of these endeavours. Even if the 1745 campaign had succeeded, it is questionable whether Bonnie Prince Charlie's Presbyterian supporters would have accepted a Catholic monarch; and had he been forced to choose between the Church and the British throne, the prince would almost certainly have chosen the latter.

On the continent, Spain, formerly the supreme military and naval executor of the Church, had been reduced to lame-duck status; and by 1704, Europe's other great powers, indifferent altogether to Rome, were fighting over whether the increasingly decrepit Spanish Empire was to be ruled by a Bourbon or a Habsburg. Austria remained nominally Catholic and managed to repel a major Islamic thrust westwards. By the mid eighteenth century, however, her influence in central Europe was being challenged and neutralised by the advent of a new and dangerous Protestant power to the north, the fledgling Kingdom of Prussia, created in 1701. During the wars of the period, Russia, too, made her début on the chessboard of European politics, bringing a further threat to Rome in the form of the Orthodox Church.

Of the Catholic powers that had formerly been the Church's executive in secular spheres, only France remained. However, France fiercely maintained her independence from Rome. And though still nominally Catholic, she now began to pose the greatest threat of all – a threat in the world of ideas and values, and thus more difficult to oppose than any military or political edifice. Under the influence of Cartesian rationalism, France, by the mid eighteenth century, had assumed the vanguard of anti-clerical sentiment and become a veritable hotbed of hostility – towards organised religion in general and towards Catholicism in particular. In the writings of '*les philosophes*' – men such as Montesquieu, Diderot and, supremely, Voltaire – the once august and unassailable Church was not only repudiated, but openly, scandalously and blasphemously mocked. To the mortification of the ecclesiastical hierarchy, Rome became a species of running joke, the object of merciless derision. In consigning the authors of this derision to the Index, the Holy Office only contrived to look more puerile, more humiliatingly impotent.

If Cartesian rationalism and the writings of *les philosophes* represented major challenges to the Church, a challenge of comparable magnitude was presented by the dissemination of Freemasonry. The institution now known as Freemasonry had coalesced, at least in something like its modern form, in Scotland and England during the early seventeenth century. By the end of Cromwell's Protectorate and the restoration of the Stuarts to the British throne in 1660, Freemasonry seems to have been widespread throughout the British Isles, and increasingly supportive of the ruling dynasty. Had it remained confined to Britain, a lost cause anyway in Rome's eyes, 'the Craft', as it was called, might have been ignored. But when the Stuarts were driven into exile, they took Freemasonry with them; and in the years that followed, it proceeded to proliferate rapidly across the continent.

According to the documentation now available, the first Lodge outside the British Isles was founded in Paris in 1726 by Charles Radclyffe, later Earl of Derwentwater, an illegitimate grandson of Charles II. In 1746, Radclyffe would be executed

FREEMASONRY AND THE INQUISITION

in London for his role in Bonnie Prince Charlie's bid for the British throne. Before his death, however, he founded additional Lodges in France, and Freemasonry acquired an irresistible momentum of its own. The Austrian Empire's first Lodge was established at Prague in 1726, shortly after Radclyffe's in Paris. In 1736, having been initiated as a Mason five years earlier, François, Duke of Lorraine, married Maria Theresa von Habsburg, thus becoming joint ruler of the Austrian Empire. He founded a Lodge in Vienna and extended his protection over Freemasonry throughout the Habsburg domains.

The first Lodge was founded in Italy in 1733, in Holland in 1734, in Sweden in 1735, in Switzerland in 1736. The first German Lodge was established at Hamburg in 1737. A year later, the future Frederick the Great of Prussia was initiated and subsequently founded his own Lodge at his castle of Rheinsberg. In 1740, a Lodge was founded in Berlin. By that time, the number of Lodges in Holland and Sweden had become sufficiently great to warrant the creation of a national Grand Lodge. By 1769, there were ten Lodges in Geneva alone. In the very teeth of the Inquisition, Lodges were also established in Spain and Portugal.

By the mid eighteenth century, Freemasonry had reached every corner of western Europe. It had already spread across the Atlantic to the Americas. It was soon to extend eastwards into Russia, as well as to European colonies in Asia, the Indian subcontinent and the Pacific. In addition to Frederick the Great and the Holy Roman Emperor François of Lorraine, the ranks of Freemasonry included such crowned heads as Stanislaus II of Poland, Adolphus Frederick of Sweden and, according to unconfirmed reports, Louis XV of France. They also included many 'founding fathers' of the future United States, such as Benjamin Franklin and George Washington. They included prominent literary figures such as Montesquieu, Diderot, Voltaire and, by the end of the eighteenth century, Goethe and Schiller. In Britain, prominent members of the Hanoverian ruling dynasty were Masons, as were Pope, Swift, Boswell and Hogarth.

The threat posed to the Church by Freemasonry was manifold. In the first place, many if not most Lodges of the time subscribed in at least some measure to Cartesian rationalism, and thus served as a conduit for modes of thought inimical to Catholicism. Freemasonry never pretended to be a rival or alternative religion; but it raised spiritual questions and thereby presented challenges to the dogmatic, docile and obsequious faith demanded by Rome. While Rome clung stubbornly to dogma that had not changed for centuries, Freemasonry embraced the rapidly changing world of the eighteenth century, with its commerce, industry and scientific progress. That world also included significant social reform, with an unprecedented emphasis on egalitarianism and the rights of man. While the Church looked backwards, Freemasonry looked forwards; and when Rome contemplated the future, that future seemed more likely to be influenced by the Lodge than by the pulpit.

There were other grounds for concern. Until the Reformation, the Church, if only in theory, had represented the supreme arbiter of western Christendom. In effect, it served, or was supposed to serve, as an international forum – the equivalent for the time of the League of Nations, or the United Nations. If only in theory, secular disputes between rival potentates, for example, were subject to arbitration and judgement by the Church. The Church was authorised and mandated to act as negotiator, as peace-broker and facilitator of reconciliation.

This role had been dramatically restricted by the

Reformation. Protestant churches were hardly prepared to accept Catholic authority in either spiritual or temporal matters. But Catholicism still retained enough currency on the continent – in France, in Austria and southern Germany, in Italy, in Spain and Portugal – to offer at least some common ground on which *rapprochement* might be established. It was precisely in this area that Freemasonry threatened to encroach on the Church's traditional functions, possibly even to usurp them.

Unlike the Church, the network of Lodges transcended denomination, enabling Catholics and Protestants to talk to each other without the fetters of doctrine and dogma. The proliferating web of Lodges afforded both a conduit for the transmission of messages and a forum for high-level inter-governmental and international contacts, for off-the-record discussion of treaties, for delicate diplomatic negotiations. Thus, for example, Protestant Prussia, under Frederick the Great, and Catholic Austria, under Maria Theresa and François of Lorraine, might be at war – as indeed they were on two separate occasions between 1742 and 1763. But both Frederick and François were Freemasons, as were many of their ministers and military commanders. Through the Lodges, peace feelers might be extended and common ground established in a way that was no longer possible through the Church. Through the Lodges, new alliances might be formed, new alignments and configurations to maintain the balance of power in equilibrium. This undoubtedly complemented the fluidity of the era's politics, whereby developments such as the famous 'Diplomatic Revolution' could be instigated. During the War of the Austrian Succession (1742–8), Austria was aligned with Britain against Prussia and France. As a result of the 'Diplomatic Revolution', the antagonists changed partners. During the Seven Years War (1756–63), Austria was aligned with France against Prussia and Britain.

It goes without saying, of course, that the potentialities offered by the Lodges were not always actualised, and as often as not, remained purely theoretical. But the Church's capacity for arbitration had seldom been more than theoretical either; and the Lodges were at least as successful as the Church at turning theory into practice. Even if war could not be averted, it could be made to conform, insofar as possible, to scrupulously observed rules and certain premises of the Enlightenment promulgated by the Lodges. And in fact, the wars of the eighteenth century, unlike those of the seventeenth, were conducted in as 'civilised', 'chivalrous' and 'gentlemanly' a fashion as any war can be conducted, in rigorous adherence to internationally agreed and accepted tenets and standards of behaviour. In part, this reflected a revulsion from the excesses of such conflicts as the Thirty Years War, but it also stemmed from an absence of religious hatred and fanaticism, and a recognition of certain increasingly respected codes. These codes owed more than a little to the ideas, attitudes and values disseminated by the Lodges.

Attacks upon Freemasonry

Alarmed by the vigorous spread of Freemasonry and by the threats the institution posed, the Church proceeded to act. On 25 July 1737, a secret conference of the Holy Office was convened in Florence, probably under the auspices of Pope Clement XII himself. The conference was attended by three cardinals, the heads of the primary Papal Congregations and the Inquisitor General. Their sole topic of discussion was Freemasonry.[1]

High-level leaks of information were almost as prevalent then as they are now, and reports of the secret conclave were published soon after in a Berlin journal. According to these reports, the assembled ecclesiastics were convinced that Free-masonry was but a façade for some much vaster, all-encompassing, clandestine heresy of an altogether new kind. It is difficult to imagine what the clerics believed such a heresy might entail to generate such extreme anxiety. In any case, the Berlin journal reported, Freemasons were already being arrested. Later in the year, anti-Masonic riots instigated by unseen hands erupted in a number of towns. It was growing increasingly clear that powerful interests behind the scenes were beginning to mobilise against Freemasonry.

Nine months after the conference in Florence, on 28 April 1738, Pope Clement issued the first of what was to become an increasingly belligerent sequence of Bulls on the subject. The Bull, *In eminenti*, began:

> Condemnation of the Society, Lodges ... (of) Free Masons, under pain of excommunication to be incurred *ipso facto*, and absolution from it being reserved for the Supreme Pontiff.[2]

In the text that followed, the Pope proceeded to state that

> it is our will and charge that as well Bishops or higher or Prelates, and other local Ordinaries as the deputed Inquisitors of Heretical Depravity everywhere take action and make inquisition against transgressors, of whatever status, grade, condition, order, dignity or eminence they may be, and inflict upon them condign punishment, as though strongly suspected of heresy, and exercise con-straint upon them.[3]

The 'constraint' in question – the imprisonment and attendant punishment – was, if necessary, to be implemented and effected with 'the aid of the secular branch'.

Being reluctant to antagonise the Church, a number of European regimes acted at once. As early as the previous summer, the police in France had begun to arrest Lodge members and confiscate their literature – from which much of our knowledge of French Freemasonry at the time derives. In Poland, Freemasonry was banned throughout the kingdom. In Sweden, participation in Masonic rituals was declared punishable by death. Encouraged by this response, the Church hardened its position. On 14 January 1739, Cardinal Joseph Firrao, Secretary of State for the Vatican, published a new edict. All Freemasons everywhere were threatened with the confiscation of their possessions, excommunication and death.[4]

In February 1739, a Masonic text – written in French but published in Dublin – was condemned, placed on the Index and officially burned in the Piazza Santa Maria Minerva in Rome. Shortly thereafter, a number of Freemasons in Florence were arrested, imprisoned and tortured. One of them managed to obtain his freedom when certain English Lodges made a 'financial donation' – that is, paid a fine – to the Holy Office. Others were released through the intervention of François of Lorraine, whose titles included that of Grand Duke of Tuscany.

In 1751, Pope Clement XII's successor, Benedict XIV, issued a second Bull against Freemasonry, repeating the condemnation of the first but adding even more stringent penalties. Despite such measures, however, and to the profound consternation of the Holy Office, Catholics continued to join Lodges in substantial numbers. More worrisome still, the Lodges were beginning to attract not only lay Catholics, but priests as well, and even several high-level clergy. A Lodge in Mainz, for example, was composed almost entirely of clergy. Another, in Münster, included the presiding bishop's own officials. At Erfurt, the future bishop founded a Lodge himself, which convened in the rooms of the abbot at a prominent monastery. A Lodge in Vienna included two royal chaplains, the rector of the theological college and two other priests. Another Viennese Lodge counted no fewer than thirteen priests among its membership. By the end of the eighteenth century, the list of high-ranking Catholic Freemasons was augmented by numerous abbots and bishops, one imperial chaplain, one cardinal and at least five archbishops.[5] Freemasonry was rapidly becoming as hydra-headed, and as irrepressible, as Protestantism had been 200-odd years before. And the Church, increasingly bereft of secular armies to impose its authority, was significantly more impotent than it had been at the time of the Reformation.

Where the Holy Office's writ still ran enforceably, however, Freemasons were fair game, and pursued as assiduously as witches had been in the past. This was particularly so in Spain and Portugal, where a national Inquisition, accountable to the Crown, still operated. Shortly after the first Papal pronouncement against Freemasonry in 1738, the Spanish Inquisition raided a Lodge in Madrid and arrested its members, eight of whom were sentenced to the galleys. In 1748, the Inquisition completed a four-year investigation into Freemasonry. All Freemasons, it concluded, were subject to automatic excommunication as 'perverse reprobates acting contrary to the purity of the Holy faith and public safety of the realm'.[6] Three years later, in 1751, the Inquisition procured a decree from the Crown which sanctioned an automatic death penalty for Freemasons and denied them even the right of trial. In that same year, one Inquisitor, Father Joseph Torrubia, joined a Lodge himself in order to spy, to collect information and denounce members. According to his reports, there were ninety-seven Lodges in Spain at the time.[7] Despite the draconian measures instigated against them, their number was to increase and their struggle against the Inquisition's persecution to continue for another three-quarters of a century. In the end, they would emerge triumphant. After the Napoleonic Wars and the restoration of the Spanish monarchy, it was the Inquisition that was dismantled. The Lodges survived and thrived, both in Spain and the Spanish colonies of Latin America.

A similar story obtained for Portugal. In certain of his works, the novelist José Saramago, winner of the Nobel Prize for Literature in 1998, depicts the omnipresence of the Portuguese Inquisition well into the eighteenth century. Like its counterpart in Spain, it needed a scapegoat to justify its continued existence, and Freemasonry was an obvious candidate for the role. One particularly notorious case was that of John Coustos, a Swiss-born diamond cutter resident in England since childhood, naturalised and duly initiated as a Freemason.

In 1736, Coustos had established a Lodge of his own in Paris. In 1741, impelled by the discovery of diamonds in Brazil, he moved to Lisbon and founded a Lodge there. It included no Portuguese members, only other foreign diamond cutters, traders, merchants, goldsmiths and a ship's captain. It was nevertheless denounced to the Portuguese Inquisition, which, in March of 1743, proceeded to act. The first member of the Lodge to be arrested was a French jeweller. On a pretext of business, agents of the Inquisition visited him at noon, just as he was closing his shop for siesta. He was summarily arrested, searched for weapons and forbidden to speak. He was then hustled out into a small closed carriage, driven off and imprisoned in the dungeon of the Inquisition's palace without being allowed to contact anyone. To account for his disappearance, the Inquisition disseminated a rumour that he had absconded with a quantity of diamonds.

Four days later, on 5 March 1743, Coustos himself was

arrested. At ten in the evening, he emerged from a coffee house where he had been chatting with two friends. Outside, nine officers of the Inquisition were waiting with the customary small closed carriage. His sword being taken from him, he was handcuffed and driven rapidly to the Inquisition's palace, where he, too, was consigned to the dungeon. Here he was left in solitude for two days, receiving no visitors, hearing only moans and cries from the surrounding cells and corridors. At last, there began a prolonged sequence of torture and interrogation. The Inquisition, it transpired, desired to know everything possible about Freemasonry and the extent of the Lodges' activity in Portugal.

Not being a masochist or a particularly heroic individual, Coustos endeavoured to satisfy his persecutors. In the course of several sessions of interrogation, he volunteered a good many details on the rituals and practice of Freemasonry and named twelve other members of his Lodge, all foreign nationals, most of them French. Despite having taken down pages of information and confession, however, the Inquisitors were not convinced they had learned everything Coustos had to tell. What was more, they insisted that he convert to Catholicism. This he refused to do, even when English and Irish monks resident in Lisbon at the time were brought in to exhort him.

The Inquisition's files on Coustos's case still exist and run to some 600 pages. They include the text of an exhaustively detailed confession. Despite this confession, the tribunal decided to 'proceed to Tortures, to extort from him a Confession . . . that the several Articles of which he stands accused are true'.[8] In other words, Coustos was to be tortured in order to obtain a confession attesting to the validity of his previous confession. According to the surviving Inquisition documents, Coustos, on 6 March 1744, nearly a year after his first confession, was 'given a turn on the rack'.[9] Coustos himself later described what this apparently insouciant phraseology entailed. He was conducted to a square tower-like room with no windows and no illumination save that of two candles. The doors were padded to muffle all sound. The victim was seized by six assistants, who stripped him of most of his clothes and fastened him to the rack with an iron collar around his neck and an iron ring on each foot, two ropes around each arm and two around each thigh. Four men then proceeded to stretch his limbs by drawing the ropes tight – so tight that the ropes cut through his flesh and caused him to bleed from all eight lacerations. When he fainted, he was returned to his cell to recover.[10]

Six weeks later, on 25 April 1744, Coustos was subjected to a second session of torture. The Inquisition's documents describe the punctiliousness with which the legal niceties were observed. Thus

the Doctor and Surgeon and the other Ministers of the torture approached the Bench where they were given the oath of the Holy Gospels, on which they placed their hands, and promised faithfully and truly to carry out their duties, and the torture prescribed for the accused was then ordered to be executed, and stripped of those clothes which might impede the proper execution of the torture, he was placed on the rack and the binding commenced and he was then informed by me, the notary, that if he died during the operation, or if a limb was broken, or if he lost any of his senses, the fault would be his, and not of the Lords Inquisitors.[11]

On this occasion, Coustos's arms were stretched backwards over a wooden frame, dislocating his shoulders and making blood run from his mouth. The process was repeated three times, after which he was returned to his cell. Here, a physician and a surgeon reset his bones, giving him 'exquisite pain' in the process.[12]

Some two months later, Coustos was subjected to his third session of torture. A thick chain was wound around his stomach and attached at each arm to a rope, which was progressively tightened by means of a windlass. His stomach was severely bruised, his shoulders were dislocated again and his wrists as well. When a surgeon had reset his bones, the whole procedure was repeated. For some weeks afterwards, he was unable to lift his hand to his mouth.

On 21 June 1744, Coustos's public trial was held. Along with other victims, he was made to walk in procession to the Church of Saint Dominic, where the king, the royal princes, members of the nobility and a substantial crowd waited in attendance. Coustos was accused of

> not confessing the heretical, disturbing and scandalous purpose for which he intended to introduce a new doctrine into the Catholic Realm, nor has he made true declaration in connection with the matters for which such inviolable secrecy is required.[13]

He was sentenced to four years in the galleys, but quickly became so ill that he was obliged to spend two months in an infirmary. Here, he was again visited by Irish monks, who promised him release in exchange for conversion to the Church. Coustos again refused; but from the infirmary, he managed to smuggle out a letter to his brother-in-law, who worked in the household of a prominent Freemason, the Earl of Harrington. The earl spoke to a secretary of state at the time, the Duke of Newcastle, who instructed the British ambassador in Lisbon to effect Coustos's release. This finally occurred in October. There were no British ships in the vicinity; but a small Dutch fleet happened to be at anchor in the harbour, and Coustos was granted passage on a Dutch vessel by the admiral in command. The Inquisition was still sniffing about, looking for an excuse to rearrest him. He was accordingly allowed aboard immediately. For the next three weeks, he remained there, while agents of the Inquisition rowed repeatedly around the fleet, trying to locate the ship on which he had found refuge. His health severely impaired, he arrived back in London on 15 December 1744. Of his ordeal, he wrote:

> I have but too much Reason to fear, that I shall feel the sad Effects of this cruelty so long as I live; I being seized from time to time, with thrilling Pains, with which I never was afflicted till I had the misfortune of falling into the merciless and bloody Hands of the Inquisitors.[14]

He was to die two years later. Before that he wrote an account of his experience, *The Sufferings of John Coustos for Freemasonry*, which was published at the end of December 1745, when the Jacobite rebellion instigated by Bonnie Prince Charlie was still in progress. Not surprisingly, Coustos's book was seized upon for purposes of anti-Catholic, and thus anti-Jacobite, propaganda. It continued to exert an influence long afterwards, establishing an indelible portrait of the Inquisition in the minds of English readers and the English public. One can discern traces of this portrait in some of the 'Gothic fiction' of the late eighteenth and early nineteenth centuries, such as Matthew Lewis's novel, *The Monk*.

Cagliostro and Casanova

Supported by the judicial, civic and military authority of their respective crowns, the Spanish and Portuguese Inquisitions continued to operate with vigour throughout the eighteenth century, not only at home, but in colonies abroad as well. Both were dismantled during Napoleon's occupation of the Iberian Peninsula and the campaign of reconquest that followed under the future Duke of Wellington; and Freemasons in the British army, as well as the French, displayed little sympathy towards the institution that had formerly persecuted them. Towards the end of the Peninsular War, the Inquisition was reestablished by the restored and restabilised monarchies in Spain and Portugal. Its reestablishment, however, was to be short-lived. By the end of the first quarter of the nineteenth century, the Spanish and Portuguese Inquisitions were both defunct; and in the former colonies of Latin America, republics dominated largely by Freemasons were founded.

Elsewhere in Catholic Europe, the Holy Office, lacking the secular support of its Spanish and Portuguese counterparts, functioned in a more desultory fashion. Tenuous though its position was becoming, it did continue to flail out against Freemasonry; and in Italy especially, Freemasons continued to suffer from its ministrations. Among the more prominent victims was Joseph Balsamo, better known as Count Cagliostro. Born in Palermo in 1743, Cagliostro travelled widely and was initiated into Freemasonry in London in 1777. He subsequently proceeded to devise his own brand, or rite, of Freemasonry, which he then attempted to disseminate across Europe. In 1789, he arrived in Rome to seek an audience with Pope Pius VI, whom he imagined would be sympathetic towards his Masonic rite and embrace it to the benefit of the Church. This might appear to have been naive; but Cagliostro in fact found the Roman clergy extremely receptive to his evangelism, and he made friends with high-ranking figures in a number of Catholic institutions, including the Knights of Malta. Encouraged by his success, he established his own Lodge in the Eternal City, which supposedly met at the palace of the Knights of Malta. Its membership is reported to have included not only knights and nobles, but also clerical officials, ecclesiastics and at least one cardinal.

The Pope, however, had already passed files pertaining to him on to the Holy Office. At the end of December 1789, some seven months after his arrival in Rome, Cagliostro was arrested along with eight members of his Lodge, one of them American. For the next eighteen months, he was subjected to 'examination' in the Castel Sant' Angelo. On 21 March 1791, the Holy Office condemned him to death for heresy – a sentence commuted by the Pope to life imprisonment. On 4 May 1791, the Pope ordered all Cagliostro's documents and manuscripts, Masonic regalia and accoutrements, to be burned in the Piazza Santa Maria Minerva by the public hangman. One dossier, containing stray papers, personal notes and letters, apparently escaped the flames. In the early 1970s, an Italian author, Roberto Gervaso, requested permission to examine this material, but was denied access to it by the head of the Holy Office.[15] Cagliostro himself, still imprisoned, died in 1795.

Another well-known Freemason to run foul of the Holy Office in Italy was Cagliostro's contemporary, Giacomo Girolamo Casanova di Seingalt (1725–98). After being expelled from seminary for allegedly outrageous conduct, Casanova, like Cagliostro, travelled widely and was initiated into Freemasonry in 1750. He was later to write that induction into a Lodge was a mandatory step in the education, development and career of any intelligent and well-bred young man who desired to make a mark in the world. When he returned to his native Venice, Casanova was pounced on by the Holy Office, who accused him of impiety and magical practices. After first being coerced into spying on Masonic and other suspect activities, he was imprisoned. Eventually, in circumstances worthy of a swashbuckling thriller by Dumas, he managed to escape, and embarked on the career for which he subsequently became famous.

Casanova's posthumously published memoirs established his reputation as an adventurer, a hustler, a confidence man, a seducer and amorist on a scale worthy of Don Juan. But he was also a gifted self-publicist, with an ego that cast a shadow the size of a blimp; and his memoirs unquestionably contain much exaggeration, much hyperbole, much poetic licence. Quite apart from their lavish self-advertisement, however, they offer a profoundly insightful and revealing panorama of the manners and mores of the age. What is more, Casanova was a talented writer. He produced historical works in Italian and one phantasmagorical novel of some literary merit in French. In 1788, he published a detailed account of his imprisonment by the Holy Office and his escape, *Histoire de ma fuite des prisons de Venise*, which constitutes one of the most valuable sources available on the workings of the Holy Office during the latter part of the eighteenth century.

Papal Paranoia

It is extraordinary to reflect that as late as the 1790s – after the American War of Independence, during the French Revolution, when western Europe had embarked on the 'Modern Age' – the Holy Office still possessed the power to imprison people, even to impose the death penalty. That power, however, was soon to be curtailed and abrogated. The French Revolution, the revolutionary movements that ensued in Italy and Napoleon's invasion of the peninsula all left the Church, the Papacy and the Holy Office badly shaken. So, too, did the French plundering of the Vatican's archives, much of which remains to this day in Paris, in the Arsenal Library. In several Italian cities, Freemasons sought vengeance on their former persecutors, and more than a few Inquisitors were obliged to flee lynch mobs.

With Napoleon's fall, the Church, instigated by the Holy Office, resumed its self-proclaimed vendetta against Freemasonry, a campaign that would become progressively more rabid and more paranoid as the nineteenth century unfolded. In 1814, after Napoleon's first abdication, a new Bull against Freemasonry was promulgated. Further denunciations would follow, by Pope Pius VII (1800–23), by Leo XII (1823–9), by Pius VIII (1829–30) and by Gregory XVI (1831–46). Pope Pius IX, who was subsequently to declare himself infallible, issued an encyclical condemning Freemasonry in 1846, his first year of office, and followed it with further condemnations on no fewer than seven separate occasions. Freemasonry was denounced as 'the synagogue of Satan' and a 'damnable sect of depravity'.[16]

Pius IX's successor, Leo XIII, ascended the Papal throne in 1878 and occupied it until 1903. In 1884, he published an encyclical that constituted the most virulent denunciation of Freemasonry ever to issue from the Church. Read before all church doors at the Pope's explicit orders, the encyclical begins:

> The human race is divided into two different and opposing
> parties . . . The one is the Kingdom of God on earth –

that is, the Church of Jesus Christ; the other is the kingdom of Satan.[17]

The text than focuses specifically on Freemasonry:

In our days . . . those who follow the evil one seem to conspire and strive all together under the guidance and with the help of that society of men spread all over, and solidly established, which they call Free-Masons.[18]

The Pope goes on to enunciate explicitly the source of the Church's paranoia – the fear of a supposed rival. Freemasons

say openly what they had already in secret devised for a long time . . . that the very spiritual power of the Pope ought to be taken away, and the divine institution of the Roman Pontificate ought to disappear from the world.[19]

In his 1914 narrative *Les caves du Vatican* (published in Britain as *The Vatican Cellars* and in America as *Lafcadio's Adventures*), André Gide dramatises in fictionalised form an episode reportedly rooted in historical fact. In the late nineteenth century, during the pontificate of Leo XIII, two ingenious confidence tricksters are seen wandering about the provinces of southern France. They are dressed in clerical garb and carry with them a carefully prepared and detailed list of wealthy Catholics residing in the vicinity. They present themselves at the doors of these victims, gain admission and recount – in what purports to be the most urgent and portentous secrecy – a horrifying story.

The figure seen at intervals on the balcony of Saint Peter's is not, they report, the Pope. He is in fact a double, a lookalike, an impostor installed by means of a pernicious Masonic conspiracy. The real Holy Pontiff has been kidnapped by

Freemasons. He is being held hostage under strict guard at some undisclosed location. Unless a stipulated ransom is raised in time, he will be executed, and the entire Papacy will be taken over by Freemasonry. In consequence, loyal and devout Catholics are being approached discreetly to make donations to the Pope's ransom. Not surprisingly, the two confidence tricksters make off with a tidy fortune.

Such stories were not uncommon at the time. There is no way of knowing which of several Gide might have had in mind, or how much artistic licence he took with the actual facts of the scam. But his narrative bears eloquent testimony to the trepidation about Freemasonry fostered by the Holy Office at the time, and the delusional paranoia to which the Church and its adherents were prone. That paranoia has continued to the present day. As recently as the early 1990s, lavishly printed four-page broadsheets from a hardline Catholic organisation were shoved through letter-boxes in London's Belgravia, once again alleging a nefarious Masonic conspiracy bent on world domination – and erroneously citing as Freemasons men such as Earl Mountbatten of Burma, who were never Freemasons at all.

10

The Conquest of the Papal States

B y the last third of the nineteenth century, the Church, and the Holy Office with it, had become uncomfortably beleaguered. Since Diderot's novel *The Nun*, published more than a century earlier in 1760, priests, monks, abbots, bishops, cardinals and especially Inquisitors had been cast with increasing frequency as arch-villains, figuring in such 'Gothic novels' as *The Monk* by Matthew Lewis and the more serious literary work of writers such as Stendhal. And in 1879–80, in *The Brothers Karamazov*, Dostoevsky's Grand Inquisitor seared into both Russian and Western consciousness an indelible and definitive image of a cynically ruthless patriarch prepared to send Jesus himself to the stake in order to preserve the vested interests of the Church and its hierarchy.

Nor was it only through 'high culture' that Rome was receiving a distinctly bad press. The Church had always inspired hostility in substantial segments of the population. Now, through increasing freedom of speech, the dissemination of education and the proliferation of newspapers, journals and popular literature, such hostility was becoming ever more effectively equipped to express itself; and it received additional reinforcement from the attitudes and values percolating down from the cultural summits. In largely Protestant countries such

as Britain and Germany, antipathy to the Church's aggrandise-
ment of power was an accepted given. In the United States,
despite the influx of Catholic immigrants from Italy and Ireland,
anti-Catholic prejudice was rife.

The Church found itself subject to other threats as well. In
1859, Charles Darwin published *The Origin of Species*. This
was followed in 1871 by *The Descent of Man*, an even more
theologically explosive work, which questioned scriptural
accounts of the Creation. For nearly three centuries, the scales of
Western values had swayed in precarious equilibrium between
science and organised religion. Now, seemingly at a single
stroke, they tipped decisively in favour of science, and Western
civilisation assumed a secular dimension that would have
appeared unthinkable only a short time before. In the past, any
deviation from religious orthodoxy, not to mention atheism,
had been a criminal and punishable offence. As recently as the
end of the eighteenth century, in Protestant England, Shelley
had been expelled from Cambridge for atheism; and penalties
in spheres where the Church exercised influence were consider-
ably more severe. Now, however, a mere sixty-odd years later,
atheism, and the agnosticism promulgated by Thomas Huxley
and Herbert Spencer, had become not just respectable, but
eminently fashionable. So, too, in ever more vociferous quarters, had the 'dialectical materialism' of Karl Marx, with its
repudiation of organised religion as 'the opiate of the people'
– even though Marxism itself was ultimately to prove a no
less deadly opiate. As such inimical ideas were diffused across
Christendom, the Church, stripped of its power to suppress
them, could only look on with enraged impotence. The Inquisitors of the Holy Office, who had formerly rampaged like
bloodhounds, were now leashed and kennelled.

A further threat was posed by the development of German

historical and archaeological scholarship, and the methodology it employed. Until the mid nineteenth century, the methodology and procedures of historical and archaeological investigation, which we take more or less for granted nowadays, simply did not exist. There were no generally accepted standards, no premises for establishing a coherent discipline and training. There was no real awareness that such research might constitute a form of 'science' – or that it might demand the rigour, the objectivity, the systematic precision that any science does.

Under the auspices of Germanic scholarship, this state of affairs altered dramatically. The change was illustrated conspicuously by Heinrich Schliemann (1822–90), born in Germany and naturalised as an American citizen in 1850. Since boyhood, Schliemann had been captivated by the Homeric epics of the Trojan War, the *Iliad* and the *Odyssey*. He became increasingly persuaded that these poems were not mere fictitious fables, but mythologised history – chronicles exalted to legendary status yet based on events, people and places that had once actually existed. The Siege of Troy, Schliemann insisted, had been a genuine historical occurrence. Troy was not just the product of a poet's imagination. On the contrary, it had once been a real city.

Schliemann proceeded on the assumption that Homer's poems could be used as a map, whereby certain recognisable geographical and topographical features could be identified. The approximate speeds of travel at the time could be computed and distances thereby estimated between one point and another cited in the Greek texts. By such techniques, Schliemann insisted, the itinerary of the Greek fleet in the *Iliad* could be retraced and the actual site of Troy located. After performing the appropriate calculations, Schliemann was convinced he had found 'the X that marked the spot'.

Through his commercial activities, Schliemann had become immensely wealthy. With the vast financial resources at his disposal, he embarked on what seemed to his contemporaries a quixotic enterprise – to undertake a full-scale excavation of the 'X' he had located. In 1868, starting from Greece and using a two-and-a-half-millennia-old poem as his guide, he set about retracing the route ascribed by Homer to the Greek fleet. At what he concluded to be the relevant site in Turkey, he began to dig. And to the world's amazed admiration, Schliemann there found Troy – or, at any rate, a city that conformed to Troy in Homer's account. In fact, Schliemann found a number of cities. During four campaigns of excavation, he exhumed no fewer than nine, each superimposed on the ruins of its predecessor.

Schliemann proved triumphantly that archaeology could do more than just confirm or disprove the historical validity behind archaic legends. He also demonstrated that it could add flesh and substance to the often skeletal, starkly simplistic chronicles of the past. It could provide a comprehensibly human and social context for such chronicles, a framework of daily life and practices that revealed the mentality and milieu whereby they had been engendered. What was more, he demonstrated the applicability to archaeology of rigorous scientific methods, such as the careful observation and recording of data. In exhuming the nine superimposed cities of Troy, Schliemann utilised the same approach that had only recently come into favour in geological studies. This led him to a recognition of what the modern mind might find self-evident – that one stratum of deposits can be distinguished from others on the basic premise that the lowest is the earliest. Schliemann thus pioneered the archaeological discipline now known as 'stratigraphy'. Virtually single-handedly, he revolutionised the entire sphere of archaeological thought and methodology.

It was quickly appreciated that Schliemann's scientific orientation could productively be employed in the field of biblical archaeology. Within a few years, British investigators were vigorously at work in Egypt and Palestine, burrowing, among other sites, beneath the Temple of Jerusalem. Sir Charles Wilson, then a captain in the Royal Engineers, here found what were believed to have been Solomon's stables.

The scientific methodology that had proved so dramatically effective in archaeology was also applied to history. Schliemann's discoveries, after all, had derived in large part from his meticulous scrutiny of Homer's epic poems, his rigorous scientific insistence on separating fact from fiction, his application of a discipline systematic enough for geological studies. It was inevitable that other men should bring the same sort of ruthless and uncompromising scrutiny to bear on scripture.

The man most responsible for this process was the French historian and theologian Ernest Renan. Born in 1823, Renan had originally imagined himself destined for the priesthood and enrolled at the seminary of Saint Sulpice. In 1845, however, he abandoned his supposed vocation, having been prompted by Germanic biblical scholarship to question the literal truth of Christian doctrine. In 1860, he undertook an archaeological journey to Palestine and Syria. In 1863, he published his highly controversial *La vie de Jésus*, which was translated into English a year later. Renan's book endeavoured to demystify Christianity. It depicted Jesus as 'an incomparable man', but nothing more than a man – an altogether mortal and non-divine personage – and adumbrated a hierarchy of values that might be comfortably accommodated by the 'secular humanism' of today.

Renan's book was almost immediately placed on the Index. In the years that followed, no fewer than nineteen of his works were to be banned by the Holy Office. But Renan was no obscure academician. Neither was he a sensationalist hack. On the contrary, he was one of the most profoundly respected and prestigious intellectual figures of his era. As a consequence, *The Life of Jesus* provoked one of the greatest traumas in the course of nineteenth-century thought. It became one of the half-dozen or so bestselling books of the entire century, and has never since been out of print. For the 'educated classes' of the age, Renan was as much a household name as Marx, Freud or Jung might be in our own century; and, given the absence of cinema and television, he was probably much more widely read. At a single stroke, *The Life of Jesus* revolutionised attitudes towards biblical scholarship to a degree that would have been unthinkable only shortly before. And for the next thirty years, Renan was to remain a self-appointed gadfly to the Church, publishing controversial examinations of the Apostles, of Paul and of early Christianity in the context of imperial Roman culture. In effect, Renan loosed from its previously sealed bottle a genie which Christianity has never since contrived to recapture or tame.

Garibaldi and the Unification of Italy

Through Darwin and his followers, science presented an increasingly serious threat to the Church. A further threat was posed by the newly applied rigour and scientific methodology of biblical archaeology and scholarship. There were also influential and widely read philosophers – Schopenhauer, for instance, and Nietzsche, proclaiming the 'death of God' – who challenged, even blasphemously assaulted, conventional Christian ethical and theological assumptions. Under the French writer Théophile Gautier's doctrine of '*l'art pour l'art*', 'art for art's sake', the arts were becoming a self-contained religion of their own, moving increasingly into sacred territory which organised religion seemed increasingly to have abdicated. Thus, for example, Wagner's theatre at Bayreuth became in effect the temple of a new cult; and well-educated Europeans deemed it quite as acceptable to be 'a Wagnerian' as to be a Christian. By the end of the century, the artist would have usurped the role of the priest, becoming, in Joyce's famous phrase, 'a priest of the imagination'.

And then there was the ever more volatile political situation. Between 1805 and 1808, Napoleon had established his own regime in Italy, dividing the country into kingdoms ruled by himself and one of his brothers, then one of his marshals, Joachim Murat. In 1809, Napoleon had abolished all temporal holdings and power of the Papacy. On being excommunicated by Pope Pius VII, the 'Corsican monster' had responded by having the pontiff thrown into prison. The Papacy was never wholly to recover from this humiliation.

In the wake of Napoleon's final downfall in 1815, attempts were made to restore the old order in Europe, and the continent embarked on a period of conservative reaction that prevailed in most quarters for some twenty years. In Italy, however, the old order had been definitively ruptured. Most of the peninsula was ruled directly or indirectly by the Austrian Habsburgs; but the Habsburgs themselves had become increasingly enfeebled. The rest of the country was divided between Habsburg and Bourbon duchies, the Papal States nominally ruled by the Pope, the Bourbon Kingdom of Naples and the Two Sicilies which encompassed the south and, in the northwest, the fledgling Kingdom of Piedmont, ruled from Turin by the House of Savoy. The Italian peninsula was thus as fragmented as it had been before the French Revolution and the Napoleonic Wars, and even less stable. It could hardly be expected to retain whatever precarious equilibrium it possessed. The nationalism and desire for unification that swept across the whole of Europe during the nineteenth century were soon to erupt in Italy as well. By 1815, events were already in motion that would lead some fifty-five years later to the unification of the country and the emergence of a new European power.

One of the key factors in this process was the Carbonaria, a network of secret societies dedicated to revolution, to the expulsion of all foreign powers from Italian soil, to the unification of the country and the establishment of democratic independent government. The Carbonaria were organised along Masonic lines. Indeed, many commentators have described them as an essentially Masonic institution. Certainly there was considerable overlap between the Carbonaria and Freemasonry, with prominent members of the former also belonging to the latter. One such was Giuseppe Mazzini, exiled to France in 1830 where, two years later, he created a new secret society, 'Young Italy'. In the following year, Mazzini was joined by a twenty-six-year-old revolutionary, Giuseppe Garibaldi. By this time, the joint membership of 'Young Italy' and the Carbonaria numbered more than 60,000. So far as the Papacy and the Holy Office were concerned, they were all Freemasons, and their activities were deemed to constitute evidence for an alleged Masonic conspiracy. Papal pronouncements against Freemasonry began to increase in both frequency and vehemence.

In 1848, virtually the whole of Europe was swept by revolution, and Italy did not escape the contagion. On 9 January, Palermo revolted, and the remainder of Sicily rapidly followed. In March, the Habsburg territory in the north, Lombardy and Venetia, declared its independence, and Piedmont, seeking to annex it, declared war on Austria. By May, the Piedmontese invasion of Lombardy had been rebuffed by Austrian troops, and conservative troops from Naples had embarked on the reconquest of Sicily. In November, however, the Papal Prime Minister was assassinated in Rome and Pope Pius IX was forced to flee the city in disguise. The following February, Mazzini, aided by Garibaldi, proclaimed a Roman republic in place of the old Papal States.

From then on, civic and political turbulence was to continue almost uninterrupted. For a time at least, the forces of the old order gained an ascendancy. A second Piedmontese attack on Austria was defeated, and the Roman republic of Mazzini and Garibaldi was toppled by French troops dispatched by Louis Napoleon, subsequently the Emperor Napoleon III. Towards the latter part of 1849, however, a new king, the moderate Victor Emmanuel II, ascended the throne of Piedmont. A year later, he brought into his cabinet a dynamic moderniser and progressive, Camillo di Cavour. For the duration of his life, Cavour was to dedicate himself to the creation of a united Italy. By 1857, he had established a monarchist and unionist political party. Garibaldi had become his vice-president.

In 1859, Piedmont again went to war with Austria for control of northern Italy. This time, however, by dint of Cavour's clandestine machinations, Piedmont's ineffectual forces were reinforced by a full-sized French army under the command of Napoleon III in person. Two major battles ensued, at Magenta and Solferino, and the defeated Habsburgs were expelled from Lombardy. In January of the following year, Garibaldi, discreetly supported by Cavour, sailed from a port near Genoa with a force of volunteers known as 'the Thousand'. In May, they landed in Sicily and quickly conquered the entire island. In August, they captured Naples. On 26 October 1860, Victor Emmanuel met Garibaldi in what had formerly been Neapolitan territory, and Garibaldi proclaimed the Piedmontese monarch

King of Italy. The Kingdom of Italy was officially proclaimed on 17 March 1861, at the Piedmontese capital of Turin. With the exception of the Papal States, the whole of Italy was now united.

In July 1862, Garibaldi dispatched a circular letter to all Masonic Lodges in Sicily, urging that

> Brethren, as citizens and as Masons, must cooperate so that Rome will be an Italian city, and the capital of a great and powerful Nation. And it is their duty not only to help the patriotic undertaking with every means at their disposal but also to persuade the non-initiated that without Rome the destiny of Italy will always be uncertain and that with Rome all sorrows will end.[1]

To advocate the conquest of Rome and the Papal States was one thing, to translate this aspiration into practice quite another. The Papacy was still protected by the French army, deemed at the time to be invincible. And Napoleon III had no desire to see the European balance of power upset by a united and potentially dangerous Italy. When Garibaldi attempted to annex the Papal States by force in 1867, he was thwarted by French troops.

Another opportunity was soon to present itself, however. On 19 July 1870, Napoleon III – grievously overestimating his own military resources and underestimating those of his adversary – was lured into war with Prussia. As one French disaster followed another in catastrophic succession, the troops protecting the Papacy were recalled. Their transfer to the front made scant difference. In less than three months, the Franco-Prussian War was effectively over. On 1 September 1870, the sequence of French reverses culminated in the débâcle at Sédan. The French army surrendered, Napoleon III abdicated

A mass burning of witches in Toulouse in 1577; over 400 were burned that year. A Papal Bull of 1484 had established the reality of witchcraft to the Church's satisfaction.

A sixteenth-century woodcut of three witches being burned
in the Harz mountains, Germany.

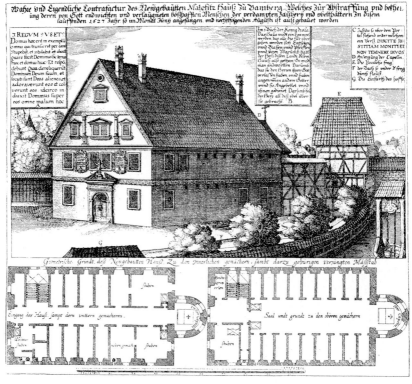

A seventeenth-century illustration of the Malefitz House built at Bamberg
specifically for the interrogation and torture of suspected witches.

Top and above The use of torture was recommended to all Inquisitors and secular judges when seeking confessions to support accusations of witchcraft.

Testing the guilt of a witch in Sweden by ducking: if she drowned, she was presumed innocent; if she survived, it was presumed to be with the devil's aid and so she would be burned.

Interrogation of a witch: any faint or fit was taken as
proof of demonic possession.

ABOMINATION DES SORCIERS

Gaspar Isac exc.

Est il rien qui soit plus damnable,
Ny plus digne du feu d'enfer,
...e cette engeance abominable
...es ministres de Lucifer?

Ils tirent de leurs noirs mysteres
L'horreur, la hayne le debat,
Et font de sanglans caracteres
Dans leur execrable Sabat.

C'est la que ces maudites a...
Se vont preparer leur tou...
Et qu'elles attisent les flan...
Qui bruslent eternellem...

Above and top right Illustrations depicting the general attitude towards
witchcraft in the eighteenth century and earlier.

Above Nine women burned for witchcraft at Dumfries,
Scotland, 13 April 1659.

Matthew Hopkins, the self-appointed 'Witchfinder-General'
in East Anglia during the English Civil War, who was responsible for
many false accusations of witchcraft.

and the Second French Empire collapsed. Three weeks later, on 20 September, Italian soldiers marched triumphantly into Rome, brushing aside the largely symbolic, token resistance of the Pope's miniature army. Refusing to accept the defeat, the Pope, sulking, withdrew into the Vatican. The Kingdom of Italy now encompassed the entire peninsula, and its capital was soon to be moved from Turin to Rome.

The threats posed to the Church by science, by archaeology and biblical scholarship, by the 'cult' of the arts exemplified by Bayreuth were all real enough. The unification of Italy, however, was an altogether different matter, a veritable and definitive *coup de grâce* to the Church of former centuries. The Papacy was now entirely divested of all temporal power, was left incapable of imposing authority by physical force, was bereft of the capacity to inflict physical punishment on those who professed defiance. For all its wealth, majesty, pomp, circumstance and tradition, the Roman Catholic Church was now as impotent in the secular world as it had been in the semi-legendary days of the 'early Christians'.

Who Holds the Power in the Church?

In addition to the array of external pressures, the Church was also threatened by dissension within. As so often in the past, this dissension stemmed in large part from France. And when it did not actually arise from France, it was conditioned by events there.

France had traditionally been regarded as the 'eldest daughter of the Church', but had often been a recalcitrant and rebellious daughter. In the early fourteenth century, Philippe IV had kidnapped the Pope, established the Papacy at Avignon and effectively turned it into an instrument of his own policy.

The resulting schism had lasted for 108 years and irrevocably compromised Papal authority. In the seventeenth century, two French cardinals, Richelieu and Mazarin, had ruthlessly subordinated the Church's interests to those of the French Crown. At the end of the eighteenth century, the French Revolution had exterminated an estimated 17,000 priests and twice that many nuns, had destroyed or confiscated Church buildings and lands, had plundered Church treasures and, if only briefly, installed a regime that did not even pay lip service to Rome. Shortly thereafter, Napoleon had treated the Papal States as just another conquered territory, had imprisoned the Pope, had made off with the treasures of the Holy See and the Vatican's secret archives, had dismantled the Holy Roman Empire which represented the Church's temporal dominion, had driven the Knights of Saint John from their abode on Malta and had definitively ruptured the relationship in France between Church and State.

During the Second Empire of Napoleon III, the Church in France, though no longer yoked to the government, had managed to regain a measure of equilibrium. By 1870, however, that, too, had become precarious. By 1870, the Second Empire and the stability it had afforded were in process of collapse; and that collapse would be complete by the end of the year. No one, of course, could foresee the precise sequence of events that would follow – the Prussian investment and siege of Paris, the fratricidal days of the Commune, the tentative emergence of the Third Republic, the triumphant creation of the German Empire. But even by the middle of 1870, it was clear that the Church, whatever happened, would suffer. Four years earlier, after all, the Prussian war machine had almost casually crushed Habsburg Austria, the only remaining Catholic power of consequence on the continent, in a mere six weeks. Whether the

Second French Empire could withstand a similar onslaught was doubtful; but even if it could, the Church's position would be severely shaken. And so far as military might was concerned, there would soon be only one 'superpower' in Europe, a monolithic martial state to the north where Rome enjoyed no official currency whatever and where the hated Lutheran Church was effectively an adjunct of the War Office.

Against this backdrop, French ecclesiastics had begun to agitate within the Church itself. Since the Middle Ages, there had been incessant dispute about where ultimate authority in the Church lay. Did it reside with the Papacy and with the individual personage of the Pope? Or did it reside with the scattered bishops of Christendom, expressing their collective voice through Church councils? Was the Pope ultimately subordinate to councils of bishops? Or were the councils of bishops subordinate to the Pope? What would happen, for example, if the throne of Saint Peter were to be occupied by an heretical pontiff? Who would have the power to remove him? Rome, needless to say, insisted on the supremacy of the Papacy. The bishops of France, supported by many in Germany, advocated the supremacy of their councils.

The contingency of an heretical Pope had been confronted and addressed by Church lawyers since the thirteenth century. To protect the Church from such a possibility, the lawyers had argued that supreme authority resided ultimately with a 'General Council'. The persuasiveness of their argument was reinforced during the so-called Avignon Captivity, when two or even three rival Popes and Antipopes contended with, condemned and excommunicated each other. In 1378, John Wycliffe had observed from England: 'I always knew the pope had cloven feet. Now he has a cloven head.'[2]

At last, in 1414, the Council of Constance was convened –

a General Council of the sort advocated by Church lawyers – to resolve the intractable and embarrassing situation. On 6 April 1415, the assembled ecclesiastics resolved by decree that 'the council is above the Pope'.[3] All Christians, *including the Pope*, were declared subject to the decisions of a General Council, which was deemed to derive its authority directly from God:

> This holy Synod of Constance, which forms an ecumenical council . . . declares the following:
>
> First, this synod, legitimately assembled in the Holy Spirit, which forms an ecumenical council and represents the Catholic Church in dispute, has its authority directly from Christ; everyone, of whatever estate or dignity, even if this be papal, is bound to obey it in matters relating to the faith.[4]

According to the modern theologian Hans Küng: 'Authority in the church does not lie in a monarch but in the church itself, of which the Pope is the servant, not the master.'[5] As Küng explains, 'the legitimacy of . . . all subsequent Popes to the present day depends on the legitimacy of the Council of Constance'.[6] And he adds that

> the fundamental binding character of the decrees of Constance may not be evaded. No Pope has ever dared to repeal the decree . . . or to declare that it is not generally binding.[7]

The decrees of Constance, which established the supremacy of a General Council over the Pope himself, were embraced with particular enthusiasm by the Church in France. In 1682, a council of French bishops and other clergy enunciated their position – subsequently known as 'Gallicanism' – in four central points, the so-called 'Gallican Articles'. The 'Gallican Articles' stated that the Pope had no authority over temporal affairs and that kings were not subject to Papal rulings. The decrees of the Council of Constance were endorsed, and General Councils were declared to have greater authority than the Pope. The traditional independence of the Church in France was reasserted, and certain of its prerogatives – the right to appoint its own bishops, for example – were declared beyond the Papacy's power to rescind. And finally, the 'Gallican Articles' stated that no Papal decision was irrevocably fixed until a General Council had consented to it.

Through the ensuing vicissitudes of French history, 'Gallicanism', with its adherence to 'Conciliar' authority, was to characterise the Church in France. By its very nature, it was potentially inimical to the Papacy. Pursued to its logical conclusion, 'Gallicanism' would effectively demote the Pope to what he had originally been – merely the Bishop of Rome, one among numerous bishops, enjoying some kind of nominal or symbolic leadership, but not any actual primacy or power. In short, the Church would be decentralised.

The opposing position, which advocated the Pope's supremacy over bishops and councils, became known as 'Ultramontane', because it regarded authority as residing with the Papacy in Rome, 'on the other side of the mountains' from France. By 1870, the developments of the nineteenth century had brought the 450-year antagonism between 'Gallican' and 'Ultramontane' positions to a head. Out of this situation, the modern Papacy, the Papacy as we know it today, would emerge.

11

Infallibility

Writing in the 1950s, an historian and Catholic apologist described the Papal States of the immediate post-Napoleonic period as 'a benevolent theocracy'.[1] Between 1823 and 1846, some 200,000 people in this 'benevolent theocracy' were consigned to the galleys, banished into exile, sentenced to life imprisonment or to death. Torture by the Inquisitors of the Holy Office was routinely practised. Every community, whether small rural village or major city, maintained a permanent gallows in its central square. Repression was rampant and surveillance constant, with Papal spies lurking everywhere. Meetings of more than three people were officially banned. Railways were banned because Pope Gregory XVI believed they might 'work harm to religion'.[2] Newspapers were also banned. According to a decree of Pope Pius VIII, anyone possessing a book written by a heretic was to be considered a heretic himself. Anyone overhearing criticism of the Holy Office and not reporting it to the authorities was deemed as guilty as the critic. For reading a book on the Index, or for eating meat on Friday, one could be imprisoned.

In 1846, Pope Gregory XVI died and a new pontiff ascended the throne of Saint Peter under the name of Pius IX. It was a volatile moment in European history. Since 1815 – since

Napoleon's final defeat at Waterloo and the order imposed by the Congress of Vienna – Europe had passed through thirty years of relative stability, characterised by extreme reactionary conservatism. Now, the continent was stirring restlessly again. Among the diverse forces in the wind, two were particularly virulent – revolution and nationalism.

Strangely enough, given his subsequent career, Pius IX began his reign with the reputation of a reformer. He was sympathetic to at least some form of Italian unification and nationalism. He envisioned himself, in his capacity of pontiff, serving as a divinely ordained conduit and instrument for Italy's rebirth. He dreamed of presiding over a confederation of Italian states. He even elicited hopeful appeals for support from Mazzini and Garibaldi, who in their naivety fancied they might find a new ally in the Church.

Whatever illusions Pius may initially have fostered, they quickly evaporated, along with his popularity. It soon became apparent that the Italy the Pope had in mind bore little relation to any constitutional state. In 1848, he doggedly refused to lend his support to a rebellious military campaign against Austrian domination of the north. His studied neutrality was perceived as a craven betrayal; and the resulting violent backlash obliged him to flee Rome in ignominious disguise, as a priest in the carriage of the Bavarian ambassador. In 1850, Papal rule was restored by the arrival of French troops and Pius returned to his throne. His political position, however, now made no concessions of any kind to liberalism or reform; and the regime he established in his own domains was to become increasingly hated.

As a result of the war between Austria and France in northern Italy in 1859, all the former Papal States were annexed by the new Kingdom of Italy except for Rome and the countryside immediately surrounding the city – a region of some 120 by 30 miles. Even in this shrunken domain, the Pope's position was precarious and had to be protected – in effect, guaranteed – by a perpetual French military presence. Thus shielded, Pius took advantage of developments in transport and communications to weaken further the authority of Catholic bishops and to centralise control increasingly in his own person. Alois Hötzl, for example, a distinguished Franciscan lecturer in philosophy and theology, was peremptorily summoned from Munich to Rome for having defended a writer the Pope and the Holy Office deemed inappropriate. Hötzl was promptly condemned and sentenced to a regimen of solitary spiritual exercises in a Roman monastery. His release was secured only by repeated appeals by the Bavarian ambassador, acting on the express orders of King Ludwig II; and even then, Hötzl was obliged officially to recant.

Within his own domain, Pope Pius IX ruled as an absolute monarch. The old restrictions, such as those curbing the right of assembly, still applied. No independent newspapers were allowed. Dispatches from reporters and correspondents working within the Papal State were intercepted by the police before they could be sent abroad. Any adverse criticism was censored or suppressed, and critics themselves were often banished. Undesirable books and journals were denied entry. All writings advocating ecclesiastical reform, or even the 'Gallican' position, were automatically placed on the Index.

The values and attitudes of the age could not, however, be altogether ignored. Thus, for example, the Holy Office no longer enjoyed the prerogative of burning people. There were also some curbs on torture. But the Holy Office, by Papal decree, still retained the powers of 'excommunication, confiscation, banishment, imprisonment for life, as well as secret execution in heinous cases'.[3] Papal police and spies continued to be ubiquitous and were quick to act against political or theological transgressions. Arrests were common and numerous. Political offences were heard by special courts and judged solely by priests exercising unchallenged authority. 'In the best traditions of the Inquisition', those accused were never allowed to meet witnesses brought against them by the prosecution, nor were they permitted to be defended by a lawyer. Doctors were forbidden to continue treating any patient who, after a third visit, did not consult with his confessor. Jewish doctors were prohibited from practising at all. By dint of pressure from the Pope, they were also banned from the adjacent territory of Tuscany.

Such was the temporal regime of Pius IX. As if to surround himself with an army of celestial enforcers as well, the Pope proceeded to create an unprecedented number of new saints. In 1862, for example, he created twenty-six of them at once by canonising twenty-six missionaries killed in Japan in 1597. He packed the episcopate with bishops of like mind to his own and established more than 200 new dioceses. Acting on his own authority – without, that is, the consent of a General Council supposedly required by the Council of Constance – he elevated to the status of official dogma the doctrine of the Immaculate Conception. Contrary to the misapprehension of non-Catholics, this did not refer to Jesus's alleged virgin birth. It posited, rather, that Mary, in order to serve as vessel for God's incarnation in Jesus, had herself to have been born free of original sin. By virtue of the Pope's declaration, her purity became retroactively 'true'.

In 1864, as the American Civil War attained its bloody climax and the Prussian military machine under Bismarck crushed Denmark in six days, the Pope declared his own war against 'progress, liberalism and modern civilisation'. These things were officially denounced in an encyclical letter issued to all Roman Catholic bishops, in which the pontiff expressed his dream of seeing the entire world united under one religion – that of Rome.

Appended to the encyclical letter was a formal 'Syllabus of Errors', a catalogue or inventory of all the attitudes and beliefs the Pope deemed dangerous, wrong and heretical. Not surprisingly, the 'Syllabus' condemned rationalism, secret societies and Bible societies. According to the Pope, it was also an error to believe that every individual 'is free to embrace and profess that religion . . . he shall consider true'.[4] Equally erroneous was the belief that 'it is no longer expedient that the Catholic religion should be held as the only religion of the state, to the exclusion of all other forms of worship'.[5] It was wrong to believe 'that persons . . . shall enjoy the public exercise of their own peculiar worship'.[6] The eightieth and last error condemned by the Pope was the belief that he himself, the Roman pontiff, 'can and should reconcile himself, and come to terms with progress, liberalism and modern civilisation'.[7]

The 'Syllabus of Errors' was accompanied by a short introduction from Cardinal Antonelli, Secretary of State for the Papal States and one of the cardinals presiding over the Holy Office – which had now taken to referring to itself as the Sacred Roman and Universal Inquisition. Antonelli wrote that the Pope

has willed that a syllabus of the same errors should be compiled, to be sent to all the Bishops of the Catholic world, in order that these Bishops may have before their eyes all the errors and pernicious doctrines which he has reprobated and condemned.[8]

One historian has commented that 'the Syllabus was widely regarded as a gesture of defiance hurled by an outraged Pope against the nineteenth century'.[9] Such a conclusion is apt. In effect, the Pope was trying to outdo King Canute. His ultimate desire was for God to abrogate and annul the nineteenth century in its entirety. When God failed to comply, the Pope attempted to commandeer and usurp the divine prerogative by declaring himself infallible.

For some years prior to this step, Pius IX had been implementing measures that would transform the Papacy. At a time when even the most autocratic secular regimes had begun to inch their way towards representative democracy, the Church, under Pius, was moving in precisely the opposite direction – towards neo-feudal absolutism. It was as if the Pope and the rebranded Inquisition sought to compensate for the increasing loss of temporal power by arrogating an ever greater psychological and spiritual authority. If the Grand Inquisitor could no longer legally send people to the stake, he would now undertake to penalise them from within, working through their consciences by means of techniques similar to those of voodoo. In effect, the spirit of the Papacy sought to 'possess' the faithful. Having been dispossessed of worldly sovereignty, the Church now endeavoured to establish a new domain for itself primarily within the vulnerable confines of the Catholic mind.

This shift in the Church's 'theatre of operations' was inaugurated by the First Vatican Council, which convened under the auspices of Pius IX in December 1869. It continued for some ten and a half months, and when it ground to a halt on 20 October 1870, the Papacy had been transformed.

The Council began in a predictable enough fashion, with more or less conventional condemnation of atheism, materialism and pantheism. Before long, however, its real thrust was to become apparent – to resolve definitively the centuries-old struggle for authority between bishops, who wanted a more decentralised Church, and the Papacy, which sought supreme and autocratic power. By the time the Council concluded, it was the Papacy's aspirations that had emerged triumphant.

Vatican I was not a free Council. On the contrary, it was characterised by bullying, intimidation and coercion. It was dominated entirely by the Pope's wishes, and there were no secret ballots to protect dissenters. Those who opposed Pius's will were under no illusions about what they would incur. At best, they would be forced to resign or simply be removed from their posts. At worst, they could expect to be arrested by the Papal police, who operated in accordance with the Inquisition.

At first things did not come to anything so extreme or so dramatic. After all many bishops were financially dependent on the Vatican and thus on the goodwill of the Pope. More than 300 of them had been brought to Rome at the pontiff's expense. Having thereby placed them in his debt, he could feel confident enough about their loyalty in any ensuing controversy.

Having stacked the odds in his favour, the Pope could deal swiftly, ruthlessly and decisively with any dissent. When, for example, a Croatian bishop dared to assert that even Protestants were capable of loving Jesus, he was loudly shouted down. When he dared further to 'dispute the feasibility of deciding dogmatic questions by majority rule', the majority erupted with the rabid fury of a lynch mob, screaming across the floor of the Council: 'Lucifer! Anathema! A second Luther! Throw him out!'[10]

Nor was the Pope himself above personal intimidation. When the Chaldean Patriarch, for example, presumed to challenge a proposed Bull that augmented the Papacy's power to appoint ecclesiastics, he was angrily summoned to a private meeting in one of the Pope's chambers. No sooner had he entered than the pontiff, shaking with rage, bolted the doors behind him. He must either consent to the Bull in writing or resign. Unless he did one or the other, he would never leave the room. On this occasion, the Patriarch submitted. When he defied the Pope again later in the Council, he was summarily dismissed from his position.[11]

In this atmosphere of bullying and menace, few ecclesiastics possessed sufficient courage to protest openly. Many of them left the Council before it had finished its business. The Pope encouraged their flight, pleased to be rid of rebellious voices.

It soon became apparent that the ultimate objective and governing purpose of the First Vatican Council was to promulgate the doctrine of Papal infallibility. This issue, however, was not announced in advance. Indeed, it was kept rigorously secret. The Prefect of the Vatican Secret Archives was sacked for allowing certain friends to see the Pope's rules for debate; and lest he had a key he might pass on to his successor, the door affording access from his rooms to the archive was walled up.[12]

The Inquisition, in contrast, was privy to the Pope's plans. It was instrumental in keeping them secret until the appropriate moment and then in railroading them through whatever opposition might arise. Of the five men presiding over the First Vatican Council, three were cardinals, all of them members of the Inquisition. Of the various commissions operating behind the Council, the most important was the one devoted to theology and dogma. On the advice of Cardinal Giuseppe Bizzari, also a member of the Inquisition, it was established 'that the Holy Office must form the core of the commission entrusted with doctrinal matters'.[13] When one cardinal expressed anxiety about introducing the question of Papal infallibility, he was told not to worry, to leave everything to the Inquisition and let the Holy Spirit take care of the rest.[14]

In the Bull that announced the gathering of the Council, there was no mention whatever of Papal infallibility. There was no mention either in any preparatory literature or preliminary agenda. The issue was not even raised until February 1870, by which time the Council had already been in session for a full two months and the ranks of the Pope's opponents thinned. When the matter of Papal infallibility was finally introduced, therefore, most of the assembled bishops were caught by surprise and off guard. Many of them were profoundly shocked. More than a few were genuinely horrified.

As in matters of lesser consequence, dissenters were subjected to extreme pressure and intimidation. Some were threatened with curtailment of financial support. When an abbot-general of an Armenian monastic order spoke out against infallibility, he was told he would be dismissed, then sentenced by the infuriated Pope to a regimen of 'compulsory spiritual exercises' in a local monastery – a form, in effect, of house arrest.[15] Another Armenian ecclesiastic received a similar sentence. When he defied it, the Papal police attempted to arrest him in the street, and the ensuing brawl escalated into a riot. Immediately thereafter, all the Armenian bishops requested permission to leave the Council. When this was refused, two of them fled.[16]

Altogether, 1,084 bishops were eligible to attend and vote at the First Vatican Council, of whom some 700 were actually present. Approximately fifty were fervent supporters of the Pope's desire to arrogate infallibility to himself, some 130 were militantly opposed to it, and the remainder were initially indifferent or undecided. By the time it came to a vote, the Papacy's strong-arm tactics had tipped the balance decisively. In the first vote, on 13 July 1870, 451 declared themselves in favour and eighty-eight opposed.[17] Four days later, on 17 July, fifty-five bishops officially stated their opposition but declared that, out of reverence for the Pope, they would abstain from the vote scheduled for the following day. All of them then left Rome, as a good many others had already done. The second and final vote occurred on 18 July. The number of those supporting the Papacy's position increased to 535. Only two voted against, one of them Bishop Edward Fitzgerald of Little Rock, Arkansas. Of the 1,084 bishops eligible to vote on the issue of Papal infallibility, a total of 535 had finally endorsed it – a 'majority' of just over 49 per cent.[18] By virtue of this 'majority', the Pope, on 18 July 1870, was formally declared infallible in his own right and 'not as a result of the consent of the Church'.[19] As one commentator has observed, 'this removed all conciliarist interpretations of the role of the Papacy'.[20]

The decisive vote of 18 July occurred against a background of increasingly turbulent political events. On the very next day, 19 July, the French Empire under Napoleon III suicidally declared war on Prussia. The chaos that ensued in France distracted attention from religious affairs and no doubt blunted what might otherwise have been a rebellious reaction from the independent-minded French clergy. Elsewhere a backlash did occur. Prejudice against the Church seemed to have acquired a new justification; and anti-Catholic sentiment erupted across the whole of Europe and North America. In Holland, there was virtual schism. In the Habsburg imperium of Austria-Hungary, a concordat previously concluded with the Papacy was abrogated by the government. The Papal Nuncio in Vienna reported to the Vatican's Secretary of State that 'almost all the bishops of

Austria–Hungary now returned from Rome are *furious* over the definition of infallibility';[21] and two of them publicly demanded that a debate be opened to reverse the decision of the Council. For more than a year, the bishops of Hungary refused to accept the Council's ruling.

The Bishop of Rottenburg openly branded the Pope the 'disturber of the Church'.[22] In Braunsberg, a distinguished professor published a manifesto castigating the pontiff as 'heretic and devastator of the Church'; and the local cardinal and the local bishop both tacitly concurred in this condemnation.[23] In Prussia, Bismarck introduced laws that radically altered the Church's status and relationship with the state. Jesuits were effectively banned from the kingdom. Legal proceedings were instituted for the appointment of clergy. Civil marriage ceremonies were made obligatory. All schools were placed under state supervision.

In the face of such reactions, the Papacy simply became more aggressive. All bishops were ordered to submit in writing to the new dogma; and those who refused were penalised or removed from their posts. So, too, were rebellious teachers and professors of theology. Papal nuncios were instructed to denounce defiant ecclesiastics and scholars as heretics. All books and articles challenging, or even questioning, the dogma of Papal infallibility were automatically placed on the Index. On at least one occasion, attempts were made to suppress a hostile book through bribery. Many records of the Council itself were confiscated, sequestered, censored or destroyed. One opponent of the new dogma, for example, Archbishop Vincenzo Tizzani, Professor of Church History at the Papal University of Rome, wrote a detailed account of the proceedings. Immediately after his death, his manuscript was purchased by the Vatican and has been kept locked away ever since.[24]

Against the tide of history, however, the Pope's newly acquired infallibility proved of little avail. At the beginning of September, the French army surrendered at Sédan, Napoleon III abdicated and the Second Empire collapsed. In a hopelessly belated attempt to avert catastrophe, the French troops protecting the Vatican were recalled. On 20 September, Italian soldiers marched triumphantly into Rome. Deliberations of the First Vatican Council juddered to a halt, and the Council itself closed a fortnight later. In July 1871, Rome became the capital of the newly unified and newly secularised Kingdom of Italy. The monarch, Victor Emmanuel, installed himself in the former Papal palace of the Quirinal.

Two months earlier, in May, the Italian government had enacted the Law of Guarantees. According to this measure, the Pope's safety was assured and he was accorded the status of a reigning sovereign in the Vatican. Vatican City – a tract of land totalling some 108.7 acres within the ancient walls of the Vatican itself – was declared an independent principality, not part of Italian soil.

Unappeased, the Pope embarked on a highly publicised sulk. Refusing to leave the Vatican, he complained that he was being held prisoner. Within the confines of his own miniaturised domain, he endeavoured to remain oblivious to the external world; and there is some evidence that infallibility by then had gone to his head. In the account of one commentator at the time:

> The pope recently got the urge to try out his infallibility. While out on a walk he called to a paralytic: 'Get up and walk.' The poor devil gave it a try and collapsed, which put God's viceregent very much out of sorts . . . I really believe that he's insane.[25]

For the next fifty-eight years, the Papacy persisted in refusing to acknowledge the Italian state. During the whole of that time, no Pope visited Rome or deigned to set foot on Italian soil. At last, in February 1929, the Lateran Treaty was concluded. Vatican City was officially recognised and ratified as a sovereign state under international law, and Catholicism was proclaimed the state religion of the Italian people. In return, the Papacy formally recognised the Italian government – the government of Benito Mussolini.

By that time Pope Pius IX was long dead. He had died in 1878. He had been one of the most influential of modern Popes, but also one of the most unpopular. In 1881, his body was moved in an elaborate funeral procession from Saint Peter's across the Tiber and through Rome. Mobs gathered and yelled abuse: 'Long live Italy!' 'Death to the Pope!' 'Throw the pig in the river!' Along the route of the procession, stones were hurled and six individuals were arrested – apparently for attempting to seize the dead pontiff's coffin and tip it into the Tiber. They were charged with 'disturbing a religious function', and the reigning Pope, Leo XIII, lodged a formal protest with the Italian government for the 'outrage' to the Papacy's dignity.[26] Despite such hostility, however, Pius IX had made an indelible mark on history:

> When he died, he had effectively created the modern papacy, stripped ... of its temporal dominion but armed with vastly enhanced spiritual authority in compensation.[27]

12

The Holy Office

As the last third of the nineteenth century unscrolled, the Church was more bereft of temporal power than it had been for more than a millennium and a half. Nor was there much to be done about the situation. In certain quarters there was sporadic talk of a new Holy League, similar to that of the sixteenth century, which united the Catholic powers of Europe. Subsequent to 1870, however, there were few officially Catholic powers left on the continent. The most important was the Habsburg dual-monarchy of Austria-Hungary; but she, as Robert Musil later said, 'spent only enough on her army to ensure her position as the second weakest of the great powers'. The weakest of all was the recently unified Kingdom of Italy, whose population was still largely Catholic but whose government, having finally wrested control from the Church, was hardly prepared to become the Church's sword arm. Neither could the Kingdom of Italy be expected to enter into alliance with the old Austrian enemy.

Like Italy, France remained largely Catholic in her population; but the Third French Republic had rigorously preserved the old revolutionary separation of Church and State. And after the cataclysmic defeats of the Franco-Prussian War, the fragile French government was in no position to pose a challenge to the newly created German Empire, the Second Reich, now the supreme military power on the continent. Spain and Portugal were still officially Catholic, but they no longer ranked as major powers. At the same time, a new threat had arisen in the east. For centuries, the Eastern Orthodox Church had played second fiddle to Rome in temporal might. Now, as the official Church of Tsarist Russia, she could muster far greater temporal resources than Rome; and in such Balkan principalities as Bosnia, she was actively encroaching on what had been Catholic territory. The friction between Catholic and Orthodox Churches intensified. By 1914, that friction had contributed more than a little to the shots in Sarajevo that precipitated the First World War.

If it was painfully vulnerable in the secular world, however, the Church believed itself newly armed and equipped in other spheres. The doctrine of Papal infallibility provided, if nothing else, a seemingly impregnable bulwark against the advances and trespasses of science. For the faithful at least, Papal infallibility preempted and precluded all argument. While the Church could not defeat its adversary, it was spared defeat itself by being prevented from even entering the arena. For devout Catholics, Papal infallibility constituted a new 'rock' against which the tide of infernally driven science could only break in vain.

Against science, the Church could therefore engage in a species of sustained holding action. Against its other chief opponent in the world of ideas – against, that is, the researches of historical, archaeological and biblical scholarship – it believed it could move on to the offensive. This conviction was to lead to the mortifying embarrassment of the Catholic Modernist Movement.

The Modernist Movement arose out of the specific desire

to counter the depredations being wrought on scripture by commentators like Renan, and by Germanic biblical scholarship. Through Modernism, a new Church Militant – a Church Militant in the sphere of the mind – attempted to launch its counter-offensive. The Modernists were originally intended to employ the rigour, the discipline and precision of Germanic methodology not to challenge scripture, but to defend and support it. A generation of Catholic scholars was painstakingly trained and groomed to provide the Papacy with the equivalent of an academic strike force, a cadre purposefully formed to fortify the literal truth of scripture with all the heavy ordnance of the most up-to-date critical techniques and procedures. Like the Dominicans of the thirteenth century, like the Jesuits of the sixteenth, the Modernists were mobilised to launch a crusade that reclaimed lost territory.

To Rome's discomfiture and humiliation, however, the campaign backfired. The more the Church endeavoured to equip younger clerics with the tools necessary for combat in the modern polemical arena, the more those same clerics proceeded to desert the cause for which they had been recruited. Meticulous scrutiny of the Bible revealed a plethora of discrepancies, inconsistencies and repercussions that were alarmingly inimical to official dogma – and cast the doctrine of Papal infallibility in an ever more dubious light. Before anyone quite realised what was happening, the Modernists themselves had begun with their doubts and questions to erode and subvert the very positions they were supposed to be defending. They had also begun to challenge the Church's centralisation of authority.

Thus, for example, Alfred Loisy, one of the most distinguished and respected Modernists, asked publicly how certain of Rome's doctrines could possibly still be sustained in the wake of contemporary biblical and archaeological research. 'Jesus proclaimed the coming of the Kingdom,' Loisy stated, echoing Dostoevsky's Grand Inquisitor, 'but what came was the Church.'[1] Loisy demonstrated that many points of dogma had crystallised as historically determined reactions to specific events, at specific places and times. They were not, therefore, to be perceived as fixed and immutable truths, but at best as symbols. According to Loisy, such basic premises of Christian teaching as the Virgin Birth and Jesus's divinity were no longer tenable as literal.

In 1893, Loisy was dismissed from his teaching position, but that did little to salvage the situation because he remained vociferous and prolific. In relation to Loisy and his Modernist colleagues, the Church was in the dilemma of an arsonist trapped in the building he has himself set alight. Modernism was no longer merely embarrassing. It was displaying a capacity for becoming genuinely disruptive and destructive.

In 1902, nine months before his death, Pope Leo XIII created the Pontifical Biblical Commission to supervise and monitor the work of Catholic scriptural scholars. Officially the Commission's task was 'to strive . . . with all possible care that God's words . . . will be shielded not only from every breath of error but even from every rash of opinion'.[2] It was to ensure that scholars 'endeavour to safeguard the authority of the scriptures and to promote their right interpretation'.[3]

Leo XIII died in July 1903, to be succeeded by Pius X. The new Pope promptly established his position by making two appointments that were to have a prominent influence in determining the character of the twentieth-century Church. One of these was Cardinal Rafael Merry del Val (1865–1930), a cold and sinister personality, born in London to an English-woman and an aristocratic Spanish diplomat. He had worked in the Vatican's diplomatic service, and in 1898 had become a consultant to the department entrusted with maintaining the Index of prohibited books. Merry del Val had played a key role in orchestrating the election of Pius X as pontiff and exercised an enormous influence over the new Pope, who raised him to cardinal and appointed him Vatican Secretary of State – a position he continued to hold until Pius's death in 1914. His personal and doctrinal rigidity shaped the entire tenor of Pius's reign. He was vehemently hostile to Modernism and devoted himself to destroying it, even helping to establish a network of informers to denounce clerics and teachers who displayed Modernist tendencies. When Pius died, Merry del Val became Prefect of the Holy Office, or Grand Inquisitor, a post he retained until his own death in 1930.

Pius's second important appointee was Cardinal Mariano Rampolla del Tindaro (1843–1913), a scion of the Sicilian nobility. In 1887, he had been made a cardinal and Merry del Val's predecessor as Vatican Secretary of State. Under Pius X, he became Secretary of the Holy Inquisition. He was also made a member, then President, of the Pontifical Biblical Commission – which was thus brought under the Inquisition's authority. Between them, Rampolla del Tindaro and Merry del Val transformed the Commission into what one commentator has described as 'a militant mouthpiece for their own interests'.[4] In 1905, it officially declared that biblical texts were to be regarded as absolutely and literally 'true' history. It also published formal decrees on 'the right way to teach . . . scripture'[5] – decrees which, in 1907, Pope Pius X made obligatory throughout the Church.

On his election as pontiff in 1903, Pius X, supported by Rampolla del Tindaro and Merry del Val, had immediately placed the Modernist works of Alfred Loisy on the Index of forbidden books. In 1904, the new Pope issued two encyclicals opposing any scholarship that presumed to explore the origins and early history of Christianity. Seminaries and theological schools began to receive visits of inspection from the Vatican's minions. All Catholic teachers suspected of Modernist tendencies were summarily suspended or dismissed from their posts.

The Modernists, the best-educated, most erudite and articulate enclave in the Church, had few compunctions about fighting back. They received eloquent support from secular quarters – from prominent thinkers, from acclaimed cultural and literary figures, such as Antonio Fogazzaro in Italy and Roger Martin du Gard, subsequent winner of the Nobel Prize for Literature, in France. In 1896, Fogazzaro had become a senator. He was also revered as 'the leading Catholic layman of his day' and, by his contemporaries at least, as the greatest novelist Italy had produced since Manzoni. In *The Saint*, published in 1905, Fogazzaro wrote:

> The Catholic Church, calling herself the fountain of truth, today opposes the search after truth when her foundations, the sacred books, the formulae of her dogmas, her alleged infallibility, become objects of research. To us, this signifies that she no longer has faith in herself.[6]

Fogazzaro's work, needless to say, was itself promptly placed on the Index. And the Church's campaign against the movement it had fostered and nurtured was intensified. In 1907, the Pope issued an encyclical that formally condemned Modernism. In the same year, the Inquisition published a decree that castigated Modernist presumption in questioning Church doctrine, Papal authority and the historical veracity of biblical texts. In September 1907, Modernism was declared a heresy and the entire Modernist movement was officially banned. The quantity of books on the Index suddenly increased dramatically. A new, much more stringent censorship was introduced. Ecclesiastical commissars monitored teaching with a doctrinaire inflexibility unknown since the Counter-Reformation. At last, in 1910, a decree was issued compelling all Catholics involved in preaching or teaching to swear an oath repudiating 'all the errors of Modernism' – an oath that was not to be abolished until 1967. A number of Modernist writers were excommunicated. Students at seminaries and theological colleges were even prohibited from reading newspapers.

In originally endorsing and sponsoring the Modernist movement, the Church had attempted to enter the modern world, availing itself of the modern world's intellectual resources and scholarly methodology. Given the result of the experiment, one might well be justified in concluding the Church and the modern world to be incompatible. That, certainly, seemed to be the Church's conclusion. Rome withdrew into a bunker of its own and remained there until the 1960s.

Its public image scarred by the battle with Modernism, the Inquisition was in urgent need of a facelift. In 1908, the word 'Inquisition' was officially dropped from its title and it became the Sacred Congregation of the Holy Office.

Monsignor Benigni's Intelligence Network

The influence of Cardinal Merry del Val, Prefect of the Holy Office or Grand Inquisitor, continued to radiate as the twentieth century unfolded. When he died in 1930, the eleven cardinals who comprised the ruling council of the Holy Office were all his protégés. One of them, Cardinal Eugenio Pacelli, eventually became Pope Pius XII in 1939. Another, Cardinal Donato Sbarretti, became the new Prefect and presided in that capacity throughout the 1930s and early 1940s. Among the consultants to the Holy Office under Merry del Val were the two figures who succeeded Sbarretti and presided as Prefect from the early 1940s until 1982. One of the consultants under Sbarretti was Giovanni Battista Montini – who became Pope Paul VI in 1963. Thus did Merry del Val's shadow brood over the Holy Office and the Papacy throughout most of the twentieth century. As we will see shortly, it has still not been exorcised.

Not surprisingly, the cardinal and his disciples also endeavoured to extend their influence, insofar as possible, into politics. In the political arena, one of Merry del Val's most sinister protégés was Monsignor Umberto Benigni (1862–1934), described by a contemporary as a 'strange character and without scruples'.[7] A native of Perugia, Benigni was ordained in 1884 and became a teacher of ecclesiastical history at a local seminary. He then took up journalism of sorts, founding a popular Catholic publication. In 1901, he moved to Rome to continue teaching there, but soon abandoned that in order to work in the Curia, becoming a secretary at the Congregation for the Propagation of the Faith. Then, in 1906, he joined the press office of the Vatican's Secretary of State, Merry del Val. For the next five years, Benigni worked under the auspices of the future Grand Inquisitor. At last, in 1911, he left, and, with Merry del Val's blessing, devoted himself entirely to the administration of the secret society he had founded two years earlier, *Sodalitium pianum* ('Pius Society').

Its original objectives were to help implement and enforce Pope Pius X's strictures against Modernism. In 1907, Pius had 'urged bishops to supervise closely seminary teaching and writing by priests and to establish in each diocese vigilance committees'.[8] In accordance with this injunction, Benigni had created his secret society as an international network of informers to spy, collect and collate information on suspected Modernist sympathisers, who would then be publicly exposed and condemned. Acting as a species of *ad hoc* and self-appointed Inquisition, *Sodalitium pianum* employed codes, pseudonyms and all the other devices associated with an intelligence agency. Many of its activities remain unknown to this day, as do the undercover links it forged with a spectrum of religious and political institutions. All papers pertaining to *Sodalitium pianum* are locked away in the Vatican's archives and have never been released.

In parallel to his clandestine network, Benigni produced a regular publication, *Corrispondenza di Roma* which, to reflect its orientation and primary audience, subsequently adopted the French version of its name, *Correspondance de Rome*. Like *Sodalitium pianum*, *Correspondance* devoted itself to exposing Modernism and Modernist sympathisers, to denouncing teachers, scholars and clerics who had allegedly deviated from doctrinal orthodoxy. Both Benigni's enterprises were openly endorsed by Pope Pius X, as well as by Merry del Val. With Pius's death, however, some wider support began to wane. In 1913, *Correspondance* was closed down. Shortly after the outbreak of the First World War in 1914, German troops in Belgium captured an archive of documents belonging to *Sodalitium pianum*. The documents contained compromising evidence, and pressure was brought to bear on the Vatican to curb Benigni's activities. Eventually, *Sodalitium pianum* was suppressed by Pope Benedict XV, in 1921.

In Merry del Val, however, Benigni possessed a powerful protector, under whose auspices he proceeded to engage in other dubious undertakings. For centuries, the Church had dreamed of establishing a foothold in Russia and gradually displacing or subsuming Russian Orthodoxy. Were anything of that sort to occur, the Greek Orthodox Church would be increasingly marginalised, and Rome would be strategically positioned to repair the schism with Byzantium that had split Christendom a millennium and a half earlier. Accordingly, Pius X had created an 'exarchate' of the Russian Rite in 1907 and appointed a Uniate Archbishop of Lvov in what is now Poland. Immediately thereafter, Benigni had begun to meddle in Russian affairs. By 1910, he was on intimate terms with pan-Slavic – that is, hardline right-wing – Russian diplomats and politicians.

Whatever schemes he may have been hatching were shelved by the outbreak of the First World War, then definitively thwarted by the Revolution and the bloody civil conflict that followed. As the Bolsheviks emerged triumphant, it must have been apparent to him that Russia was a lost cause, for his lifetime at least. He accordingly turned his attention elsewhere.

In 1920, still under the protection of Merry del Val, Benigni began to produce a bulletin in French called *Antisémite*. Despite this title, the cardinal insisted that he was not really anti-Semitic. He was merely opposed to the alleged international Judaic conspiracy that dominated banking, Freemasonry and Bolshevism. If pressed, he would no doubt have pleaded that some of his best friends were Jews. Or perhaps not, since he referred to the Jewish people as the 'Elect of the Antichrist'.[9]

In 1923, two years after the suppression of Benigni's *Sodalitium pianum*, a new organisation appeared in France under the name of ERDS – *Entente romaine de défense sociale*. Some commentators have suggested that ERDS was in fact a resurrection of *Sodalitium pianum* under a new appellation. To join the ranks of ERDS, one had to be Christian, belong to an 'aryan or aryanised nation' and embrace the motto 'Religion, Family, Homeland',[10] a motto revived and being promulgated by a certain Catholic organisation today. One of the primary spokesmen for ERDS was a certain Abbé Boulin, who wrote belligerently of the 'assault' on Europe by international Jewish banking.[11] In 1924, Boulin co-hosted, in Paris, a meeting of a self-styled 'Anti-Jewish International'. A second such meeting was convened a year later in Austria, and Benigni attended it.[12]

From what is known of it, ERDS would appear to have had much in common with *Action française*, the hardline right-wing nationalist movement whose cult of 'blood and soil' was similar to that of National Socialism in Germany. Benigni was a vigorous supporter of *Action française*, whose membership is believed to have included certain of the French leaders of the old *Sodalitium pianum*.[13] Unfortunately for the cardinal, relations with *Action française* tended to be uneasy. In 1926, a rift opened between them that was never subsequently repaired.

On 11 February 1929, the Lateran Treaty was signed between the Vatican and Benito Mussolini, Italian Prime Minister since 1922, establishing the Vatican City as an independent and sovereign state, a self-contained enclave that was not part of Italian soil. The Church was indemnified for the loss of the old Papal States and Catholicism was adopted as Italy's official religion. In return, the Papacy deigned to recognise Italy as a kingdom and Rome as its capital. For the first time since 1870, the Pope ventured to set foot in the Eternal City.

Monsignor Benigni was pleased. Later he would collaborate closely with the OVRA, the Italian equivalent of the Gestapo. One can imagine the enthusiasm with which, had he lived to see it, he would have embraced Franco's Phalangist movement in Spain.

13

The Dead Sea Scrolls

The traumatic events of the first half of the twentieth century – the two world wars, the clash of ideologies, the revolutions and civil conflicts in Mexico, Russia, Spain and elsewhere – demonstrated the extent to which the Church had become marginalised from the course of Western history. Except in such isolated cases as Ireland, Western history had become increasingly secular. And Rome, ever more bereft of secular power and influence, was reduced to the status of one plaintive voice amid a greater chorus. It is true, of course, that the Church had been ineffectual enough on numerous occasions in the past – during the Napoleonic Wars, or before that, during the struggle for empire and continental dominance in the eighteenth century. In the past, however, the West had still, if only nominally, been 'Christian'; and as long as it remained so, the Church could still claim a role. But as the twentieth century unfolded, Christianity became progressively less relevant; and in consequence, the Church was reduced to a new nadir of impotence. Among the unseemly scrum of 'isms' contending for supremacy, Catholicism was one of the more feeble.

Such, at any rate, was the situation so far as the corridors of power were concerned, the decision-making machinery that determined public policy and the march of events. Among the hapless multitudes at the mercy of such machinery, the Church retained a substantial congregation – a congregation more numerous, indeed, than that of any other religious denomination in the world. If this congregation could no longer be mobilised for crusades or holy wars, it could still be influenced in the realm of the psyche and the spirit. In the realm of the psyche and the spirit, it remained vulnerable. And in the realm of the psyche and the spirit, the Church still possessed weapons to deploy. One of these was the age-old measure of excommunication.

Nearly a millennium before, Pope Gregory VII (1073–85) had turned excommunication into a finely honed political instrument. It could be exploited even in the deposing of princes, kings, emperors. During the centuries that followed, however, the overuse of excommunication had debased and devalued its currency. During the nineteenth century, for example, young people were routinely excommunicated by the Holy Office for not denouncing parents who ate meat on Fridays, or for reading a book prohibited by the Index.[1] In the aftermath of the Second World War, Pope Pius XII threatened to excommunicate any member of the Church who voted for a Communist in an election rather than for a Catholic candidate. Such profligacy in its utilisation could only render excommunication increasingly puerile, increasingly drained of puissance.

For most Catholics, however, excommunication remained – and, indeed, still remains – a potential source of terror, and thus a potent instrument for intimidation. To be 'excommunicant' – ejected, that is, from the community of the Church and the communion it offers – is to be rendered an outcast, with all the sense of isolation and loneliness that such status entails. The excommunicant individual is forbidden to participate in the Mass or any other public worship. He cannot receive any sacraments other than last rites. He cannot be married by a priest or bishop, cannot enjoy any benefit of the Church, cannot continue to enjoy any spiritual privileges previously granted. In the more severe of the two forms of excommunication, one must be completely shunned by all other Catholics. Technically speaking, excommunication can only exclude the individual from the Church, the body or congregation of the faithful. It does not and cannot sunder a person from God. For many believers, however, this distinction is blurred, and excommunication is perceived as tantamount to damnation. The resulting psychological impact can often be devastating.

Modern Canon Law specifies a number of offences punishable by excommunication. These include abortion, apostasy, heresy, schism, discarding or misusing a consecrated host, physically attacking the Pope and consecrating a bishop without the Pope's permission. It has also been used to muzzle dissent or opposition within the Church. Thus, for example, the Modernist Alfred Loisy was excommunicated in 1908; more recent Catholic writers and commentators have also suffered. Investigations and tribunals for possible excommunication would be conducted officially by the Holy Office. On its recommendation, the sentence of excommunication would then be pronounced by the Pope.

Excommunication was one instrument by means of which the Church, working through the Holy Office, exercised control over its congregation. A second instrument, for the first half of the century at least, was the Index, which effectively denied Catholics access to any material Rome deemed inimical – including historical studies of Freemasonry and of the Inquisition itself. As has been seen, the Index was first instituted in 1559 and remained in force for the next 400-odd years. As recently as the early 1960s, Catholic students and scholars at universities were restricted from reading not only established classics by writers like Voltaire and Stendhal, but also the topically relevant works of such figures as Sartre, Simone de Beauvoir and André Gide – works that would appear on almost every university syllabus of the period.

By this time, however, the Index was becoming increasingly untenable. Texts previously banned by secular authorities – *Ulysses, Lady Chatterley's Lover, Lolita,* even the works of the Marquis de Sade – were readily available in any well-stocked city bookshop, not to mention those of the universities. Literature itself was becoming ever more explicit, and four-letter words, as well as graphic sexual or blasphemous passages unprintable a few years before, were now almost obligatory. In *The Last Temptation*, Nikos Kazantzakis not only portrayed Jesus in a highly heterodox light, but also depicted him, if only in a dream sequence, engaging in sexual union with the Magdalene. Despite endorsements from such luminaries as diverse as Thomas Mann and Albert Schweitzer, Kazantzakis' novel was promptly added to the Index. But there were too many other works, often of high literary quality, for even the most fanatically zealous Inquisitors to keep pace. In 1966, the Index was formally abolished by Pope Paul VI.

Control over the Dead Sea Scrolls

To some extent, the abolition of the Index was a mere formality. For some time previously, it had been doomed by trends of modern secular culture. Literate Catholics had inevitably been incurring sustained exposure to theologically unacceptable material, regardless of the prohibitions of the Church. But there were other spheres in which the Church still remained capable of regulating, controlling and restricting both access to knowledge and the flow of information, as rigorously as it had done in the Middle Ages. Perhaps the most notorious such instance was that of the Dead Sea Scrolls. In its handling of the Scrolls, the Holy Office, working on behalf of the Church through the Pontifical Biblical Commission, perpetrated what one scholar has called 'the academic scandal *par excellence* of the twentieth century'.[2]

In the 1880s, the fledgling Modernist movement had not yet become subversive, not yet fallen into disrepute. Among the young Modernist scholars of the era, there was a naive credulity and idealistic optimism, a complacent assumption that disciplined archaeological research would validate, not contradict, the literal truth of scripture. The Ecole Biblique et Archéologique Française de Jérusalem – which eventually came to tyrannise and manipulate Dead Sea Scroll scholarship – was spawned by the first generation of Modernism, before the Church recognised how vertiginously close it had come to undermining itself. The school had its inception in 1882, when a French Dominican monk on pilgrimage in the Holy Land determined to establish a Dominican house in Jerusalem, comprising a church and a monastery. He selected a location where the ruins of an earlier church had been revealed by excavations. On this spot, according to tradition, Saint Stephen, supposedly the first Christian martyr, had been stoned to death.

Rome not only endorsed the idea, but proceeded to elaborate and expand on it. Pope Leo XIII recommended that a school of biblical studies also be created. It was duly founded in 1890 by Father Albert Lagrange and opened officially in 1892, containing living accommodation for fifteen resident students. The institution was one of many typically Modernist ventures of the time. Within its precincts, Catholic scholars were to be equipped with the academic expertise required to fortify the faith against the challenge posed by advances in historical and archaeological research.

Ten years later, disillusionment prevailed and Modernism had fallen under a cloud of official opprobrium. In 1903 Pope Leo had created the Pontifical Biblical Commission, an institution devised to work in tandem with the Holy Office in supervising and monitoring the work of Catholic scriptural scholarship. By this time, the mere suggestion of historical and archaeological research was sufficient to incur condemnation; and Father Lagrange along with his biblical school were duly investigated by the Commission. It was quickly confirmed, however, that Lagrange remained loyal to official doctrine and tradition, and that his heart was still in the right place so far as the Church was concerned. Indeed, much of his writing had endeavoured systematically to refute Modernist contentions. Lagrange was consequently appointed a member, or 'consultant', of the Pontifical Biblical Commission. His journal, *Revue biblique*, became the Commission's official publication; and this arrangement continued until 1908, when the Commission launched a journal of its own.

Despite the endorsement he had received, Lagrange continued to attract accusations of Modernism from the lower echelons of the clerical hierarchy. These accusations so demoralised him that in 1907 he abandoned his work in Old Testament studies. In 1912, he determined to relinquish biblical scholarship entirely and decamped from Jerusalem. But the Pope hastened to support him, ordered him back to his post and urged him to resume his work. Under his obedient auspices, the Ecole Biblique, originally founded as an adjunct of Modernism, now became a bulwark against it. Such, half a century later, was the institution that contrived to establish a virtual monopoly over the Dead Sea Scrolls.

In 1947, the first of these ancient texts – documents dating from the dawn of the Christian era and before – were discovered in a cave near Qumran, a forty-minute car drive east of Jerusalem, on the shores of the Dead Sea. The cave, subsequently known as Cave 1, proved to contain more than one Scroll. During the ensuing decade, another ten caves were found nearby to contain additional Scroll material, sometimes in substantially complete form, sometimes in fragments that had to be assembled like a jigsaw puzzle. American and Israeli scholars were quick to publish their findings, which generated immense excitement across the world. The Qumran texts were the earliest such documents ever to come to light in the Holy Land. They clearly dated from some time around the beginning of the Christian era. They bore testimony to a messianic, apocalyptic religious community that had occupied the site some 2,000 or more years before.

As long as the Scrolls could be associated exclusively with an isolated Judaic sect, the Church and the Holy Office remained indifferent to them, regarding them merely as interesting historical and archaeological material. In 1950, however, a professor at the Sorbonne, André Dupont-Sommer, gave a public lecture that caused an international sensation. He described one of the Dead Sea texts as depicting a 'Sect of the New Covenant'. The leader of this sect was a messianic figure known as the 'Teacher of Righteousness', who suffered persecution and martyrdom. His followers believed the end of the world to be imminent. Only those having faith in the 'Teacher' would be saved. To worldwide consternation, Dupont-Sommer concluded that the 'Teacher of Righteousness' was in many respects 'the exact prototype of Jesus'.[3]

The Church promptly panicked. Documents pertaining to an isolated Judaic sect were one thing, documents that might cast a compromising or equivocal light on the origins of Christianity quite another. Catholic scholars had previously been offered access to Scroll material and expressed little interest. Now, however, an operation in damage limitation had to be launched and a cover-up instituted. Control of research and scholarship on the Scrolls had to established. At all costs the Qumran texts had to be presented to the public in a manner that distanced them from the origins of Christianity, that rendered them incidental or irrelevant to Catholic tradition, teaching, doctrine and dogma. Although he possessed no archaeological qualifications whatever, the Dominican director of the Ecole Biblique, Father Roland de Vaux, embarked on a concerted campaign to arrogate authority over as much Scroll material as possible.

Between 1951 and 1956, de Vaux undertook his own excavations at Qumran. His objective was to find – or if necessary contrive – proof that the Scrolls were indeed irrelevant to early Christianity, that they pertained merely to an isolated and unrepresentative desert community divorced even from the 'official' Judaism of the time. As a matter of course, dating of the Scrolls had to be brought into accord with this interpretation. In consequence, de Vaux had to engage in some distinctly dubious archaeological procedures – such as, for example, inventing walls where none existed by the simple expedient of leaving sections of a site unexcavated.[4] By means of such devices, he endeavoured to establish his own chronology for the Scrolls, dating them safely and uncontroversially from *before* the Christian era.[5]

In the meantime, additional Scrolls and Scroll fragments were continuing to come to light – sometimes in substantial quantity at some locations. A picture was coalescing that threatened to become even more embarrassing for the Church than had first been supposed. There were indeed disturbing parallels between early Christianity and the community at Qumran to which the Scrolls bore witness. At the same time, the community at Qumran was emerging not as a remote desert enclave, but as a centre that had figured with some prominence in New Testament times, playing a significant role in the period's events. Worse still, it was emerging not only as messianic and apocalyptic, but also as militant and revolutionary, intent on wresting the Holy Land from the yoke of the Roman Empire and restoring the Judaic monarchy of the Old Testament. In other words, its orientation was as much political as religious.[6] Such an orientation was increasingly difficult to reconcile with the meek lamblike Saviour of Christian tradition, who rendered unto Caesar what was Caesar's and urged his followers to turn the other cheek in pacific martyrdom. To establish control and management over the Scrolls, and over the awkward revelations they might contain, was thus becoming a matter of intensifying urgency for the Church.

By dint of dexterous machiavellian politicking, de Vaux contrived to get himself appointed head of an international team of scholars assigned to assemble, translate and publish the texts found at Qumran. He also contrived to bring the international team, and thus all work on the Dead Sea Scrolls, under the auspices of the Ecole Biblique – a Dominican institution, it must be remembered, accountable through the Pontifical Biblical Commission to the Holy Office. He further consolidated his authority by publishing the official academic journal devoted to the material found at Qumran. And he got himself appointed editor-in-chief of the supposedly definitive translation of Qumran texts, *Discoveries in the Judaean Desert*, issued under the imprint of Oxford University Press. By these means he was able to exercise control over what was and was not published, how it was edited and translated. As a result he was able to establish an ostensibly unimpugnable orthodoxy of interpretation over all Qumran documents. De Vaux and his protégés thus became the internationally recognised experts on the Dead Sea Scrolls; and there seemed no reason for the world at large to doubt their integrity.

Such were the circumstances in which Dead Sea Scroll scholarship proceeded for some forty-five years. In a previous publication, *The Dead Sea Scrolls Deception* (1991), the authors of this book chronicled the story in detail. Here, it is sufficient to note that until the early 1990s, the Ecole Biblique maintained a virtually exclusive monopoly over Dead Sea Scroll research and over all new discoveries. Access to the texts was restricted to scholars whose interpretations would not embarrass the Church or its doctrinal teachings. When John Allegro – a non-Catholic member of the team entrusted with custody of the Scrolls – presumed to challenge the 'official' interpretation, he was systematically marginalised and academically discredited.

For forty-five years, the Scrolls remained in effect a private fiefdom – the exclusive domain of a team of predominantly Catholic scholars accountable to the Ecole Biblique, the Pontifical Biblical Commission and the Holy Office. This team equivocated, prevaricated and procrastinated. The release of certain material potentially embarrassing to the Church was inexplicably delayed. Other material was not released until a consensus of orchestrated interpretation had been established that cast it in the least compromising light. Questionable dating was deliberately promulgated, so as to distance the Scrolls from Christianity and prevent them from seeming to pertain in any way to Jesus, Saint Paul, Saint James or the movement that coalesced into the early Church of Christian tradition. Passages that bore too close a textual similarity to the New Testament were mistranslated and, in at least one dramatic instance, held back for decades.

On 9 July 1958, to cite but one example, de Vaux's team of scholars obtained a new Scroll fragment containing a bit of text. It was duly assigned an identifying number, 4Q246, denoting fragment 246 from Cave 4 at Qumran. The text proved easy and straightforward enough to translate. Indeed, a researcher present at the time told one of the authors of this book that a basic translation was completed by the following morning – by which time all the members of de Vaux's team had read it or knew what it said. But what it said was potentially explosive: 'He will be called son of God, and they will call him son of the Most High . . . His kingdom will be an eternal kingdom.'[7]

The parallels with Christian scripture are obvious enough. This meagre fragment of text could undo all the efforts of de Vaux's team to distance the Dead Sea Scrolls from early Christianity. In consequence, its very existence was kept a closely guarded secret for fourteen years. It might have remained a secret, had not one of de Vaux's team of scholars let slip a reference to it during a lecture at Harvard University in December 1972. Even then, he refused to let any other researcher make a copy for independent study. Another eighteen years were to pass before the text was anonymously leaked to a journal of popular biblical exploration, *Biblical Archaeology Review*, which published it in 1990.[8]

For thirty-two years after it was first translated, then, the text in question had been known to de Vaux's team of scholars but withheld from everyone else. Without breathing a word about it, Church commentators had in the meantime blithely dissembled and equivocated. In 1968, for example, Xavier Leon-Dufour, a friend of de Vaux and a member of the Pontifical Biblical Commission, wrote disingenuously: 'None of the

Qumran texts speaks of a "son of Man".[9] He said nothing whatever of a reference to a 'Son of God' and proceeded to argue that the leader of the Qumran community, as depicted in the Scrolls, had nothing in common with the figure of Jesus. Eleven years later, in 1979, Cardinal Jean Danielou, another of de Vaux's friends, published an English translation of his own book, *The Dead Sea Scrolls and Primitive Christianity*. He continued to echo what had become the official 'party line'. Ignoring the existence of the 'Son of God' text, he, too, argued that no connection could exist between Jesus and the leader of the Qumran community.

Not until the early 1990s did the circumstances governing Dead Sea Scroll scholarship begin at last to change. This change was due largely to the stubborn perseverance of Professor James Robinson, head of the team that had translated the so-called 'Gnostic Gospels' found at Nag Hammadi in Egypt, and Professor Robert Eisenman of the University of California at Long Beach, who had long spearheaded the campaign for release of the Qumran texts. Drawing on negatives obtained from an anonymous source, Robinson and Eisenman issued a two-volume set of photographs, *A Facsimile Edition of the Dead Sea Scrolls*. For the first time, the entire corpus of Qumran texts was made available to independent researchers.

The sluice gates had finally opened. The Huntington Library in California was one of several institutions holding photographs of all the Dead Sea Scrolls – for insurance purposes, in case the originals were destroyed in a new Middle East conflict. Within three months of the publication by Robinson and Eisenman, the Huntington defied the Ecole Biblique by announcing its intention to make its collection available to scholars. Eisenman was first to gain access to the material. He and Professor Michael Wise of the University of Chicago quickly assembled two teams, one at each of their respective universities, to embark on a translation of the fifty most significant unpublished texts. These appeared in 1992 as *The Dead Sea Scrolls Uncovered*.

Nowadays the Church no longer controls access to the texts found at Qumran, but it still endeavours to control interpretation. Catholic scholars continue to promulgate their own established orthodoxy of interpretation – and in the process attempt to shout down all opposition. So far as the Church is concerned, the Dead Sea Scrolls must remain distanced from the origins of Christianity, lest Christianity emerge in a light inimical to official doctrine and dogma.

14

The Congregation for the Doctrine
of the Faith

In 1962, the cover-up involving the Dead Sea Scrolls was
still intact and effectively unknown to the world at large.
The Church at the time had other, more immediate and more
contemporary issues with which to contend; and these were
of more dramatic and discernible interest to the ecclesiastical
hierarchy, to the congregation of the faithful, to the media and
to the general public. Under Pope John XXIII, the most liberal,
lucid, progressive and dynamic pontiff of the twentieth century,
the Church undertook to put its own house in order and
integrate itself constructively and creatively with the modern
age. This enterprise took the form of the Second Vatican
Council, which convened on 11 October 1962, and remained
in session until the end of 1965.

John XXIII had first suggested the idea of the Council to a
conclave of cardinals in January 1959. He desired, he said, a
reformist Council which would renew the Church and bring
it into accord with the post-Second World War world. He
wanted to inaugurate a process of healing which would draw
together the diverse churches of Christendom. He sought a
new *rapprochement* with Protestantism. He also wished to repair
the rift between the Roman Catholic and the Eastern Orthodox

Churches, which had been separated by mutual pronouncements of excommunication in 1054.

The Curia promptly went into shock. Assiduous efforts were
made to prevent the Pope's Council from occurring – or, if
that failed, at least to delay it. Despite such opposition, however,
the pontiff proceeded with his plans, employing to constructive
effect the authority arrogated by his predecessors. The thrust
of the Council he envisioned was to be international and
ecumenical. He set about laying the groundwork accordingly,
establishing conduits of communication not only with other
Christian churches, but with other religions as well. For the
first time since the creation of the Church of England, a
Roman pontiff met personally with an Anglican Archbishop
of Canterbury. Similar contacts were established with the
Greek and Russian Orthodox Churches. For the first time,
Catholic representatives were allowed to attend a meeting
of the World Council of Churches. And a dialogue was inaugurated with Judaism, which was to culminate in an encyclical
exonerating the Jewish people from any culpability in Jesus's
death.

John XXIII also enlarged the College of Cardinals, creating
new members from every continent in the world and making
the Curia more truly international than it had ever previously
been. In 1960, he formed an official department within the
Curia to foster the unification of all Christian churches. In
March 1962, he embarked on a comprehensive revision of
Canon Law, which was eventually published in 1983.

Such were the preparations for the Second Vatican Council.
When it convened in October 1962, it conducted its business
openly, not with the paranoid secrecy that had characterised
Church affairs in the past. Indeed, observers from no fewer
than eighteen non-Catholic churches were present in an official

capacity. This provoked certain members of the Curia and of the Holy Office to complain that the Pope was communicating with heretics – a crime, according to Canon Law.

Throughout the proceedings of the Council, opposition to the Pope was led, not surprisingly, by the Prefect of the Holy Office at the time, Cardinal Alfredo Ottaviani. He attempted repeatedly to ensure that the Council be controlled by the Curia. The Pope's own charisma, however, and the new cardinals he had created, decisively tipped the balance. The Curia's attempt to establish authority over the Council was thwarted. To the assembled ecclesiastics, as well as to the world at large, it became shockingly apparent that the Curia, contrary to popular belief, no longer represented the Church as a whole.

As the Council progressed, the belligerent 'Old Guard' were forced into retreat on virtually every measure, and radical new reforms were introduced. One of the most immediately obvious was in the Mass, no longer to be conducted in Latin but in the vernacular. At the same time, the notorious 'Syllabus of Errors', promulgated through the Holy Office by Pius IX, was discarded as outmoded and no longer relevant. Before the Council ended, the mutual excommunication of the Roman and Orthodox Churches was to be lifted. In an encyclical published during the spring of 1963, Pope John XXIII explicitly embraced and endorsed the progress his nineteenth-century predecessors had explicitly condemned. And in a statement unique from a Roman pontiff, the encyclical asserted the right of every human being 'to worship God in accordance with the dictates of his own conscience'.[1]

On 3 June 1963, shortly after the publication of this encyclical, John XXIII died. On 21 June, Giovanni Battista Montini, a consultant of the Holy Office, was elected to succeed him and took the name of Paul VI. By that time, the Council's programme of reform had acquired too much momentum to be arrested altogether. There was, however, a noticeable deceleration; and the progress optimistically anticipated by the world at large, Catholic and non-Catholic, was gradually to grind to a halt. It has subsequently gone into reverse.

In certain spheres, the progressive spirit of the Second Vatican Council has remained intact. Mass, for example, is still conducted officially in the vernacular. The Index was abolished, and no serious attempt has been made to revive it. Neither has there been any effort to resuscitate the 'Syllabus of Errors'. But in many issues of immediate practical relevance to the Church's congregation, the spirit of the Council has indeed been betrayed. Abortion remains a sin punishable by excommunication. And while such prospects as overpopulation and the depletion of natural resources brood like spectres over the planet, the Church plays ostrich, doggedly refusing to acknowledge the threat and maintaining an intransigent position on birth control that keeps it disastrously out of step with the age, alienates many Catholics and creates agonising crises of conscience for many others.

At the beginning of the Second Vatican Council, Pope John XXIII had created a commission to examine the question of birth control. Was the use of artificial contraception indeed a mortal sin, punishable by mandatory condemnation to hell? Unfortunately the pontiff died before the issue could be addressed by the Council. When it did come up for debate in October 1964, a substantial number of ecclesiastics were manifestly in favour of a more flexible attitude. As this became apparent, the debate was summarily curtailed by Cardinal Agagianian, a prominent member of both the Holy Office and the Pontifical Biblical Commission. The vexed question, which should have been decided by the Council, was instead referred to the new Pope, who asserted his own authority and arrogated the decision to himself.

When the Council inclined towards the commission's recommendations for greater flexibility, Paul VI added his own amendments, which effectively diluted any proposed reform. These amendments were vehemently opposed by the majority of the commission's members. The Pope responded by publishing his infamous encyclical of 25 July 1968, which, with all the authority of his infallibility, definitively banned artificial contraception. The old 'Syllabus of Errors' had been discarded, but something no less blinkered, anachronistic and reactionary was promulgated in its stead.

In November 1963, during one of the debates at the Second Vatican Council, Cardinal Frings of Cologne presumed to criticise the Holy Office itself. Its methods, he said,

> are out of harmony with modern times and are a cause of scandal in the world . . . No one ought to be judged and condemned without being heard, without knowing what he is accused of.[2]

Cardinal Alfredo Ottaviani, in charge of the Holy Office at the time, was intent on maintaining the regime of his predecessor and mentor, the sinister Merry del Val. Any attack on the Holy Office, Ottaviani replied, was a 'direct insult to the Pope'.[3]

In the age of television and mass media, however, not even the Holy Office could remain entirely indifferent to matters of image and public relations. In 1965, under the auspices of Pope Paul VI, the institution shed the name that had provoked fear and revulsion for centuries. Directed by its new Prefect, the Yugoslavian Cardinal Franjo Seper, it became – less menacingly if also more sententiously – the Congregation for the Doctrine of the Faith. Under this ponderous appellation, the former Inquisition has continued to operate ever since, as if a sanitised title could distance it from its bloody and incendiary past. In 1997, however, Dr Paul Collins, a Harvard graduate and priest, wrote that

> the Holy Office may have changed its name, but the ideology underpinning it has survived. It has certainly not changed its methods. It still accepts anonymous accusations, hardly ever deals directly with the person accused, demands retractions and imposes silences, and continues to employ third-rate theologians as its assessors. This body has no place in the contemporary Church. It is irreformable and therefore should be abolished.[4]

Dr Collins goes on to observe that the faults of the Congregation for the Doctrine of the Faith are essentially the faults of the entire Roman Curia – which exists solely 'to prop up papalism . . . to serve papal power, not the ministry of the Church'.[5]

According to a somewhat less critical commentator, the Congregation

> is the instrument through which the Holy See promotes the deepening of faith and watches vigilantly over its purity. Accordingly, it is the custodian proper of Catholic orthodoxy. Not by chance does it occupy first place on the official list of the Congregations of the Roman Curia.[6]

The Congregation was ratified in its precedence by Pope Paul VI, who stated that it 'deals with questions of greatest importance' in the wake of the Second Vatican Council. It is not at present a large institution. No longer can it dispatch squadrons of aggressive Inquisitors across the globe. It is believed to number perhaps some thirty individuals who work for it on a full-time basis. While their declared *raison d'être* is to safeguard the 'purity' of the faith, their real purpose is to protect the power of the Papacy and to stifle dissent. To this end, they have become adept at what their Prefect calls the 'art of *soprassedere*' – the Italian word for postponing decisions – in order to let situations 'ripen'.[7] In other words, the Congregation will act when it is confident of being able to do so with impunity, on its own terms – to muzzle, investigate, suppress or even excommunicate a dissident theologian, for example. When it cannot act with impunity – when, for instance, there is a threat of a backlash from the faithful – the Congregation will hold both change and the decision-making process at bay, and play for time. While doing so, it will store up and nurture rancour, resentment and vindictiveness, bringing its grudges almost lovingly to fruition. During the mid-1990s, a joke made the rounds of the Vatican's officials: a newly born infant is found in the chambers of the Congregation for the Doctrine of the Faith and the Congregation's Prefect is scandalised, thinking one of his own priests responsible. A monsignor takes him aside, however, and endeavours to assuage his anxiety: 'Surely it is not by us. In this office nothing is completed in nine months.' Another functionary concurs and adds: 'A child is a very fine thing, it is the fruit of love. Therefore it is surely not by us.'[8]

Of all the so-called Congregations, or departments, of the Curia, the Congregation for the Doctrine of the Faith is the most important. It dominates the Curia. It is always listed first. In effect, it is the single most powerful department of the Vatican. Its official president is the Pope. Its chief executive, the modern incarnation of the Grand Inquisitor, is known as the Prefect. According to the *Catholic Encyclopaedia*, the Congregation's 'primary function has always been to assist the Pope in his task of preserving the integrity of the Church's

doctrine of faith and morals'.[9] According to a more independent
commentator, the Papacy, since the First Vatican Council of
1870 if not before, 'has been determined to bring theology under
its control';[10] and the Congregation is its primary instrument for
doing so.

The Congregation is housed in what used to be the Palace
of the Inquisition, the Casa Santa, a large edifice with an
impressive gateway situated in the Via del Sant'Ufficio, close
to Saint Peter's. The former dungeons have been converted
into offices and archives. It is from these headquarters that the
Congregation conducts its business, much of it technically
judicial. The head of the Congregation's judiciary and at least
two of its associate judges are always Dominicans, thus preserving the traditional link to the original Inquisition of the thirteenth century.

In 1967, when the Congregation for the Doctrine of the
Faith adopted its current name, another body was created
to operate in tandem with it, the International Theological
Commission. The Commission's role was to act in an advisory
capacity to the Congregation. In 1976, the Commission urged
the Congregation to employ methods that were less 'inquisitorial' and more conciliatory. In its proceedings up to the
present the Congregation has taken little heed of this advice.
One commentator has summarised its recent activities:

In addition to reviewing faculty appointments and pro-
motions at ecclesiastical faculties, the Congregation for
the Doctrine of the Faith also examines the writings of
theologians brought to its attention by bishops, nuncios,
or other theologians. Greater attention is given to those
theologians who become popular in the mass media and
whose books are read by a wide audience. The Vatican

also focuses on theologians who deal with certain topics: sexual ethics, birth control, abortion, clerical celibacy, divorce and remarriage, papal authority, episcopal authority, the resurrection, and the divinity of Christ. Liberation theologians in Latin America and Africa have received attention because of their writings on church authority and on class conflict. Asian theologians writing on the relation between Christianity and Asian religions, have been investigated as well. The Vatican is also concerned about feminist theologians writing on sexuality, patriarchy in the church, and women priests.[11]

The Congregation for the Doctrine of the Faith investigates any theologian, teacher or ecclesiastic whose pronouncements, whether written or oral, might be seen to deviate from official orthodoxy. Denunciations of any such transgressor from other theologians, teachers or ecclesiastics are also welcomed. As soon as the Congregation commences its investigation, a file is opened containing all relevant material – statements by the individual under scrutiny, newspaper clippings, other media reports, letters of complaint from colleagues or parishioners. According to procedures established in 1971, staff and high functionaries of the Congregation meet on Saturdays to study the case in question. If they decide an error of faith is indeed involved, an ineluctable course of action ensues – always with great secrecy.

The Congregation begins by contacting the accused's immediate superior, for instance the local bishop, who exhorts him to retract or modify his assertions. If the Congregation decides that false or dangerous opinions are being promulgated in writing, the author may be contacted directly. A warning from his superior or from the Congregation itself will be the first indication the accused receives that he is under investigation. He will be granted one month in which to respond to the accusations against him. He may also be summoned perfunctorily to Rome in order to explain himself in person.

In 1978, shortly after the election of John Paul II as pontiff, the Congregation investigated and clamped down on a French Dominican, Jacques Pohier, and forbade him to teach. A year later, Hans Küng, one of the most distinguished of modern Catholic theologians, had his licence to teach theology revoked. Immediately afterwards, he was dismissed from his faculty post at the University of Tübingen. On being offered another position, which did not require a licence from Rome, Küng commented:

> I have been condemned by a pontiff who has rejected my theology without ever having read one of my books and who has always refused to see me. The truth is that Rome is not waiting for dialogue but for submission.[12]

In 1983, the new Code of Canon Law stated that all teachers of theological material in institutions of higher learning were required to possess a mandate or sanction from 'the competent ecclesiastical authority' – meaning, at very least, the local bishop. In other words, according to one commentator, 'theologians are to serve, not to challenge'.[13] Shortly thereafter, more than 500 German theologians appended their signatures to a protest known as the 'Cologne Declaration'. It announced their distress at the increasing number of qualified individuals who were being denied permission to teach. According to the 'Cologne Declaration': 'The power to withhold official permission to teach is being abused; it has become an instrument to discipline theologians.'[14]

The Congregation for the Doctrine of the Faith remained

indifferent to such protests. In September 1984, a Brazilian Franciscan, Father Leonardo Boff, was summoned to Rome – where, having appeared before the Congregation, he was condemned to a year of silence. In November of the same year, the eminent Dutch Dominican writer, Father Edward Schillebeeckx, received a similar summons – the third such he had received since 1979 – and was ordered to explain himself before the Congregation. In March 1986, Father Charles Curran, a theologian at the Catholic University of Washington, had his teaching licence revoked and was dismissed from his post a year later. In 1987, too, Archbishop Hunthausen of Seattle, a prominent exponent of the spirit of the Second Vatican Council, was subjected to a hostile investigation. In 1988, an Indian Jesuit, Luis Bermejo, was condemned. An American Jesuit, Father Terence Sweeney, was commanded to cease his research on ecclesiastical attitudes towards clerical marriage and to burn all his papers. Rebelling against this attempt to re-ignite the old Inquisition's traditional bonfires, Father Sweeney defected from the Jesuits. His indignation at his treatment was equalled by that of a German moral theologian, Father Bernard Häring. Father Häring found his examination by the Congregation more offensive than the four occasions on which he had formerly been forced to appear before a Nazi court.[15]

In 1989, the Congregation officially demanded that new appointees to seminaries and Catholic universities – rectors, presidents, professors of theology and philosophy – not only make a profession of faith, but also take an oath of fidelity. A similar oath was made obligatory for new pastors. The standard profession of faith was amended to include an additional sentence: 'I also firmly embrace and hold each and everything that is definitively proposed by the same Church concerning the doctrine of faith or morals.'[16] These measures were instituted by the Congregation entirely on its own initiative. There had been no previous consultation with the theological community or with participants at any episcopal conferences. They came as a surprise and a shock even to other offices of the Curia. Within the Catholic academic world, there was an immediate reaction of 'deep and profound disquiet'.[17]

In May 1990, the Congregation produced the first draft for a proposed new *Universal Catechism of the Catholic Church*. In its 354 pages, papal infallibility was vigorously reaffirmed, and the *rapprochement* with other faiths and denominations inaugurated by the Second Vatican Council was implicitly repudiated. According to the Congregation's text:

> The task of giving an authentic interpretation of the Word of God, whether in its written form or in the form of tradition, has been entrusted to the living teaching office of the Church alone.[18]

Condemnation of artificial birth control and of abortion was, of course, reiterated. Cohabitation before marriage was also condemned, as was euthanasia. Divorce was condemned as immoral and conducive to social disorder. Masturbation was condemned as morally reprehensible, homosexuality as sinfully degrading.

The proposed *Catechism* was sent with a request for comments to all the 2,421 Roman Catholic bishops across the globe. Inevitably it was leaked to the media and extracts from it were published in newspapers. An overwhelming number of people, Catholic and non-Catholic alike, were shocked and horrified by the document's doggedly obtuse, psychologically naive and rabidly reactionary nature. Hopes of a more progressive Church evolving from the reforms of the Second Vatican Council were rudely disappointed, even dashed. The Congregation for the Doctrine of the Faith seemed adamantly bent on undoing those reforms, rolling history back and further dissociating the Church from the contemporary world around it.

Shortly after the draft text of the new catechism was circulated, Cardinal Ratzinger, the Congregation's Prefect, hastened to erect a bulwark against possible dissent. This took the form of a twenty-seven-page document written by Ratzinger himself and published officially by the Congregation for the Doctrine of the Faith, *The Ecclesial Vocation of the Theologian*. In his text, Ratzinger condemned not only personal dissent, but equally 'that public opposition to the magisterium also called dissent'.[19] The cardinal categorically denied that anyone possessed a 'right to dissent'. On the contrary, the text stated explicitly that Catholic theologians have no right to dissent from the established teachings of the Church and that 'the theologian should be an instrument of the faith rather than its analyst'.[20] Indeed, dissent itself was to be regarded as a certifiable sin: 'To succumb to the temptation of dissent . . . (allows) infidelity to the Holy Spirit.'[21] The Church made no pretence to democracy. 'Standards of conduct appropriate to civil society or the workings of a democracy cannot be purely and simply applied to the Church.'[22] Neither could whatever personal relationship one enjoyed with the sacred. 'Appealing to the obligation to follow one's own conscience cannot legitimate dissent.'[23] The text of the document ended with a warning:

> The freedom of the act of faith cannot justify a right to dissent. This freedom does not indicate freedom with regard to the truth, but signifies the free determination of the person in conformity with his moral obligation to accept the truth.[24]

In other words, insofar as this exercise in obfuscation and casuistry can be deciphered at all, one is free only to act in accordance with the Church's teachings. To act otherwise is not a manifestation of freedom, but of error. Freedom consists solely of accepting the 'truth', and 'truth' is the exclusive monopoly of the Papacy, to define as it wishes.

In 1992, for example, an American Dominican, Father Matthew Fox, was dismissed from his post in Chicago for having founded an institution in California devoted to creative and spiritual studies that included on its faculty a self-proclaimed 'witch'. In 1993, three German bishops were forced by the Congregation to retract their assertion that Catholics who remarried without Church approval might still receive communion. In 1995, Bishop Jacques Gaillot of Evreux was dismissed from his position for supporting a priest who had married, endorsing the use of condoms as a defence against AIDS and simply entertaining the possibility of blessing homosexual 'marriages'. When he refused to resign, the Vatican forcibly ejected him. More than 20,000 people attended his valedictory Mass.

In the same year, a Brazilian nun, Ivone Gebara, was exiled to an Augustinian convent in Belgium for two years of so-called 'study', in order that her 'theological imprecisions' might be 'corrected'. During this time, she was forbidden to write or engage in any public speaking. In 1995, too, an American nun, Carmel McEnroy, was dismissed from her institute of theology in Indiana for having signed a statement endorsing the ordination of women. In January 1997, the Sri Lankan Father Tissa Balasuriya – a graduate of the Gregorian University in Rome, founder and director of the Centre for Society and Religion in Sri Lanka and founding member of the Ecumenical Association of Third World Theologians – was excommunicated for an essay, published seven years earlier, on the Virgin Mary and women's rights in the Church. Father Balasuriya had dared to suggest that women might enjoy a status equal to that of men within the community of the Church.

Such is a representative selection of the activities of the Congregation for the Doctrine of the Faith during the last twenty years. It speaks eloquently for itself. As Hans Küng has said: 'Cardinal Ratzinger is afraid. And just like Dostoevsky's Grand Inquisitor, he fears nothing more than freedom.'[25]

The Grand Inquisitor

Cardinal Joseph Ratzinger is the Grand Inquisitor of today, the currently presiding Prefect of the Congregation for the Doctrine of the Faith. He was born in Bavaria in 1927 and ordained as a priest in 1954. Having served at Freising, in the diocese of Munich, he wrote a dissertation on Saint Augustine, then lectured on dogma at a spectrum of German universities – Bonn, Münster, Tübingen and Regensburg. He attended the Second Vatican Council and published a number of books. In 1977, he was made a cardinal by Pope Paul VI, then Archbishop of Munich. In January 1982, Pope John Paul II appointed him to the helm of the Congregation.

Cardinal Ratzinger is a close personal friend and trusted confidant of the present Pope. They meet for discussions reportedly every Friday. By virtue of their relationship, as well as by virtue of his professional position as Prefect of the Congregation, the cardinal is the Pope's proverbial 'right-hand man'. Commentators are repeatedly astonished by – and prompted to remark upon – the reactionary nature of the current Papacy, its ostrich-like tendency to bury its head in the sand and render itself wilfully oblivious to developments in the surrounding world. These characteristics are generally and not without justification attributed to John Paul II; but they should also be attributed at least as much to Ratzinger. He is in effect the Vatican's 'Theologian in Chief' and, as such, responsible for much of the Church's policy.

As one might expect from a high-ranking prelate and former theology professor, Ratzinger is extremely clever, if not particularly imaginative. He is articulate, frequently even eloquent. His arguments are pointed, focused, lucid, consistent and – within their own circumscribed frame of reference – ostensibly persuasive, even if they do involve elements of sophistry. Circular reasoning is seldom promulgated with such a patina of urbane sophistication. Unlike Dostoevsky's Grand Inquisitor, Ratzinger is no world-weary cynic. On the contrary, there is no reason to doubt the sincerity with which he issues his pronouncements, no reason to doubt that he believes deeply and fervently in what he says and does. Indeed, his sincerity and intensity of belief would appear at times to verge on fanaticism. One is tempted to wonder whether fanaticism is better or worse in a Grand Inquisitor than machiavellian cynicism. Both traits can conduce equally to arrogant ruthlessness and the dehumanised single-mindedness of a cruise missile.

Ratzinger is authentically and profoundly concerned about the current and future affairs of the Church. He is anxious to avert a number of crises – of faith, of trust in dogma, of morality – by which he sees the modern Church beleaguered. He believes the Church must be spared such awkwardness. By existing in a lofty and rarefied sphere of its own, the Church should be immune and insulated from the taint and controversy of 'merely' human institutions. For Ratzinger the Church is quite literally the 'mystical body of Christ'. He dismisses any suggestion that it might ultimately be man-made. On the contrary, the Church's

> fundamental structures are willed by God himself, and therefore they are inviolable. Behind the *human* exterior stands the mystery of a *more than human* reality, in which reformers, sociologists, organisers have no authority whatsoever.[26]

So fervid is Ratzinger's belief in the Church that he appears prepared, when expedient, to place it above scripture:

> A group cannot simply come together, read the New Testament, and say: 'We are now the Church, because the Lord is present wherever two or three are gathered in his name.'[27]

Faith in itself for Ratzinger is not sufficient. There must also be the organisation, the structure, the hierarchical edifice:

> The Church is really present in all *legitimately organised* local groups of the faithful, which, *in so far as they are united to their pastors*, are . . . called Churches.[28]

It goes without saying, of course, that 'legitimately organised' in this context means created by and subject to Rome. For the faithful to be 'united to their pastors' means receiving communion from a priest of the authorised and correct apostolic succession – a priest who has been ordained by the hands of a bishop in communion with the apostolic succession supposedly descended from Saint Peter. The sacraments of the Church are legitimised for Ratzinger by virtue of being passed down from hand to hand through history. If this chain of transmission is broken, the sacrament is no longer valid. That the chain of transmission has indeed often been broken – and often twisted and corrupted as well – is not relevant for Ratzinger.

> The Church is not something one can make but only something one can receive from where it already is and where it really is: from the sacramental community of (Christ's) body that progresses through history.[29]

In consequence, Ratzinger's concept of the Church cannot accommodate any personal experience of the numinous, any mystical experience or individual revelation. Indeed, Ratzinger states explicitly: 'Revelation terminated with Jesus Christ.'[30] And, further: '"Revelation" is closed but interpretation which binds it is not.'[31] Interpretation, of course, is the Church's exclusive prerogative. One cannot attempt to interpret for oneself. One must not think. One must simply accept the interpretation proffered by those legitimately sanctioned to do so.

From this conviction stems Ratzinger's intolerance of criticism or dissent. 'Even with some theologians,' he complains, outraged and incredulous, 'the Church appears to be a human construction.'[32] He contrives to forget that the Church, as it exists today and has existed throughout its history, is indeed a human construction. He contrives to forget, for example, that the Council of Nicea in AD 325 *voted* Jesus divine by a majority of 217 to 3. He contrives to forget that the Pope was *voted* infallible in 1870 – by only 535 of the 1,084 ecclesiastics eligible to cast a ballot. Serenely oblivious to these facts, Ratzinger stresses that 'authority is not based on the majority of votes'.[33] It derives solely from 'the authority of Christ' – who himself never dreamed of establishing a church, let alone the dogmatic complexities of Rome's. Without any apparent sense of irony, Ratzinger asserts that 'truth cannot be created through ballots'.[34] The Church makes no pretence to democracy. 'On matters of faith and morals no one can be bound by majority decisions.'[35] Indeed,

> even ecumenical councils can only decide on matters of faith and morals in moral unanimity, since one cannot establish the truth by resolution but can only recognise and accept it.[36]

With typical sophistry, Ratzinger uses rhetoric to blur crucial distinctions. 'We sin,' he declares, 'but the Church ... the bearer of faith does not sin.'[37] He does not clarify how the Church can remain sinless while implementing the decisions of the sinful individuals who compose it. Neither is it clear whether he concedes that the Church, if it cannot sin, can at least err – though recent rehabilitations of individuals like Galileo suggest a reluctant preparedness to acknowledge some such concession. In that case, presumably, the hundreds of thousands whose bodies were forcibly sacrificed for the alleged sake of their souls may come to be regarded as merely victims of error, or oversight.

It is self-evident and generally acknowledged that the Church has survived only through a readiness, however grudging, to adapt. Only by modifying its structures, its policies, its teachings, its attitudes to each successive generation, each successive century, has it managed to last as long as it has. With sovereign obliviousness to this obvious and elemental fact, Ratzinger states that Catholic dogma, as we have inherited it, 'is a message that has been consigned to us, and we have no right to reconstruct it as we like or choose'.[38] In consequence, he sees no value whatever in ecumenism:

> We must beware of a too-easy ecumenism which can lead Catholic charismatic groups to lose their identity and, in

the name of the 'spirit' . . . uncritically associate with forms of Pentecostalism of non-Catholic origin.[39]

Ratzinger remains adamant in prohibiting Catholics from receiving communion in any other Christian church:

> The Catholic confession is that without the apostolic succession there is no genuine priesthood, and hence there can be no sacramental Eucharist in the proper sense.[40]

If the cardinal is hostile to other Christian denominations, he is positively alarmed by the dissemination of interest in other religions and other spheres of professedly spiritual activity. He voiced this alarm in an indignant interview:

> Visiting a Catholic bookshop . . . I noticed that . . . the spiritual treatises of the past had been replaced by the widespread manuals of psychoanalysis . . . in many religious houses (of both men and women) the cross has at times given up its place to symbols of the Asiatic religious tradition. In some places the previous devotions have also disappeared in order to make way for yoga or Zen techniques.[41]

In the same vein, Ratzinger laments 'an exaggerated shift of emphasis towards non-Christian religions', which he describes as 'realms of fear and unfreedom' – as if the Church never trafficked in either.[42] According to the cardinal's obsessively rigid and medieval dogmatism, there is no room in the terrestrial Kingdom of God for Judaism, Islam, Hinduism, Buddhism or anything else. There is only the Church of Rome, the one true living embodiment of God. All else is either ignorance – the condition of the 'benighted heathen' of other creeds – or heresy. In modern Canon Law, heresy, still deemed a principle of evil, is defined as 'the obstinate denial or doubt, after baptism, of a truth which must be believed by divine and catholic faith'.[43] To that extent, all forms of Protestantism would qualify as heresy.

For Catholics today, Ratzinger maintains, one of the most pressing needs is to hold the modern world at bay. In August 1984, he stated to a journalist:

> I am convinced that the damage that we have incurred in these twenty years is due . . . to the unleashing *within* the Church of latent polemical and centrifugal forces; and *outside* the Church it is due to a confrontation with a cultural revolution in the West.[44]

And further:

> Among the most urgent tasks facing Christians is that of regaining the capacity of nonconformism, *i.e.*, the capacity to oppose many developments of the surrounding culture.[45]

What is extraordinary is the cardinal's preparedness to offer, without any apparent sense of irony, so novel a definition of 'nonconformism'. In his context, the rebellion that led many young people of the sixties to turn away from Christianity and look to psychology, Eastern thought and so-called 'esoteric' tradition would be presumably classified as 'conformity'. 'Nonconformism' is redefined to mean nothing other than embrace of the Church of Rome.

Veneration of Mary

Pope John Paul II is eager to make new saints. To justify the making of new saints, he wants more miracles. In order to accelerate the entire process, the Pope has changed the rules.

The number of miracles an individual must perform to qualify for sainthood is no longer two, but one.

All candidates for sainthood, at least since 1940, must be awarded a certificate of spiritual cleanliness, a written declaration that 'nothing objectionable' about them exists in the Vatican's archives. The files containing all relevant information on such matters are held by the Congregation for the Doctrine of the Faith. This is hardly surprising. Where else but in the records of the former Inquisition would one look for both family skeletons and family jewels? On one occasion, the process of canonisation was abruptly curtailed when the candidate was discovered to be deficient in the moral qualities generally associated with sainthood. Incontrovertible evidence revealed that he had been a committed and unrepentant child molester.

Strictly speaking, the assessment of candidates for sainthood is not the business of the Congregation for the Doctrine of the Faith, but of another department, the Congregation for the Causes of Saints. Neither does Ratzinger's Congregation generally concern itself with the investigation and authentication of miracles. But apparitions of the Virgin Mary, and miracles associated with her, are of special interest to the cardinal and his Congregation. Indeed, one section of the Congregation is devoted exclusively to assessing the validity, or lack thereof, of Marian manifestations and miracles.

In one of his few genuinely sane and psychologically astute convictions, Ratzinger regards the Madonna as vital to the survival of the Church. In his eyes, worship of Mary is crucial. Without it the Church is incomplete. She is necessary for 'the equilibrium and completeness of the Catholic faith'.[46] She provides Rome with 'the right relationship, the necessary integration between Scripture and tradition'. The cardinal elaborates on this point:[47]

The correct Marian devotion guarantees to faith the co-existence of indispensable 'reason' with the equally indispensable 'reasons of the heart' . . . For the Church, man is neither mere reasoning nor mere feeling, he is the unity of these two dimensions. The head must reflect with lucidity, but the heart must be able to feel warmth: devotion to Mary . . . this assures the faith its full human dimension.[48]

For Ratzinger Mary is also an important connecting link between Old and New Testaments, old and new dispensations:

In her very person as a Jewish girl become the mother of the Messiah, Mary binds together, in a living and indissoluble way, the old and the new People of God, Israel and Christianity, synagogue and church.[49]

And Mary functions, too, as an image or symbol of the Church itself:

In Mary, as figure and archetype, the Church again finds her own visage as Mother and cannot degenerate into the complexity of a party, an organization or a pressure group in the service of human interests.[50]

In his acknowledgement of Mary, or of the 'Feminine Principle', Ratzinger for once would seem to be in accord with the more sophisticated psychological thinking of our age. The Madonna may be an idealised, dehumanised, too-good-to-be-true image of the Feminine. But she is at least feminine; and Ratzinger's endorsement of her as a principle or conduit for integration echoes the pronouncements of C. G. Jung, as well as those of mystics, visionaries and artists for centuries. The cardinal would undoubtedly disapprove, for example, of

Goethe's pagan pantheism; but the feminine he extols in the form of the Madonna is not so very far removed from Goethe's '*Ewig-Weibliche*', the 'Eternal Feminity' that leads humanity 'ever beyond'.

Unfortunately, however, Ratzinger's acknowledgement of the feminine in Mary does not extend to other women – mortal women who inhabit the material and phenomenal world. By the Pope's infallible decree, they are still disqualified from the priesthood. And like the Inquisition of the Middle Ages, the Congregation for the Doctrine of the Faith regards them implicitly or explicitly with suspicion.

It is impossible to do justice in these pages to the history of the Church's attitude towards women. Library and bookshop shelves are crammed with entire volumes addressing the ways in which, through the centuries, women have suffered at Rome's hands. Womanhood itself has been undervalued, the 'Feminine Principle' denigrated and distorted. For a substantial part of its existence as an institution, the Church was not even prepared to allow that women possessed souls. So far as the population at large is concerned, of course, attitudes and perceptions have gradually been changing. Not even the Church has been able to insulate itself altogether from such change. Thus, for example, Father Tissa Balasuriya has stated that the priesthood 'is a spiritual function and not a biological one'.[51] In 1990, Father Balasuriya wrote:

> There is no reason, biological, psychological, pastoral, theological or spiritual, why we cannot have a yellow, brown, black or white woman Pope.[52]

Not, however, in the opinion of Cardinal Ratzinger and the Congregation for the Doctrine of the Faith. In 1996, the Congregation officially ruled that 'the Pope's ban on the ordination of women was an infallible part of Catholic doctrine and could not be disputed or changed'.[53] A year later Father Balasuriya was excommunicated.

Ratzinger and the Congregation for the Doctrine of the Faith are rather less than enthusiastic about feminism. 'I am, in fact, convinced,' the cardinal states, 'that what feminism promotes in its radical form is no longer the Christianity that we know; it is another religion.'[54] Such feminism 'announces a liberation that is a salvation different from, if not opposed to, the Christian conception'.[55] The sheer strength of this language is interesting. Feminism is placed in a relation to the Church that is not just deviant, but downright adversarial. To that extent, Ratzinger would almost seem to regard it as diabolical. In any case, he is deeply disturbed by feminism's infestation of the convents, especially in North America. 'Some,' he complains, 'have turned with great trust to those profane confessors, to these "experts of the soul" that psychologists and psychoanalysts supposedly are.'[56]

It is a cliché that politics makes for strange bedfellows. So, too, does religious dogmatism. The Church's intransigence in its attitude towards women has brought it into unlikely alignment with one of the most virulent of its traditional enemies, Islamic fundamentalism. In the past, each has regarded the other as a virtual embodiment of the devil. Each, however, is prepared to sup with its respective devil in order to keep women in their supposed place. In their joint hostility towards women, Catholicism and Islamic fundamentalism have thus paradoxically made common cause. Acting in concert, they have endeavoured to determine attitudes and policies on such issues as birth control and abortion.

In September 1994, a United Nations conference – the UN Conference on Population and Development – convened in

Cairo. The objective was to explore methods of stabilising, if not reducing, global population and to bring it under some kind of control through 'family planning', especially in countries of the Third World. The conference also addressed itself to abortion and to measures for limiting the incidence of AIDS and the alarming consequences of urban overcrowding. A total of 171 countries were represented.

For the Vatican, of course, as well as for certain Islamic factions, abortion and 'family planning' – that is, artificial contraception – were both anathema. In the weeks preceding the conference, rumours proliferated of a clandestine alliance being forged between the Muslim factions and Rome. During August, it was noted that there were Papal missions to Tehran and Tripoli. No proof of a secret accord was forthcoming until the conference had already convened. Only then did an Italian newspaper manage to obtain a three-page document in Arabic, that testified to a meeting at the Vatican three months earlier, in June, between Church functionaries and Muslim representatives. An agreement had been signed to adopt a joint strategy designed to thwart the UN's proposed measures for controlling population growth.[57]

At the conference, the Vatican and its Islamic allies refused to budge on the issue of birth control and caused the proceedings to stall hopelessly. All the other participants were prepared to compromise and make concessions – to state strongly, for example, that abortion should never be advocated as a means of birth control. For the Vatican's delegation and its allies, this was not enough. After several days of stalemate, debate had become acrimonious and tempers had begun to fray. Britain, the United States and the European Union all became exasperated with Rome. Baroness Chalker, head of the British delegation, described the Vatican's stance as 'time-wasting deadlock'.[58] Even the editor of the British Catholic newspaper, *The Tablet*, expressed frustration. 'If the Holy See was not in Cairo to negotiate,' he asked, 'why did it come?' It had done so, he concluded, for another reason. What was the 'hidden agenda'? The editor of the newspaper answered his own question:

> The conflict at Cairo is not simply over sexual ethics. It is over Western values, specifically the values of the European Enlightenment. John Paul II's doctrinal watch-dog, Cardinal Ratzinger, was explicit in his criticism of the Enlightenment.[59]

By the end of the conference, the Vatican had overstepped the bounds of prudence and provoked questions about the legitimacy of its own contribution to the debate. The Church's delegation had after all been present, technically, as representatives not of a religion, but of a sovereign state. Other nations began to complain about the delegation's undue and disproportionate influence. According to *The Times*, they also began 'to ask why one religion should have representative status at this conference whereas Islam, Buddhism and other religions do not'.[60] Implicit behind these questions, there hovered another one. Should the Vatican continue to enjoy the status of a sovereign state? Ultimately, *The Times* concluded, the 'big loser at the conference was the Vatican, which so overplayed its hand . . . that it angered most Third World delegations',[61] as well as those of the developed West.

In September 1992, the definitive version of the new *Universal Catechism* was published. Public and private mortification at the draft text had been blithely ignored, and no concessions whatever had been made. The new *Catechism*, so out of step with the modern world, inevitably produced a back-lash.

Bishops across the world, and especially in the developed West, voiced their profound concern. In Britain, the *Observer* commented that the Pope, assisted by Cardinal Ratzinger, had 'for the first time linked birth control and sexual teaching with tenets of Catholic doctrine'.[62] Personal morality was no longer allowed to be personal. It was now inextricably entangled with theology and yoked to faith. To transgress in sexual matters was to endanger one's very status as a communicant member of the Roman Catholic Church.

Subsequent statements from both the Papacy and the Congregation for the Doctrine of the Faith have only become more doctrinaire, more intransigent, more arrogantly indifferent to human needs, exigencies and aspirations. In 1994, for example, Pope John Paul II issued an apostolic letter which definitively forbade the ordination of women as priests. Later the Congregation for the Doctrine of the Faith declared that the Pope's pronouncement on the matter was to be regarded as 'infallibly taught'.

In the summer of 1998, the Pope issued a new edict which was accompanied by a commentary from the Congregation for the Doctrine of the Faith. The edict demanded complete and absolute adherence to the Papacy's official position on such matters as birth control, abortion, extramarital sexual relations and the ordination of women as priests. It was expressly forbidden to tamper with the alleged 'choice made by Christ' in accepting men alone to the priesthood.[63] Disagreement with Church rulings, on this or any other topical issue, was to be considered officially as heresy and rendered punishable by excommunication. The commentary from the Congregation for the Doctrine of the Faith stressed the 'definitive' nature of the Pope's assertions, which had perforce to be accepted by all Catholics without question. Papal infallibility was invested with a new and reinforced authority, which prohibited any debate on moral as well as on theological concerns. Dissent and heresy were now in effect synonymous.

According to the *Daily Telegraph*:

> It is believed that the Pope, nervous of the growth of liberal movements, wanted to close a loophole in Canon Law which allowed teachers to speak against the Church's moral doctrines.[64]

And further:

> It is designed to curb the activity of liberal movements and to pull into line the growing number of Catholics who do not believe they have to obey the Church's teachings to the letter.[65]

The *New York Times* described the Pope's edict as 'one of the most vivid signs yet that in the twilight of his papacy, John Paul II ... is seeking to make his rulings irreversible'.[66] In effect, future pontiffs will be shackled by the infallible character of the recent rulings; and reform of the Church in the twenty-first century will at very least be retarded, if not thwarted completely.

It is ironic that in their zeal to impose an authoritarian discipline on the Church, the Pope, Cardinal Ratzinger and the Congregation for the Doctrine of the Faith have placed themselves in violation of their own Canon Law. According to Canon 212:

> Christ's faithful ... have the right, indeed at times the duty ... to manifest to the sacred Pastors their views on

matters which concern the good of the Church. They have the right also to make their views known to others of Christ's faithful.[67]

15

Visions of Mary

B y virtue of its intransigence and dogmatism, the Church
is currently suffering one of the most severe backlashes
in its history – perhaps the most severe since the Lutheran
Reformation. In the developed West, previously its stronghold,
it is faced with an alarming defection among its congregation.
People are leaving the Roman Catholic Church in droves. By
the end of the 1980s, almost half of the seminaries in the United
States had closed; new ordinations were less than a third of
those in 1967; the number of priests had declined from 12,000
in 1962 to a mere 7,000.

Now, a decade later, the situation has dramatically worsened.
In England, Church membership has dropped by a quarter of
a million. Given the rate of defections, the Bishop of Hexham
and Newcastle has reported that by 2028, his diocese will have
no Catholics left in it at all.[1] In Ireland, traditionally the Church's
bastion in the British Isles, the number of priests in 1970 had
halved by 1998. The number of nuns had declined from 18,600
to fewer than 7,500. New entries into the seminaries are in
single figures.

There is, too, an increasing preparedness to call the priesthood to account for secular transgressions, such as sexual abuse
of minors; and this has done little to reestablish confidence. In

Austria, for example, Cardinal Groer, former Archbishop of Vienna, has been charged with criminal sexual misconduct. In Ireland, between 1980 and 1998, twenty-three members of the Catholic clergy were convicted of crimes involving sexual abuse, and another fifteen cases are currently pending before the courts.[2] It is thus hardly surprising that many former strongholds of clerical authority should have become increasingly secular in attitudes, values and orientation.

With the spread of education, moreover, a growing number of people are prepared to ask questions; and the Church's prohibition against doing so is coming to seem ever more presumptuous, tyrannical and conducive to alienation. Thus, for example, the movement known as 'We Are Church' arose in Austria, quickly assumed international proportions and now numbers more than half a million members, who still regard themselves as devout Roman Catholics. But as the name of their movement suggests, they maintain that they themselves and the millions of other Catholics across the globe constitute the real Church, not the rigid hierarchy based in Rome. The Church, they insist, is *their* Church, not the Pope's or the Curia's. They oppose the centralisation of the Papacy and wish to see the pontiff as nothing more than Bishop of Rome, perhaps with the largely symbolic status of a constitutional monarch.

Wilfully oblivious to such developments, Pope John Paul II, Cardinal Ratzinger and the Congregation for the Doctrine of the Faith remain adamant in their entrenched positions. Certain commentators have suggested that the Church has effectively 'written off' the developed West as a lost cause – especially since the collapse of Communism in Eastern Europe has left Rome without the adversary formerly cast in the role of Antichrist. The same commentators have speculated that the

Church may now be attempting to establish an entirely new centre of power in the underdeveloped countries of the so-called Third World – in Africa, in Asia and in South America. And there is indubitable evidence to suggest the existence of some such cynical design. Rome is patently mustering and concentrating resources in those regions of the globe where poverty, deprivation, meagre standards of living and a general lack of education provide fertile soil for faith.

As has already been noted, the Pope, Cardinal Ratzinger and the Congregation for the Doctrine of the Faith accord a particular and exalted status to the Virgin Mary. In the effort to establish the Church in regions beyond the developed West, apparitions, manifestations or miraculous appearances of the Madonna have played a significant role. When the Assumption of Mary was officially promulgated as dogma in 1950, C. G. Jung observed that she had been 'elevated to the status of a goddess'.[3] It is in this august capacity that she has allegedly been seen with increasing frequency in Egypt, in other parts of Africa, in Vietnam, in the Philippines, in Mexico, in the fragments of what used to be Yugoslavia, even in the Russian Federation, where Rome has sought for centuries to establish supremacy over the Orthodox Church, and where, in the general disarray following the demise of the Soviet Union, a profound spiritual longing has created a happy hunting ground for proselytisers of every persuasion. In ever swelling numbers, believers today are making pilgrimages to Marian shrines – often to new ones, as well as to the ancient sites.

But if Mary is associated with the conversion and consolidation of a new body of the faithful, she would also seem – for Ratzinger and the Congregation for the Doctrine of the Faith, as well as for Pope John Paul II himself – to be a harbinger of rather more disconcerting developments. According to some accounts, manifestations of the Virgin are supposed to portend the impending end of the world. According to other sources, such manifestations are alleged to presage the end of the Roman Catholic Church, or, at very least, of the Papacy. These rumours derive in large part from the mystery associated with the portentous 'Third Prophecy of Fátima'.

The Secrets of Fátima

In May of 1916, Western civilisation seemed engaged in a process of tearing itself apart. Since February, German and French armies were grinding each other to pieces at Verdun in a battle which would end up costing more than a million lives. On the Somme, the British army was mobilising for a bloodbath of even more staggering proportions. Portugal, however, was a backwater untouched by such traumatic events. At the village of Fátima, a young shepherdess, Lúcia dos Santos, was cavorting with some friends on a remote hill when, as she subsequently testified, a copse of trees shuddered in the wind and revealed a pure white light in the depths of the foliage. The light, she said, coalesced into the form of a transparent young man who then approached the children, identified himself as the 'Angel of Peace' and exhorted them to prayer.

During the summer, Lúcia, accompanied this time by two younger cousins, claimed to have seen the vision again. In the autumn, the apparition came once more, holding up a chalice into which a host dripped blood from above. The apparition placed the bleeding host on Lúcia's tongue and then, after a prayer, disappeared.[4]

At the same spot a year later, on 13 May 1917, another vision appeared to Lúcia, then aged ten, and her two cousins, aged nine and seven respectively. This time it assumed the form, in

Lúcia's words, of 'a lady dressed all in white', who seemed 'more brilliant than the sun, shedding rays of light'. She was young, perhaps sixteen years of age, and held a rosary of white beads. 'I am from Heaven,' she reportedly said to the children.[5] When Lúcia asked what she wanted, she replied with the request that the children come to the same hilltop on the thirteenth day of each of the months that followed. At the end of this time, she promised, she would identify herself.

Lúcia and her cousins complied with the instructions they had received, returning to the hilltop on the thirteenth day of the next six months. The vision appeared on schedule, accompanied by three flashes of light and once by a 'luminous globe', then disappeared amid claps of thunder. Not surprisingly, recent commentators have been quick to stress parallels between the children's experience and the testimony of witnesses to phenomena associated with so-called UFOs. At the time many people were sceptical of the children's accounts, and the local bishop refused to take them seriously. Local people, on the other hand, were convinced; and by the scheduled date of the last vision, 13 October 1917, a crowd of some 70,000 pilgrims had gathered from all over Portugal.

On the night of the 12th, a prodigious storm occurred. At the appointed time on the afternoon of the 13th, Lúcia and her cousins climbed their accustomed hilltop. According to Lúcia's account, the clouds parted and the woman of her previous visions reappeared. Immediately thereafter, according to an independent account:

The rain stopped suddenly, and through a rift, or hole, in the clouds the sun was seen like a silvery disc. It then seemed to rotate, paused, and rotated a second and third time, emitting rays of various colours. Then it seemed to approach the earth, radiating a red light and an intense heat. The crowd fell into a panic, thinking the world was ending, and then into tumultuous devotion.[6]

As the sun regained its wonted position, the terror of the pilgrims subsided. Whatever occurred had been witnessed by some 70,000 people, and there were reports of extraordinary solar phenomena from as far as forty kilometres away. Apart from the three children, however, no one seems to have seen anything unusual on the hilltop.

The children's accounts of their vision varied significantly. Lúcia later claimed to have seen the woman of her previous experiences appear first as 'Our Lady of Sorrows', then mutate into 'Our Lady of Carmel'. She also claimed to have seen Saint Joseph with the infant Jesus in his arms and, presumably at some point after this, 'Our Lord' blessing the assembled multitude. The older of her two cousins claimed to have seen Jesus as a child standing beside St Joseph. The youngest of the three children, a little boy, said nothing at the time. A few days later, he denied having seen the 'two Madonnas' and 'Our Lord' conferring a blessing. He had witnessed, he said, only St Joseph and the child Jesus.

The younger of Lúcia's cousins died in 1919, the elder in 1920. Lúcia herself, illiterate at the time of her visions, entered a boarding school in 1921 and acquired the elements of learning. She subsequently became a Carmelite nun. Between 1936 and 1937, she attempted to describe her experience in prose. The woman, she said, was composed 'altogether of light', waves of 'undulating' light tumbling over one another. She described the woman's veil and gown as waves of running light, the woman's face as of light rather than flesh – '*carnea luz*', or 'flesh light'.[7] The woman had identified herself as 'Our Lady of the

Rosary' – clearly, for Roman Catholic believers, the Virgin Mary. Rather prematurely, she declared the war to have ended. In fact, on the Western Front, the bloody British offensive at Ypres had only just begun, and the major German attack of 1918 was still to come. Within a week of Lúcia's vision, Austro-German forces on the Italian Front were to launch their massive assault at Caporetto, and revolution was erupting in Russia, to be followed by four years of catastrophic civil war.

Between 1941 and 1942, with the world again in conflict, Lúcia penned a second account of her vision in 1917. She stated for the first time that the apparition at Fátima had revealed three secret messages to her – or, to be more accurate, one secret message in three parts. She would disclose the first two parts of the message, she declared, but not the third.

The first part, apparently, consisted of a vision of hell – appropriate enough for the situation in October 1917, as well as for that of the winter of 1941–2. According to the second part, world peace would ensue if a special Communion were offered at the beginning of each month and if Russia were to be consecrated to the Immaculate Heart by the Pope and all Catholic bishops – a consecration which would bring about the conversion of the country. Since the message supposedly dated from the autumn of 1917, it is not clear what Russia was to be converted from – the Orthodox Church or atheistic Bolshevism. The third part of the message Lúcia declared too terrible to be revealed.

The Bishop of Leiria feared that Lúcia might die before she could reveal the whole of the message entrusted to her. At his instigation, a local cleric persuaded her to record the dreaded third part. On 2 January 1944, she began to write it down and took an entire week to do so.[8] She then slipped it into an envelope and sealed it with wax. In due course it was sent to the Bishop of Leiria, who received it on 17 June. Not daring to read it himself, he offered it to the Holy Office. The Holy Office inexplicably refused to accept it. The bishop placed Lúcia's envelope inside another and instructed that after his death it should be delivered to the Cardinal of Lisbon. At Lúcia's insistence, he promised the message would be divulged to the world in 1960, or on her death if it came before then.

In 1957, with Lúcia still alive, the Holy Office abruptly changed its mind and summarily requested the envelope containing her text. No indication was vouchsafed of who made this decision or why. In March, the envelope was delivered to the Papal Nuncio in Lisbon, who dispatched it to Rome. Holding the envelope up to the light, the bishop entrusted with carrying it could see a small sheet of paper. Whatever the portentous secret was, and despite the week Lucia had needed to transcribe it, it consisted of no more than some twenty-five lines of handwriting.

On 16 April 1957, the envelope was received by the Vatican, where Pope Pius XII placed it in his personal private archive, apparently without reading it. According to Cardinal Ottaviani, Prefect of the Holy Office under Pope John XXIII, the envelope was still sealed when John opened it in 1959, the year following his election as pontiff. Cardinal Ottaviani subsequently read the text himself. On 8 February 1960, it was announced that public disclosure of the 'Third Secret of Fátima' would be delayed indefinitely.

Until he died in 1963, John XXIII kept Lúcia's text in a drawer of his desk. Immediately following his election, Pope Paul VI demanded to see it. He read it but refused to speak about it. On 11 February 1967, Cardinal Ottaviani reiterated the Vatican's earlier decision. There would be no disclosure of Lúcia's text. The secret was to remain secret. On 13 October of that year – the fiftieth anniversary of Lúcia's vision – Pope Paul VI visited Fátima, where a shrine and a basilica had been erected during the intervening half century. In front of an audience of a million pilgrims, the Pope conducted a public Mass and offered prayers for world peace.

On 13 May 1981, the sixty-fifth anniversary of Lúcia's first vision, Pope John Paul II, on a visit to Portugal, was wounded by the bullet of a would-be assassin. In the aftermath of this trauma, he, too, read Lúcia's text, apparently requiring the aid of a Portuguese translator for some of the nuances. Cardinal Ratzinger read it as well. A year later, on 13 May 1982, the Pope visited Fátima, to thank the Virgin 'whose hand had miraculously guided the bullet'.[9]

In 1984, an Italian journalist, Vittorio Messori, was granted a lengthy interview with Ratzinger and probed the cardinal insistently on the 'Third Secret of Fátima'. When asked whether he had read Lúcia's text, Ratzinger replied curtly and without elaboration that he had. Why would it not be made public? Did it reveal something terrible? Ratzinger replied evasively:

> If that were so . . . that after all would only confirm the part of the message of Fátima already known. A stern warning has been launched from that place that is directed against the prevailing frivolity, a summons to the seriousness of life, of history, to the perils that threaten humanity.[10]

There was, then, Signor Messori pursued, to be no publication? Ratzinger this time answered somewhat more explicitly:

> The Holy Father deems that it would add nothing to what a Christian must know from revelation and also from the Marian apparitions approved by the Church in their known contents, which only reconfirmed the urgency of

penance, conversion, forgiveness, fasting. To publish the 'third secret' would mean exposing the Church to the danger of sensationalism, exploitation of the contents.[11]

When pressed on a possible political dimension to the 'secret' – one that might, for example, pertain to what was then the Soviet Union – Ratzinger replied he was not in a position to elaborate any further and firmly refused to discuss other particulars. Elsewhere, however, he stated that

> one of the signs of our times is that the announcements of 'Marian apparitions' are multiplying all over the world. For example, reports are arriving from Africa and from other continents at the section of the Congregation that is competent to deal with such reports.[12]

And he vouchsafed something purporting to be an interpretation:

> The correct evaluation of messages such as those of Fátima can represent one form of our answer: the Church heark-ening to the message of Christ, delivered through Mary to our time, feels the threat to all and to each individual and responds with a decisive conversion and penance.[13]

In a number of his own statements, Pope John Paul II echoes the foreboding that suffuses Ratzinger's words. On his visit to the site of Lúcia's vision in 1982, he declared that 'Mary's message of Fátima is still more relevant than it was sixty-five years ago. It is still more urgent.'[14] A year and a half later, in December 1983, the Pope said: 'Precisely at the end of the second millennium there accumulate on the horizon of all mankind enormously threatening clouds, and darkness falls upon human souls.'[15] In his book, *Crossing the Threshold of Hope*,

John Paul wrote that 'Mary appeared to the three children of Fátima in Portugal and spoke to them words that now, at the end of this century, seem close to their fulfilment'.[16] In a Catholic magazine he was quoted as warning that apparitions of Mary around the world are: 'A sign of the times . . . of terrible times.'[17] As for the concealed part of Lúcia's message, the Pope is said to worry about it 'daily'.

There has been no shortage of speculation about the 'Third Secret of Fátima'. In certain more extreme quarters, it has been whispered to forecast that the devil, or perhaps the Antichrist, will usurp control of the Papacy. Other commentators have suggested somewhat less apocalyptic interpretations – a general loss of faith, or a loss of faith specifically among the Catholic clergy, or a dismantling of the Papacy, or simply internal conflict within the Church. Shortly before his death in 1981 Father Joaquim Alonso, an acknowledged expert on Fátima who frequently met and spoke with Lúcia, wrote:

> It is thus entirely probable that the text of the Third Secret makes concrete allusion to the crisis of Faith within the Church and to the negligence of the Pastors themselves . . . internal conflicts in the bosom of the Church herself and of grave pastoral negligence on the part of the upper hierarchy . . . deficiencies of the upper hierarchy of the Church.[18]

Because of their importance to Cardinal Ratzinger and to recent Popes, and because of the mystery (and often spurious mystification) associated with them, the visions of Fátima enjoy a special, even sacrosanct, place in certain enclaves of the Church today. But the Church still endeavours to purvey a façade of stability, still endeavours to live up to the image of an ark breasting the sea of time; and this tends to obscure the fact that Catholicism is subject to its own forms of apocalyptic fundamentalism, which are often as extreme as those to be found in many independent fundamentalist sects. Like such sects, factions within the Church are prey to apocalyptic fears and the conviction of living through the 'Last Times', or the 'Final Days'. This sense of impending doom runs through much fringe devotional Catholic literature – and so, too, do apparitions of the Virgin acting as harbinger. Indeed, such literature often teeters on the brink of heresy, on the creation of a new goddess cult. The line dividing the Queen of Heaven from the full-fledged Mother Goddesses of antiquity can often become blurred.

It is in this context that the apparitions of the Virgin at Fátima must be placed. The visions at Fátima were not unique, not isolated phenomena. On the contrary, they conform recognisably to a pattern of Marian apparitions extending back at least to the nineteenth century. Since 1830, nearly ninety years before Lúcia's experience at Fátima, the Virgin had been uttering political pronouncements fraught with dire apocalyptic admonitions.

In Paris, in the Rue du Bac, on the evening of 18 July 1830, a nun named Catherine Labouré was awakened by the vision of a child, perhaps five years old, dressed in white. The child, she reported, led her to the convent's chapel, where, she was told, 'the Blessed Virgin is waiting for you'. On this first appearance, the Madonna's advice was wholly personal, intended merely to aid Catherine in her novitiate. Some months later, however, the Virgin appeared again, this time with streams of light issuing from her hands. She confronted the nun with a vision of two hearts – the heart of Jesus wrapped with thorns and her own, pierced by a sword to represent her suffering –

and exhorted Catherine to have a medal struck which enshrined the occasion. The medal has subsequently become known as 'the medal of the Immaculate Conception'.[19] And on this appearance, the Virgin also vouchsafed a commentary on the struggle between righteousness and wickedness then occurring in the world at large. The times, she declared, were evil. Misfortunes would fall upon France. The throne would be overturned. The entire world would be overcome by evils of all kinds.

Modern Catholic apocalyptic commentators invoke the apparition of the Rue du Bac as a defining moment. The Virgin, they believe, came to warn the world that from this point on, 'evil' would present itself to humanity as 'goodness' and subvert the divine order by deception. According to one writer,

> evil would be extolled as a modern 'good' — in the form of many liberalisms — and God would be subjugated. Little seeds of the occult, spores from certain secret societies like the Masons, would eventually germinate into a large forest, altering the landscape of politics and human thought.[20]

Such an assessment would undoubtedly have commended itself to Pope Pius IX. It might well find favour, too, with Cardinal Ratzinger.

On 19 September 1846, two peasant children — Mélanie Mathieu, aged fourteen, and Maximin Giraud, aged eleven — were minding livestock on a stony hilltop meadow overlooking the village of La Salette in the French Alps. In a ravine just below they saw a circle of bright light, within which, when they drew closer, they found a beautiful woman wearing a crown and weeping. Over her dress, according to Mélanie, she wore a pinafore which shone 'more brilliant than several suns put together', woven not of earthly cloth but of some scintillating otherworldly substance.[21] Speaking through her tears, the woman told the children she had important news to confide to them. Unless everyone submitted to God's will, she said, Christ himself might abandon them. And then:

> All the civil governments will have one and the same plan, which will be to abolish and do away with every religious principle, to make way for materialism, atheism, occultism and vice of all kinds.[22]

One wonders what two untutored and probably illiterate peasant children might have made of so weighty a pronouncement couched in so sophisticated a vocabulary. Apparently, however, the Virgin gave them no time to reflect, going on to criticise world leaders – including, seemingly, the Pope himself.

> The chiefs, the leaders of the people of God, have neglected prayer and penance, and the devil has bedimmed their intelligence. They have become wandering stars which the old devil will drag with his tail to make them perish.[23]

There then followed an apocalyptic prediction:

> God will abandon mankind to itself and will send punishments which will follow one after the other for more than thirty-five years. The society of men is on the eve of the most terrible scourges and of gravest events. Mankind must expect to be ruled with an iron rod and to drink from the chalice of the wrath of God.[24]

And the year 1864 was singled out for particularly worrisome notice:

> In the year 1864, Lucifer, together with large numbers of demons, will be unloosed from Hell. They will put an end to faith little by little . . . Evil books will be abundant on earth.[25]

Cardinal Fornari, the Papal Nuncio to France at the time, declared himself 'terrified' by these predictions. The Vatican's hierarchy appears to have shared his sentiments, but officially acknowledged and accepted the validity of the Virgin of La Salette in 1851. The revelations were not made public, however, until some time later – which may perhaps explain why, when they were, the Virgin seemed to have been speaking in a voice strikingly similar to Pius IX's. By 1864, the most 'evil' books had indeed become abundant. Darwin's *Origin of Species* had appeared in 1859, Renan's *Life of Jesus* in 1863, and the compilers of the Index had no shortage of material to keep them occupied. In other respects, 1864 was nasty enough, witnessing as it did the climax of the American Civil War and Bismarck's six-day military triumph over puny Denmark; but one might just as well point to any of a number of other years, shortly before or shortly after, which could make equally plausible claims to demonic intervention. The predicted thirty-five years of 'punishments' would have extended until 1881. In that time, traumatic events unquestionably did occur. France was defeated in the Franco-Prussian War and the Second Empire toppled. Germany and Italy were both united. The Papacy was divested of its last vestiges of secular power. But the world survived; and in compensation for his loss of temporal dominion, the Pope acquired infallibility.

On 11 February 1858, twelve years after her appearance

at La Salette, the Virgin made one of her most celebrated appearances – to the young Bernadette Soubirous at Lourdes. She identified herself as the 'Immaculate Conception' – which was convenient because Pius IX, only four years before, had officially established the Immaculate Conception as dogma, and the manifestation at Lourdes 'was the first affirmation of a declaration that Mary was conceived without original sin'.[26] At Lourdes, however, she seems to have refrained from any dire political pronouncements, confining herself to extolling penitence, the living of a pure life and the use of the rosary as a deterrent to satanic importunities.

If Marian apparitions pre-date the events at Fátima, they also post-date them. Since 1917, visions of the Virgin have occurred in Italy, Spain, Ireland, Czechoslovakia, Lithuania, Hungary, Austria, Holland, India, Japan, the Philippines, Vietnam, Russia, the Ukraine, Croatia, Egypt, Venezuela and Mexico. A significant number of these visitations were accompanied by apocalyptic messages. One such occurred on 20 December 1953, to a woman near the village of Dubovytsya in the Ukraine. Appearing during a recitation of the Mass, the Virgin announced that

> disaster is upon us as in the times of Noah. Not by flood but by fire will the destruction come. An immense flood of fire shall destroy nations for sinning before God. Since the beginning of the world there has never been such a fall as there is today. This is the kingdom of Satan. Rome is in danger of being destroyed, the Pope of being killed.[27]

The date of this prediction renders it explicable enough. Two years earlier, the Soviet Union had tested its first atomic bomb, and the spectre of nuclear holocaust had established itself as a pervasive shadow brooding over the consciousness of the age.

It has never been exorcised. On the contrary, it has since been joined by other, equally terrifying spectres.

The Cold War, international terrorism, so-called 'rogue' states or governments and the impending millennium have all, during the last half century, conduced to a sense of apocalyptic doom. Thus, in 1962, a woman in Spain experienced an apparition of the Virgin who informed her there would be only two Popes after Paul VI – which would make the present pontiff the last.

On 25 June 1981, a visitation occurred at Medjugorje, in what is now Croatia, which the Vatican is still debating whether or not to authenticate. The day after a fierce thunderstorm, two teenaged shepherdesses witnessed a mysterious light on a nearby hillside. Enclosed within the light was a woman whom the girls promptly took to be the Virgin. Since then, the apparition is reported to have appeared often. Her message, when she vouchsafes one, is frequently ominous: 'I have come to call the world to conversion for the last time. After this period I will not appear any more on this earth.'[28] On one occasion, she exhibited a commendable tolerance: 'You are not true Christians if you do not respect other religions.' Unfortunately, she then repudiated any such ecumenical spirit: 'There is only one mediator between God and man, and it is Jesus Christ.'[29] For the most part, however, her messages have been typically apocalyptic: 'The hour has come when the demon is authorised to act with all his force and power.'[30] And, even more urgently: 'Punishment will come about if the world is not converted. Call all mankind to conversion. Everything depends on your conversion.'[31]

The apparition at Medjugorje appeared jealous of other manifestations of herself, inveighing against false visions and warning that 'many pretend to see Jesus and the Mother of

God, and to understand their words, but they are, in fact, lying'.[32] The problem for Cardinal Ratzinger and for the Congregation for the Doctrine of the Faith is to determine which are indeed to be declared false and which validated. They have more than enough to keep them occupied. By the early 1990s, there had been more than 260 recent apparitions of the Virgin, and that number is constantly increasing.

The End of the Papacy?

The prophecies of Fátima and other apparitions of the Virgin are not the only such doom-laden prophecies hanging over the Church. Both Cardinal Ratzinger and Pope John Paul II are also said to be haunted by the prophecies of St Malachi. Malachi, an Irish monk, was born in Armagh in 1094 and died at Clairvaux in 1148 with St Bernard, his friend, colleague and confidant, at his side. A printed version of his prophecies first appeared in a Church history published in 1559.

In their image-clotted ambiguity, Malachi's prophecies have more than a little in common with those of Nostradamus. Starting with those of his own era, Malachi lists a total of 112 pontiffs and provides a Latin epigraph which purports to summarise or encapsulate the character and reign of each. The present Pope, John Paul II, is 111th in the sequence – the penultimate. The motto associated with him is '*De Labore Solis*' ('Of the work of the sun').[33]

Like the quatrains of Nostradamus, this can be interpreted to mean whatever one wishes. Certain commentators have endeavoured to see a parallel between John Paul II's extensive travels – more extensive by far than those of any pontiff in history – and the sun's apparent movement around the globe. Without too much difficulty one could devise other interpretations of comparable relevance (or lack thereof). That, however, is not the point. The point, regardless of interpretation, is that the present Pope, according to Malachi, is the next to last.

For the 112th pontiff, the last in the sequence, Malachi appends the motto 'Gloria Olivae'[34] – glory, or possibly fame, of the olive, or the olive tree, or the olive tree's wood, from which, perhaps, an episcopal staff might be fashioned. Here again is ample latitude in which would-be interpreters can frolic. But any disposition towards levity would be dispelled, at least for pious Catholics, by the sombre note on which Malachi concludes:

> In the final persecution of the Holy Roman Church there will reign Peter the Roman, who will feed his flock among many tribulations; after which the seven-hilled city will be destroyed and the dreadful Judge will judge the people.[35]

16

The Pope as the Problem

Confronted by the spectre of its own prospective and imminent extinction, the Church today huddles in fear. In the obtuseness with which it seeks refuge in outworn dogma, one can discern an element of desperation – an element of incipient panic verging at times on hysteria. But extinction is only one of many fears that beleaguer the Church today.

The Church fears the increasing secularisation of Western society and the defection of its congregation in such former strongholds as Ireland, southern Germany, Austria and Spain. It fears the increasing accommodation made for other faiths in multicultural societies like those of Britain, western Europe and the United States. It fears the increasing tendency of psychologically and culturally sophisticated people to seek and find a dimension of spirituality in spheres other than those controlled by the priesthood – spheres such as, for example, the arts. It fears the embryonic pantheism and Hermeticism implicit in environmental concerns, which stress the interconnected nature of reality. It continues to fear the usurpation of its authority by science and by psychology. The Church also fears ecumenical initiatives, as recently reiterated refusals to acknowledge Anglican legitimacy attest; and all Anglican ordinations continue to be regarded in consequence as 'absolutely null and utterly void'. With the collapse of Communism and the Soviet Union, the Church fears a *rapprochement* between Eastern and Western Christendom which might entail some loss of its own self-arrogated primacy. It even fears the discovery of extra-terrestrial life, and the possibility of a 'close encounter' or a 'first contact'.

They may not necessarily be fans of Mulder and Scully, but there are some Catholic clerics who seem distinctly nervous about the prospect of aliens arriving on our planet with no awareness of Jesus. Father Corrado Balducci – an official member of the Papal household and the Vatican's acknowledged expert on exorcism, demonology and the Antichrist – was quoted recently as saying he accorded some credence to accounts of 'alien abductions':

> It is reasonable to believe and affirm that extra-terrestrials exist. Their existence can no longer be denied, for there is too much evidence for the existence of extra-terrestrials and flying saucers.[1]

Not that such a belief in any way conflicted with his official faith. Invoking St Paul's acclamation of Jesus not only as 'king of the world', but also as 'king of the universe', Father Balducci explained: 'This means that everything in the universe, including extra-terrestrials and UFOs, are reconcilable with God.'[2]

Confronted on the subject by *The Times*, a spokesman for the Catholic Media Office was somewhat more cautious:

> The fundamental creation message relates to humans here on earth. If aliens are shown to exist, this would not cast doubt on the veracity of the Gospel. But we would have to ask whether the Christian atonement was applicable to them.[3]

Pope John Paul II appears to be hedging his bets. According to a report on the front page of the *Sunday Times* of 14 December 1997, the pontiff has requested a team of astronomers to probe the cosmos for 'the fingerprints of God'. There is now a Vatican project specifically dedicated to investigating the implications of contact with extra-terrestrial races. At Mount Graham in Arizona, the Vatican maintains its own observatory, staffed by Jesuits. Among the issues they address is whether Jesus's crucifixion might have saved alien races from original sin. According to Father Chris Corbally, the project's deputy director: 'If civilisation were to be found on other planets and if it were feasible to communicate, then we would want to send missionaries to save them.'[4] Father Corbally would appear to be utterly unaware of his own breathtaking arrogance.

Bishop of Rome

So numerous and pervasive are the modern Church's fears that it lives in a veritable state of siege. But there is one fear in particular that underlies, dictates and conditions all the others – the fear of change. And yet one can argue that precisely through change – and only through change – can the Church hope to ensure for itself a relevant future. In the past, the Church has maintained its own survival by virtue of its preparedness, however reluctant, to adapt to changing circumstances. To continue to survive, it must display a comparable adaptability.

Throughout the lifetimes of people today, the Church has comprised a single, ostensibly unified, monolithic edifice – a species of autocracy presiding supposedly over its self-defined sphere of 'spirituality'. This, therefore, is the image the Church enjoys in both our individual and collective psyches. But such images result merely from habits of thought, from a sort of mental inertia. For example, we think of the United States as a single monolithic entity, 'one nation indivisible' that seems to have existed from time immemorial. We tend to forget that as recently as 140 years ago, the United States came within a hair's-breadth of fragmenting into two separate nations – and that two and a quarter centuries ago the United States did not exist at all.

The same principles, the same mental processes, govern our perceptions of the Church. According to Catholic tradition, Jesus turned to Peter and stated that on this rock he would build his Church. According to the same tradition, Peter was the first Pope, the first in an apostolic succession of spiritual leaders extending in an unbroken and uninterrupted continuity from the dawn of the Christian era to the present day. In historical fact, however, such contentions are nonsense. Until the fourth century, the form of 'Christianity' we regard as 'orthodox Catholicism' was nothing of the sort. On the contrary, it was only one of numerous forms of Christian belief, each vying with the others for theological, social and political supremacy; and only when one of these systems emerged as 'orthodoxy' did the others become, by retroactive definition, 'heresy'.

Yet even after the Church of Rome had emerged triumphant over other forms of Christian belief, it bore precious little resemblance to the Church we know today. The designation of 'Pope' did not exist until the end of the fourth century, when Siricus I (384–99) adopted it for the first time. And until the middle of the fifth century, the Roman Church was the very antithesis of monolithic. In fact, it was wholly decentralised, and the so-called 'Pope' was merely the Bishop of Rome, only one of a multitude of bishops. At best, he might be regarded as the proverbial 'first among equals', roughly equivalent to a prime minister; and the bishops or patriarchs of such jurisdictions as Antioch, Alexandria and Constantinople exercised a comparable authority.

Even later, when the Papacy did emerge as the centre of the Church's power, its status as such was to a significant degree nominal. At times, it was subject and subordinate to the decisions of Church Councils. Until 1870, its possible accountability to Church Councils could at least be debated, as the controversies of the period between Gallicans and Ultramontanes demonstrate. Only in the years since 1870 – with the Church's loss of secular dominion and the concurrent compensatory promulgation of Papal infallibility – did the monolithic structure we know today begin definitively to coalesce.

With its rigid adherence to dogma and its wilful obliviousness to the realities of contemporary civilisation, that monolithic structure appears to an increasing number of people no longer adequate. To condemn birth control in an age of overpopulation and proliferating unwanted pregnancies is coming to be seen as ridiculous at best, culpably negligent at worst. To fulminate against contraceptives in the epoch of AIDS is being condemned as dangerous folly at best, at worst as criminal irresponsibility. Such criticism is being issued not only by hostile commentators or by detached and disinterested observers. It is also issuing from the Church's faithful themselves, many of whom are caused acute distress and crises of conscience by the conflict provoked within them between the inescapable pressures of the world around them and the church to which they long to remain loyal, but which seems indifferent to their dilemma.

There are too many spheres in which the Church seems not merely out of touch with the exigencies of the modern world, but in some bizarre state of psychological denial – as if it were pursuing its own agenda with the single-mindedness of a robot, while deliberately, forcibly, doctrinally blinkering itself to the very real needs of its congregation. There are too many instances in which the Church seems to have forgotten that it possesses a congregation – a congregation of human beings, with human failings, human weaknesses and human needs – and adheres with the relentless imperturbability of a machine to a naively idealistic programme of 'salvation' that might have been formulated by a computer.

In such instances as these, a decentralised Church is being ever more frequently advocated by concerned individuals as a viable alternative. Such a Church might still be able to accommodate a Bishop of Rome, who, in some redefined interpretation of 'Pope', might function as an arbiter, a chairman, a religious equivalent of a military chief of staff. In this capacity, he might still exercise some kind of administrative leadership, but he would be obliged to take cognisance of the needs of his congregation and its bishops across the globe. And those needs – differing as they do between the developed West, Africa, Asia, South America and elsewhere – would at least be accorded the hearing they deserve. Moral and spiritual authority would reside with specific bishoprics and dioceses which possessed the flexibility necessary to adapt to the requirements of their respective and often unique circumstances. In short, the Church would become centred on the diocese, and each diocese would reflect the distinctive needs of its particular flock.

This suggestion, of course, entails considerable oversimplification – more, perhaps, than those who extol it often recognise. To translate it into practice would involve a complicated, disruptive and probably prolonged process. It is not, however, the only possible solution to the question of the Church's future relevance. There are many others. But some form of change would appear patently inescapable if the Church is not to become as much an element of irrelevant history as, say, the Holy Roman Empire, which, if only in theory, once represented its secular and temporal dominion.

At its worst, the Church can constitute — as it often has in the past — a tyranny as great, as oppressive, as noxious, as monstrous as that of any secular dictatorship. At its best, it can provide solace, refuge, advice, support, charity, understanding and one of many paths — not all of them necessarily 'religious' — conducing to a sense of the sacred. But for any such institution in the modern world to claim a definitive monopoly of truth, and even more of 'salvation', is an arrogance comparable only to the sin of pride for which Lucifer, according to tradition, was banished from heaven — an arrogance that would justify the Cathar heretics of the Middle Ages in seeing Rome as the creation of the demonic 'Rex Mundi', 'King of the World', the ultimate principle of evil.

As the millennium approaches, the Church has announced its intention to acknowledge and to apologise for certain of the excesses of the past. There have even been rumours that the Church intends to apologise for the Inquisition — or, at any rate, for the zealously sadistic and pyromaniacal tendencies displayed by the Inquisition during the first few centuries of its existence — and that certain of its victims, such as Giordano Bruno, for example, are, like Galileo, to be rehabilitated.

Such measures are both welcome and encouraging. To survive it is necessary to adapt. To mature, however, it is necessary to do more than that. It is necessary to confront the past, acknowledge it and integrate it in a new unity or totality that corrects any previous imbalances. The past cannot be denied or ignored or repudiated or cavalierly consigned to oblivion. It must be brought into some kind of accommodation with the present; and both must serve as the foundation on which a new, more balanced future can be created. In previous epochs, the Church has seldom recognised this necessity. That it appears to do so now is indeed commendable, and indicative of some genuine maturation.

But the apology, as a mere gesture, can often be little more than a fashionable adjunct in our age of 'political correctness'. To offer facile apologies for past blunders and atrocities has become a vogue in our epoch. Yet while history can be rewritten, it cannot be unwritten. It is easy enough to apologise for a *fait accompli* that can no longer be undone or reversed. There is little point in apologising for the fate of long-dead Cathars when there is no one to benefit from the apology. And if the Church itself aspires to appear 'cleaner', more civilised and more humane as a result, it must do more than just apologise. It must also repent and atone. Such repentance and atonement must have repercussions that apply not only to the past, but to the present as well.

The Inquisition – or, to cite it by its current name, the Congregation for the Doctrine of the Faith – is not, of course, the whole of the Church. It is only one aspect of the Church, one office, one department. For many people today, however, including many of the faithful, the Congregation has become equated with the Church. It is often perceived as the single and definitive voice with which the Church speaks on doctrinal matters; and it does nothing to discourage such a perception. This is likely to remain a problem unless other aspects, offices and departments of the Church are seen to be accorded comparable authority – or unless the Congregation modifies its own rigidly inflexible mentality. It is the Congregation specifically, as much as the Church in general, that should repent and atone for the past. And such repentance and atonement should have some benefit for devout Catholics today.

Since its earliest crystallisation, organised religion has endeavoured to address and account for two spheres of the unknown – that which resides within humanity, and that which lies beyond, in the natural world and the cosmos at large. As Western civilisation has evolved, the terrain comprising both unknowns has been increasingly well charted, well mapped, by science and by psychology. That terrain is no longer as unknown as it once appeared to be, and organised religion has retreated from it accordingly. In the unknown that lies beyond, organised religion has reluctantly withdrawn before the apparently ineluctable advance of science. In the unknown that lies within humanity, organised religion has been increasingly challenged and thrown on to the defensive by psychology. On both fronts, organised religion has endeavoured to conduct as orderly a retreat as possible.

Yet despite the encroachments of science and psychology, despite the fighting withdrawal of organised religion, vast tracts of territory continue to be unknown, both internally and externally. The unknown may appear to recede elusively into the distance, but is unlikely ever to disappear completely, unlikely ever to be entirely and definitively charted. It is naive at best to imagine that we will one day know everything there is to know. On the contrary, there is bound to remain an element of genuine mystery, in ourselves and in the cosmos around us. Nor would we wish things to be otherwise.

Organised religion can still have a role to play in our lives, in our society, in our world. For the millions who turn to it in quest of solace, consolation, compassion, understanding and even wisdom, the Church need not be reduced to irrelevance or consigned to the obsolete debris of history like the old Holy Roman Empire. If it is to escape such a fate, however, it and the Congregation that codifies its doctrine must emerge from their bunkers. Newer and stronger bridges must be built to other Christian denominations, to the spectrum of non-Christian faiths and creeds. Such bridges must also be built to the sciences and to psychology – so that organised religion's two arch-rivals, in attempting to chart the unknown, can chart what is chartable, while not trespassing on domains of genuine, valid and necessary mystery. And bridges must be built to the arts, as well. In the past, the arts had aided organised religion in testifying to the sacred. By the mid nineteenth century, however, as Flaubert maintained, religion had abdicated all responsibility for such testimony; and the artist, as a matter of increasingly conscious and deliberate policy, had assumed the role abandoned by the priest. In attempting to comprehend and convey a sense of the sacred, the numinous, the spiritual or whatever one wishes to call it, the priest must now learn from the artist. The Pope himself, and the Congregation for the Doctrine of the Faith, must display an understanding of spirituality comparable to that of Rilke, for example, Yeats or Patrick White.

Such are the challenges confronting the Church as a whole, and the Congregation for the Doctrine of the Faith in particular, on the eve of the millennium. The extent to which the Church and the Congregation rise successfully to these challenges will determine the future of the Catholic faith in the twenty-first century.

Notes

NOTE The full bibliographical details, when not cited here, are to be found in the Bibliography.

1: A Fiery Zeal for the Faith

1. Le Roy Ladurie, *Montaillou*, p.78.
2. ibid., p.81.
3. Lea, *A History of the Inquisition of the Middle Ages*, I, p.53.
4. ibid., pp.54–5.
5. ibid., p.20.
6. Sumption, *The Albigensian Crusade*, p.93.
7. ibid.

2: Origins of the Inquisition

1. Vicaire, *Saint Dominic and His Times*, p.146.
2. Lea, *A History of the Inquisition of the Middle Ages*, I, p.329.
3. ibid., p.329.
4. Wakefield, *Heresy, Crusade and Inquisition in Southern France 1100–1250*, p.208.
5. ibid., p.211.
6. ibid., pp.211–12.

NOTES

7. ibid., p.214.
8. ibid., p.215.
9. ibid., p.216.
10. ibid., p.217.
11. ibid., p.224.
12. Chadwick, *Priscillian of Avila*, p.233.
13. Lea, op. cit., p.464.
14. Maycock, *The Inquisition*, p.157.
15. ibid., p.158.
16. Lea, op. cit., p.541.
17. ibid.
18. Maycock, op. cit., p.173.
19. Lea, op. cit., p.552.
20. ibid., p.553.
21. ibid., II, p.334.
22. ibid., I, p.494.
23. ibid., p.368.

3: Enemies of the Black Friars

1. Stoyanov, *The Hidden Tradition in Europe*, p.xvi.
2. ibid., p.193.
3. Lea, *A History of the Inquisition of the Middle Ages*, II, p.355.
4. ibid.
5. ibid., p.357.
6. For example, 4th Grand Master Bertrand de Blanchefort, 1153–70. See a discussion of this point in Baigent, Leigh and Lincoln, *The Holy Blood and the Holy Grail*, pp.44–5.
7. See discussion in ibid., p.44 referring to the work of the abbé M.-R. Mazières published in 'La Venue et le séjour des Templiers du Roussillon à la fin du XIIIme siècle et au début du XIVme dans la vallée du Bézu (Aude)', *Mémoires de*

la Société des arts et des sciences de Carcassonne, 4th ser., vol. 3, Carcassonne, 1957–9, pp.229–54.

8. Addison, *The History of the Knights Templars*, p.206.
9. See the discussion in Baigent and Leigh, *The Temple and the Lodge*, pp.56–73, especially pp.64–5.
10. Lea, op. cit., I, p.260.
11. ibid., p.295.
12. ibid., p.296.
13. ibid., II, p.171.
14. ibid.
15. ibid., p.173.

4: The Spanish Inquisition

1. Kamen, *The Spanish Inquisition*, p.139.
2. ibid., p.137.
3. ibid., p.49. The full text appears in Lea, *A History of the Inquisition of Spain*, I, pp.587–90.
4. Kamen, op. cit., p.49.
5. ibid., p.50. The full text appears in Lea, op. cit., I, pp.590–92.
6. Lea, op. cit., I, p.174.
7. Kamen, op. cit., p.69.
8. ibid., p.174.
9. ibid., p.178.
10. ibid., p.176.
11. ibid., p.186.
12. ibid., p.188.
13. Lea, op. cit., III, p.5.
14. ibid., p.22.
15. ibid., p.17.
16. Kamen, op. cit., p.20.
17. ibid., p.21.

18. Netanyahu, *The Origins of the Inquisition in Fifteenth Century Spain*, p.1090.
19. Kamen, op. cit., p.57.
20. ibid., p.301.

5: Saving the New World

1. Lea, *The Inquisition in the Spanish Dependencies*, p.233.
2. ibid., p.233.
3. ibid., p.286.
4. ibid., p.347.
5. ibid., p.455.
6. ibid., p.461.
7. ibid., p.466.
8. ibid., p.510.

6: A Crusade Against Witchcraft

1. Lea, *A History of the Inquisition of the Middle Ages*, III, pp.493–4.
2. Bede, *A History of the English Church and People*, I, 30 (pp.86–7).
3. Thomas, *Religion and the Decline of Magic*, p.521.
4. Trevor-Roper, *The European Witch-Craze of the Sixteenth and Seventeenth Centuries*, p.32.
5. Lea, *A History of the Inquisition of Spain*, IV, p.206.
6. Lea, *A History of the Inquisition of the Middle Ages*, III, p.497.
7. *Malleus Maleficarum*, p.29.
8. Lea, *A History of the Inquisition of the Middle Ages*, III, p.506.
9. ibid., p.498.
10. Kieckhefer, *Magic in the Middle Ages*, p.194.
11. *Malleus Maleficarum*, pp.30–31.
12. ibid., p.19.

13. ibid., p.24.
14. ibid., p.19.
15. ibid., p.33.
16. ibid., p.53.
17. ibid., p.203.
18. ibid., pp.205–6.
19. ibid., p.208.
20. ibid., p.117.
21. ibid., p.121.
22. ibid., p.122.
23. ibid., p.221.
24. ibid., p.253.
25. ibid.
26. ibid., pp.267–8.
27. ibid., p.268.
28. ibid., p.111.
29. ibid., p.445.
30. ibid., p.470.
31. ibid.
32. ibid., p.471.
33. ibid.
34. ibid.
35. ibid.
36. ibid., p.473.
37. ibid., p.230.
38. ibid., p.483.
39. ibid., p.482.
40. Lea, *A History of the Inquisition of Spain*, IV, p.206.
41. Lea, *A History of the Inquisition of the Middle Ages*, III, p.539.

7: Fighting the Heresy of Protestantism

1. Trevor-Roper, *The European Witch-Craze of the Sixteenth and Seventeenth Centuries*, p.66.
2. Chastel, *Art of the Italian Renaissance*, p.202.
3. ibid.
4. Kidd, *The Counter-Reformation*, p.44.
5. ibid., p.59.
6. ibid., p.57.
7. *Index Librorum Prohibitorum*, Vatican City, 1948. Thereafter issued with additions following p.509.
8. Agrippa, *The Vanity of Arts and Sciences*, p.328.
9. Thorndike, *A History of Magic and Experimental Science*, VII, p.292.
10. ibid., p.293.
11. ibid.

8: Fear of the Mystics

1. *The Cloud of Unknowing*, chapter 67, p.96.
2. ibid., chapter 13, p.31.
3. ibid., chapter 55, p.81.
4. Teresa, *The Life of Saint Teresa of Avila by Herself*, p.127.
5. ibid., p.303. See also p.139.
6. ibid., p.127.
7. ibid., p.75.
8. ibid., p.243.
9. ibid., p.298.
10. ibid., p.294.
11. ibid., p.300.
12. ibid., p.298.
13. ibid., pp.300–301.
14. ibid., p.311.

15. Lea, *A History of the Inquisition of Spain*, IV, p.3.

9: *Freemasonry and the Inquisition*

1. Lennhoff, *The Freemasons*, p.283.

2. ibid., p.284.

3. ibid., p.286.

4. Thory, *Acta Latomorum*, I, p.43.

5. Lennhoff, op. cit., pp.289–90.

6. Benimeli, *Masoneria, Iglesia e Ilustración*, II, p.234.

7. Gould, *The History of Freemasonry*, III, p.314.

8. Coustos, *The Sufferings of John Coustos for Freemasonry*, p.52.
   For a translation of the Inquisition documents on his case,
   including his 'confessions', see Vatcher, 'John Coustos and
   the Portuguese Inquisition', *Ars Quatuor Coronatorum*, 81,
   1968, pp.9–87.

9. Vatcher, op. cit., p.66.

10. Coustos, op. cit., pp.61–4.

11. Vatcher, op. cit., p.68.

12. Coustos, op. cit., pp.64–5.

13. Vatcher, op. cit., p.73.

14. Coustos, op. cit., p.67.

15. Gervaso, *Cagliostro*, p.229.

16. Lennhoff, op. cit., p.293.

17. ibid., p.297.

18. ibid.

19. ibid., p.299. A list of the major Papal attacks on Freemasonry
    is given in Read, 'The Church of Rome and Freemasonry',
    Ars Quatuor Coronatorum, 104, 1991, pp.51–73.

10: The Conquest of the Papal States

1. Stolper, 'Garibaldi: Freemason', *Ars Quatuor Coronatorum*, 102, 1989, pp.10–11.
2. Rosa, *Vicars of Christ*, p.125.
3. Küng, *Christianity*, p.466.
4. ibid., p.467.
5. ibid., p.466.
6. ibid., p.468.
7. ibid., p.471.

11: Infallibility

1. Hales, *Pio Nono*, p.164.
2. Hibbert, *Garibaldi*, p.24.
3. Rosa, *Vicars of Christ*, p.244.
4. ibid., p.343.
5. ibid., p.344.
6. ibid.
7. ibid.
8. Hales, op. cit., p.256.
9. ibid., p.274.
10. Hasler, *How the Pope Became Infallible*, p.81.
11. ibid., pp.88–9.
12. ibid., p.68.
13. ibid., p.64.
14. ibid., p.57.
15. ibid., p.97.
16. ibid., pp.97–8.
17. ibid., p.187.
18. ibid., p.189.
19. Kelly, *The Oxford Dictionary of Popes*, p.310.
20. ibid.

21. Hasler, op. cit., p.191.

22. ibid., p.192.

23. ibid.

24. ibid., p.229.

25. ibid., p.125.

26. ibid., pp.241–3.

27. Kelly, op. cit., p.310.

12: The Holy Office

1. Hasler, *How the Pope Became Infallible*, p.246.

2. *New Catholic Encyclopaedia*, vol. 11, p.551.

3. ibid.

4. Burman, *The Inquisition*, p.209.

5. *New Catholic Encyclopaedia*, vol. 11, p.551.

6. Fogazzaro, *The Saint*, p.242.

7. Poulat, *Catholicisme, Démocratie et Socialisme*, p.40. For a summary of Benigni see also Hasler, op. cit., pp.250–53.

8. Encyclical *Pascendi*, 8 September 1907. *New Catholic Encyclopaedia*, vol. 7, p.552.

9. Poulat, op. cit., p.442.

10. ibid., p.461.

11. ibid., p.460.

12. ibid., pp.444–5.

13. *New Catholic Encyclopaedia*, vol. 2, p.310; vol. 13, p.411; see also Hasler, op. cit., p.253.

13: The Dead Sea Scrolls

1. Rosa, *Vicars of Christ*, p.244.

2. Dr Geza Vermes in *Times Literary Supplement*, 3 May 1985, p.502.

3. See Baigent and Leigh, *The Dead Sea Scrolls Deception*, p.44.

4. In mid-December 1991 a heavy rainfall at Qumran washed away one of De Vaux's 'walls' to reveal a large pot sitting upon a ledge.

5. For the machinations surrounding the dubious dating of Qumran by De Vaux and others see Baigent and Leigh, op. cit., pp.151–64.

6. ibid., pp.199–210.

7. Eisenman and Wise, *The Dead Sea Scrolls Uncovered*, p.70; Garcia Martinez gives an identical translation of this text in his *The Dead Sea Scrolls Translated*, p.138.

8. *Biblical Archaeology Review*, March/April 1990, p.24.

9. Leon-Dufour, *The Gospels and the Jesus of History*, p.70.

14: The Congregation for the Doctrine of the Faith

1. Rosa, *Vicars of Christ*, p.396.

2. Collins, *Papal Power*, p.7.

3. ibid.

4. ibid.

5. ibid.

6. Ratzinger and Messori, *The Ratzinger Report*, p.10.

7. ibid., p.69.

8. Reese, *Inside the Vatican*, p.161.

9. *The New Catholic Encyclopaedia*, vol. 4, p.944.

10. Collins, op. cit., p.16.

11. Reese, op. cit., p.252.

12. *Sunday Times*, 2 December 1984, p.13.

13. Reese, op. cit., p.250.

14. ibid., p.252.

15. ibid., p.255.

16. ibid., p.259.

17. ibid.

18. *Observer*, 27 May 1990, p.1.

19. *Independent*, 27 June 1990, p.10.

20. *The Times*, 27 June 1990, p.9.

21. *Independent*, 27 June 1990, p.10.

22. ibid.

23. ibid.

24. *The Times*, 27 June 1990, p.9.

25. Reese, op. cit., p.255.

26. Ratzinger and Messori, op. cit., p.46.

27. Ratzinger, *Church, Ecumenism and Politics*, p.10.

28. ibid., pp.9–10.

29. ibid., p.10.

30. Ratzinger and Messori, op. cit., p.111.

31. Ratzinger, op. cit., p.80.

32. Ratzinger and Messori, op. cit., p.45.

33. ibid., p.49.

34. ibid., p.61.

35. Ratzinger, op. cit., p.58.

36. ibid.

37. Ratzinger and Messori, op. cit., p.52.

38. ibid., p.97.

39. ibid., p.152.

40. ibid., p.161.

41. ibid., p.100.

42. ibid., pp.138–9.

43. *The Code of Canon Law*, Canon 751 (p.175).

44. Ratzinger and Messori, op. cit., p.30.

45. ibid., p.115.

46. ibid., p.106.

47. ibid., p.107.

48. ibid., p.108.

49. ibid., p.107.

50. ibid., p.108.

51. Balasuriya, *Mary and Human Liberation*, p.91.

52. ibid.

53. Hutchison, *Their Kingdom Come*, p.439.

54. Ratzinger and Messori, op. cit., p.97.

55. ibid., p.98.

56. ibid., p.100.

57. *Independent*, 8 September 1994, p.11.

58. *The Times*, 9 September 1994, p.15.

59. *The Tablet*, 10 September 1994, p.7.

60. *The Times*, 9 September 1994, p.15.

61. ibid., 14 September 1994, p.9.

62. *Observer*, 27 May 1990, p.4.

63. *Daily Telegraph*, 3 July 1998, p.14.

64. ibid.

65. ibid.

66. *New York Times*, 1 July 1998, p.A1.

67. *The Code of Canon Law*, Canon 212:3 (p.45).

15: Visions of Mary

1. *The Times*, 3 January 1998, p.19.

2. ibid., 27 January 1998, p.4.

3. Jung, *Answer to Job*, p.399.

4. Martindale, *What Happened at Fatima*, pp.12–13.

5. ibid., p.37.

6. ibid., p.7.

7. ibid., p.11.

8. Brother Michael, *The Third Secret of Fatima*, p.4.

9. Ratzinger and Messori, *The Ratzinger Report*, pp.110–11.

10. ibid., p.110.

11. ibid.

12. ibid., pp.111–12.

13. ibid., p.118.

14. Brown, *The Final Hour*, p.211.

15. ibid.

16. Pope John Paul II, *Crossing the Threshold Of Hope*, p.221.

17. Petrisko, *The Last Crusade*, p.15.

18. Brother Michael, op. cit., p.28.

19. Brown, op. cit., pp.12–13.

20. ibid., p.14.

21. ibid., p.15.

22. ibid., p.16.

23. ibid.

24. ibid.

25. ibid., p.18.

26. ibid., p.21.

27. ibid., pp.105–6.

28. ibid., pp.214–15.

29. ibid., p.215.

30. ibid., p.225.

31. ibid., p.249.

32. ibid., p.219.

33. Bander, *The Prophecies of St. Malachy & St. Columbkille*, p.97.

34. ibid., p.98.

35. ibid., p.99.

16: The Pope as the Problem

1. *The Times*, 29 August 1998, p.1.

2. ibid.

3. ibid.

4. *Sunday Times*, 14 December 1997, p.2.

Bibliography

Addison, Charles G., *The History of the Knights Templars*, London, 1842.

Agrippa, Henry Cornelius, *Three Books of Occult Philosophy*, London, 1651.

Agrippa, Henry Cornelius, *The Vanity of Arts and Sciences*, London, 1684.

Baigent, Michael, 'Freemasonry, Hermetic Thought and The Royal Society of London', *Ars Quatuor Coronatorum*, 109, 1996, pp. 154–64.

Baigent, Michael, and Leigh, Richard, *The Temple and the Lodge*, London, 1989.

Baigent, Michael, and Leigh, Richard, *The Dead Sea Scrolls Deception*, London, 1991.

Baigent, Michael, Leigh, Richard, and Lincoln, Henry, *The Holy Blood and the Holy Grail*, London, 1982.

Balasuriya, Fr. Tissa, *Mary and Human Liberation. The Story and the Text*, London, 1997.

Bander, Peter, *The Prophecies of St. Malachy & St. Columbkille*, Gerrards Cross, 1979.

Barber, Malcolm, *The Trial of the Templars*, Cambridge, 1978.

Bede, *A History of the English Church and People*, trans. Leo Shirley-Price, Harmondsworth, 1979.

Benimeli, Jose Antonio Ferrer, *Masoneria, Iglesia e Ilustración*, 4 vols., Madrid, 1976–7.

Brown, Michael H., *The Final Hour*, Milford (Ohio), 1992.

Burman, Edward, *The Inquisition. The Hammer of Heresy*, Wellingborough, 1984.

Chastel, André, *Art of the Italian Renaissance*, trans. Linda and Peter Murray, London, 1988.

Chevallier, Pierre, *Les ducs sous l'Acacia*, Paris, 1964.

Chevallier, Pierre, *Histoire de la Franc-Maçonnerie française*, 3 vols., Paris, 1974.

The Cloud of Unknowing, ed. William Johnston, London, 1997.

The Code of Canon Law, rev. trans. by The Canon Law Society of Great Britain and Ireland, London, 1997.

Cohn, Norman, *The Pursuit of the Millennium*, Frogmore, 1978.

Collins, Paul, *Papal Power*, London, 1997.

Costa, Joseph da, *A Narrative of the Persecution of Hippolyto Joseph da Costa Pereira Furtado de Mendonça*, London, 1811.

Coustos, John, *The Sufferings of John Coustos for Freemasonry*, London, 1746.

Cross, Frank Moore, *The Ancient Library of Qumran*, London, 1958.

Denslow, William R., *10,000 Famous Freemasons*, 4 vols., Richmond, 1957–61.

Dickens, A. G., *The Counter Reformation*, London, 1977.

Drane, Augusta Theodosia, *The Life of Saint Dominic*, Rockford, 1988.

Eisenman, Robert, and Wise, Michael, *The Dead Sea Scrolls Uncovered*, Shaftesbury, 1992.

Fahy, Conor, 'The *Index Librorum Prohibitorum* and the Venetian printing industry in the sixteenth century', *Italian Studies*, 35, 1980, pp. 52–61.

Fogazzaro, A., *The Saint*, trans. M. Prichard-Agnetti, London, 1906.

Garcia Martinez, Florentino, *The Dead Sea Scrolls Translated*, Leiden, 1994.

Gervaso, Roberto, *Cagliostro*, trans. Cormac Ó Cuilleanáin, London, 1974.

Gould, Robert Freke, *The History of Freemasonry*, 6 vols. London, n.d.

Gui, Bernard, *Manuel de l'Inquisiteur*, trans. G. Mollat, Paris (Société d'Édition 'Les Belles Lettres'), 1964.

Hales, E. E. Y., *Pio Nono*, London, 1954.

Hasler, August Bernhard, *How the Pope Became Infallible*, trans. Peter Heinegg, New York, 1981.

Henningsen, Gustav and Tedeschi, John (eds.), *The Inquisition in Early Modern Europe*, Dekalb, 1986.

Hibbert, Christopher, *Garibaldi and his enemies*, London, 1987.

Hollis, Christopher, *A History of the Jesuits*, London, 1968.

Hutchison, Robert, *Their Kingdom Come*, London, 1997.

Index Librorum Prohibitorum, Vatican City, 1948.

Janelle, Pierre, *The Catholic Reformation*, London, 1975.

Jarrett, Bede, *Life of St Dominic (1170–1221)*, London, 1934.

John Paul II, Pope, *Crossing the Threshold of Hope*, trans. Jenny Mcphee and Martha Mcphee, London, 1994.

Jung, C. G. *Answer to Job*, in *Psychology and Religion: West and East*, 2nd edn, trans. R. F. C. Hull, London, 1981.

Kamen, Henry, *Inquisition and Society in Spain in the sixteenth and seventeenth centuries*, London, 1985.

Kamen, Henry, *The Spanish Inquisition*, London, 1997.

Kelly, J. N. D., *The Oxford Dictionary of Popes*, Oxford, 1986.

Kidd, B. J., *The Counter-Reformation 1550–1600*, London, 1963.

Kieckhefer, Richard, *Magic in the Middle Ages*, Cambridge, 1993.

Koudelka, Vladimir, *Dominic*, trans. Simon Tugwell, London, 1997.

Küng, Hans, *The Church*, London, 1969.

Küng, Hans, *Christianity*, trans. John Bowden, London, 1995.

Lea, Henry Charles, *A History of the Inquisition of the Middle Ages*, 3 vols., London, 1888.

Lea, Henry Charles, *A History of the Inquisition of Spain*, 4 vols., New York, 1922.

Lea, Henry Charles, *The Inquisition in the Spanish Dependencies*, New York, 1922.

Lennhoff, Eugen, *The Freemasons*, London, 1978.

Leon-Dufour, X., *The Gospels and the Jesus of History*, trans. J. McHugh, London, 1968.

Le Roy Ladurie, Emmanuel, *Montaillou*, Harmondsworth, 1980.

Malleus Maleficarum, trans. Montague Summers, London, 1986.

Martindale, C. C., *What Happened at Fatima*, London, 1950.

Matt, Leonard von, and Vicaire, Marie-Humbert, *St Dominic, A Pictorial Biography*, trans. Gerard Meath, London, 1957.

Maycock, A. L., *The Inquisition*, London, 1926.

Messori, Vittorio, *The Ratzinger Report*, trans. Salvator Attanasio and Graham Harrison, San Francisco, 1985.

Michael, Brother, *The Third Secret of Fatima*, trans. Anne Barbeau Gardiner, Rockford (Ill.), 1991.

Nauert, Charles G., *Agrippa and the Crisis of Renaissance Thought*, Urbana, 1965.

Netanyahu, B., *The Origins of the Inquisition in Fifteenth Century Spain*, New York, 1995.

Perkins, Clarence, 'The Trial of the Knights Templars in England', *The English Historical Review*, XXIV, 1909, pp. 432–47.

Petrisko, Thomas W., *The Last Crusade*, McKees Rocks (Penn.), 1996.

Poel, Mark van de, *Cornelius Agrippa, The Humanist Theologian and His Declamations*, Leiden, 1997.

Poulat, Émile, *Catholicisme, Démocratie et Socialisme*, Tournai, 1977.

Priolkar, Anant Kakba, *The Goa Inquisition*, Bombay, 1961.

Ratzinger, Joseph, *Church, Ecumenism and Politics*, Slough, 1988.

Ratzinger, Joseph, and Messori, Vittorio, *The Ratzinger Report*, San Francisco, 1986.

Read, Will, 'The Church of Rome and Freemasonry', *Ars Quatuor Coronatorum*, 104, 1991, pp. 51–73.

Reese, Thomas J., *Inside the Vatican*, Cambridge (Mass.), 1998.

Ribadeau Dumas, F., *Cagliostro*, trans. Elisabeth Abbott, London, 1967.

Rosa, Peter de, *Vicars of Christ*, London, 1989.

Roth, Cecil, *The Spanish Inquisition*, New York, 1964.

Runciman, Steven, *The Medieval Manichee*, Cambridge, 1984.

Simonde de Sismondi, J. C. L., *History of the Crusades against the Albigenses in the Thirteenth Century*, Trowbridge, 1996.

Stolper, E. E., 'Garibaldi: Freemason', *Ars Quatuor Coronatorum*, 102, 1989, pp. 1–22.

Stoyanov, Y., *The Hidden Tradition in Europe*, London, 1994.

Sumption, Jonathan, *The Albigensian Crusade*, London, 1978.

Teresa, Saint, *The Life of Saint Teresa of Ávila by Herself*, trans. J. M. Cohen, London, 1957.

Thomas, Keith, *Religion and the Decline of Magic*, Harmondsworth, 1980.

Thorndike, Lynn, *A History of Magic and Experimental Science*, 8 vols., New York, 1958.

Thory, Claude-Antoine, *Acta Latomorum ou Chronologie de l'Histoire de la Franche-Maçonnerie Française et Étrangère*, 2 vols., Paris, 1815.

Trevor-Roper, H. R., *The European Witch-Craze of the Sixteenth and Seventeenth Centuries*, London, 1988.

Vatcher, S., 'John Coustos and the Portuguese Inquisition', *Ars Quatuor Coronatorum*, 81, 1968, pp. 9–87.

Vicaire, Marie-Humbert, *Saint Dominic and His Times*, trans. Kathleen Pond, London, 1964.

Wakefield, Walter L., *Heresy, Crusade and Inquisition in Southern France 1100–1250*, London, 1974.

Walker, D. P., *Spiritual and Demonic Magic from Ficino to Campanella*, Notre Dame, 1975.

Wiesenthal, Simon, *Sails of Hope. The Secret Mission of Christopher Columbus*, trans. Richard and Clara Winston, New York, 1973.

Woodrow, Alain, *The Jesuits. A Story of Power*, London, 1996.

Woodward, Kenneth L., *Making Saints*, London, 1991.

Index

Reformation, 123–4
reincarnation, 5
religious experience, definition of, 146
Renaissance, 123
Renaissance Magi, persecution of,
    136–41
Renan, Ernest, 185–6, 211
Revue biblique, 225
Richelieu, Cardinal, 160, 192
'Rights of Man', in Americas, 88
Robert the Bruce, 53
Robin Goodfellow/Robin of the
    Greenwood/Robin Hood, 100
Robinson, Professor James, 231
Roman Empire, 99–100
Roman law, 40
Rooke, Admiral Sir George, 80
Roselli, Nicholas, 59
Rosicrucians/Rosicrucianism, 95,
    138–9, 158
Rottenburg, Bishop of, 206
Rousseau, Jean Jacques, 88
Rudolf II, Holy Roman Emperor,
    140
Rue du Bac, apparition of, 274–5
Russia, 210, 217–18
Russian Orthodox Church, 234

Sacred Congregation of the Holy
    Office, origin of, 215
Saint, The (Fogazzaro), 214
Saint John, Knights of, 192
saints, *see individual saints*
Salem witch trials, 118, 120
Salzburg, Inquisitor of, 106–7
Santiago de Chile, 90
Santiago de Compostela, 27
Saragossa, Inquisitor of, 67
Saramago, José, 170
Sardinia, 83
Sartre, Jean-Paul, 223
Satan, 102, 122–3
Savoy, 120
Sbarretti, Cardinal Donato, 215–16
Scandinavia, 41, 159
Schillebeeckx, Father Edward, 243
Schiller, Friedrich, 164
Schliemann, Heinrich, 183–5
scholarship, advocation of, 16

Schopenhauer, Arthur, 186
Schweitzer, Albert, 223
Scotland, 53, 161
Second Empire, 192–3, 207
Second Vatican Council, 233–7, 244
Selby, Hubert, 136
Seper, Cardinal Franjo, 237
Seven Years War, 165
Seville, 64
sexual transgressions, in Americas, 88
sexuality, 111–13, 122
    Saint Teresa and, 153
Shelley, Percy Bysshe, 182
Sicily, 83, 189
Sidney, Sir Philip, 140
Siricus I, Pope, 27, 285
Sixtus IV, Pope, 64–5
Sodalitium pianum (Pius Society),
    216–17
Solferino, battle of, 189
Soubirous, Bernadette, 278
Spain/Spanish, 40–41, 62–82, 161, 170
    in Americas, 83–97
    mystics in, 151–7
Spanish Inquisition
    end of, 80–82
    procedures of, 67–74
    see also Spain
Spanish Succession, War of, 80
Spencer, Herbert, 182
Spiritual Exercises, The (Loyola), 127
spirituality, definition of, 146, 147
Sprenger, Johann, 106–7
Stalin, Joseph, 131
Stanislaus II of Poland, 163
Stendhal, 181, 223
Stoyanov, Yuri, 43
strappado, 73
stratigraphy, 184
Stuart, Charles Edward (Bonnie Prince
    Charlie), 161
succubi, 103, 122
*Sufferings of John Coustos for
    Freemasonery, The*, 174
suicide, 117
Summers, Montague, 107, 108
Sweden, 163, 168
Sweeney, Father Terence, 243
Swift, Jonathan, 164